Canada Innovates: Sustainable Building

Editors
Luigi Ferrara and Emily Visser

Project Management
Emily Visser

Designer / Project Coordinator
Justin Aitcheson

Design Assistant
Eric Schmidt

Design Review
Fidel Peña and Claire Dawson
Underline Studio

Copy Editors
Elena De Marchi,
Jane Weber and Mike Barker

Cover Image
328 Euclid Avenue
Photo: Ben Rahn

Special Thanks
All of the companies and individuals
who submitted materials for inclusion
in this project.

For information on other School of Design
publications or to place an order please
contact:

Faculty of Business, Arts and Design
George Brown College—Toronto
200 King Street East
Room 313A
Toronto, ON M5T 2T9
Tel: 416.415.5000 x2137

Visit our website for more information
about the School of Design:
www.schoolofdesign.ca

E-mail: design@gbrownc.on.ca

Library and Archives Canada Cataloguing in Publication

Ferrara, Luigi
    Canada innovates : sustainable building /
    Luigi Ferrara, Emily Visser, Justin Aitcheson.

Originated as a research project conducted
    by the School of Design, George Brown College, Toronto, Ont.

ISBN 978-1-55263-957-3

    1. Sustainable architecture--Canada. 2. Sustainable buildings--
Canada--Design and construction. I. Visser, Emily, 1965-
II. Aitcheson, Justin III. Toronto City College, George Brown.
School of Design IV. Title.

TH880.F47 2007   720'.470971   C2007-901837-8

The publisher gratefully acknowledges the support of the Canada
Council for the Arts and the Ontario Arts Council for its publishing
program. We acknowledge the support of the Government of
Ontario through the Ontario Media Development Corporation's
Ontario Book Initiative.

We acknowledge the financial support of the Government
of Canada through the Book Publishing Industry Development
Program (BPIDP) for our publishing activities.

Key Porter Books Limited
Six Adelaide Street East, Tenth Floor
Toronto, Ontario
Canada M5C 1H6

www.keyporter.com

Printed and bound in China

08 09 10 11 12 6 5 4 3 2 1

SCHOOLOFDESIGN
Faculty of Business, Arts and Design
George Brown College—Toronto

CANADA INNOVATES: SUSTAINABLE BUILDING

Volume Two in a Series
Edited by Luigi Ferrara & Emily Visser
www.canadainnovates.com

With Contributions by:
Terri Meyer Boake
Ian Chodikoff
Peter Busby

In Collaboration with the Green Building Alliance:
Toronto Region Conservation Authority
Canadian Urban Institute
Sustainable Buildings Canada
Canada Green Building Council, Toronto Chapter

KEY PORTER BOOKS

TABLE OF
CONTENTS

ESSAYS
CASE STUDIES & PROJECTS
CATALOGUE
RESOURCES

OVERVIEW	CANADIAN LEADERSHIP IN SUSTAINABLE DESIGN BY LUIGI FERRARA	10
CANADA	THE LEGACY OF CANADIAN INDIGENOUS ARCHITECTURE BY EMILY VISSER	18
HISTORY	MOVING TOWARDS GREEN BY TERRI MEYER BOAKE	22
FUTURE	FUTURE DIRECTIONS AND NEEDS BY IAN CHODIKOFF	30
PRACTICE	SUSTAINABLE DESIGN: A PRACTITIONER'S PERSPECTIVE ON FUTURE BEST PRACTICES BY PETER BUSBY	36

PROJECTS	COMMERCIAL	46
	COMMUNITY PLANNING	78
	EDUCATIONAL	110
	INSTITUTIONAL	138
	RESIDENTIAL	168

| | SUPPLIER LISTING | 198 |
| | PRODUCT CATALOGUE | 205 |

	CANADIAN GREEN BUILDING RATING SYSTEMS	220
	LEED® CERTIFIED BUILDINGS	222
	DESIGN CHARETTES	223
	ARCHITECT DIRECTORY	228
	ORGANIZATIONS	234
	PRINCIPLES OF SUSTAINABLE DESIGN	235
	GLOSSARY	236

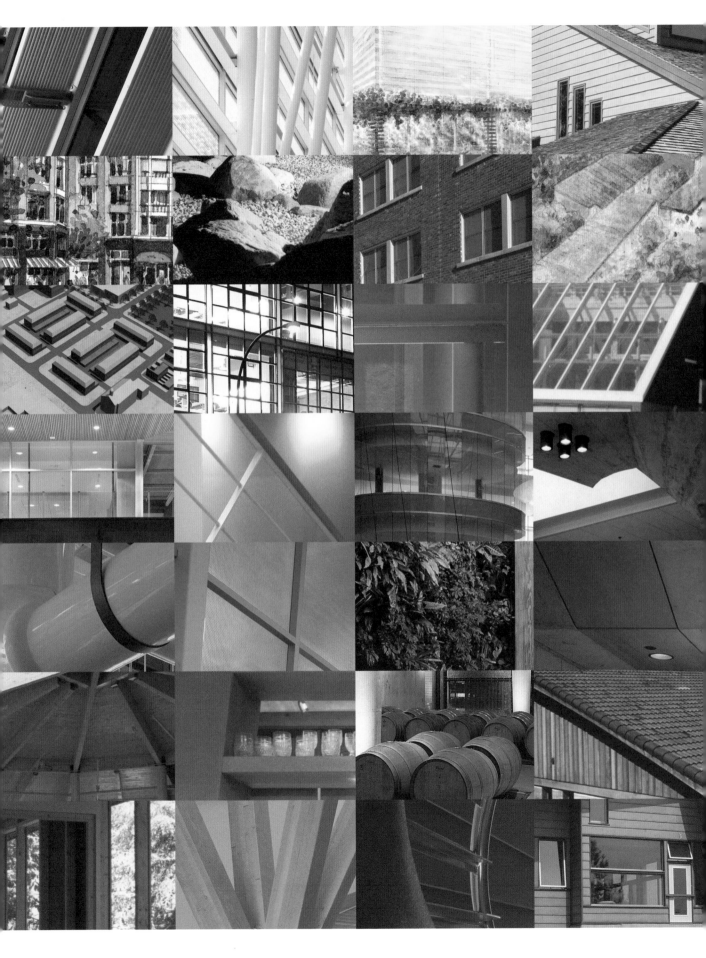

ACKNOWLEDGEMENTS

Luigi Ferrara
MRAIC, OAA, Hon. ACID O, ICSID Senator,
Director, School of Design, Faculty of Business, Arts and Design, George Brown College—Toronto

The genesis of this publication began when four individuals got together around a table to discuss how Toronto might become a more sustainable city. I want to thank Mike Singleton, Jiri Skopek and Tom Ponessa who brainstormed with me about how we could transform our city by attempting to create a green building exposition much like the one held in Berlin during the 1980's. Together our small group approached the Canadian Urban Institute where David Crombie lent support to our efforts to make a bid for the International Initiative for a Sustainable Built Environment (IISBE) conference in 2008. Before long our group grew to include Jeff Evenson, Glen Miller and Brent Gilmour. Andrew Bowerbank of the Metro Toronto Region Conservation Authority and Ian Jarvis of the Canadian Green Building Council also subsequently joined our team. While our dreams of winning the 2008 World Sustainability Conference (SB08) for Toronto were never realised, this book is one of the fruits of those labours.

Together our group founded a new organization, The Green Building Alliance, which held its first festival in 2005. This set in motion the market transformation that we had envisioned when we first came together. Many great projects are now underway as a result of this effort including an Archetype competition at the Kortright Centre as well as the World House Project at the School of Design's Institute without Boundaries Program.

This book, which has been in gestation for over two years, could not have been completed without the support and nurturing of all those involved. On a personal note, I want to thank my collaborators with whom I work on a daily basis. I want to recognize my co-editor, Emily Visser, with whom I have completed five publications including this last one, and Justin Aitcheson, a graduate of our School of Design and designer extraordinaire, who designed the book. I would like to thank Fidel Peña and Claire Dawson of Underline Studio who assisted Justin with their insightful design guidance and critiques. I also want to thank Jennifer Pavey of the Canadian Urban Institute who assisted in collecting the material and Kaeleigh Kuzma who was my right hand in communicating with the featured designers and who compiled the product catalogue. I want to thank copy editors Elena De Marchi, Jane Weber and Mike Barker for their oversight. Lastly I want to thank my Dean, Maureen Loweth, of the Faculty of Business and Creative Arts, who supports the research activities we undertake at the School of Design and the President of George Brown College, Anne Sado who has called on us to go beyond the usual in our efforts.

I also want to specially thank the individuals who contributed essays to the publication; Terry Meyer Boake, Ian Chodikoff, Peter Busby and all of the great designers across the country who, through their work and dedication, make Canada's buildings and communities more sustainable.

◄◄ University of Toronto at Mississauga
Erindale Hall Board Room
on Ground Floor
Photo: Michael Awad

CANADIAN LEADERSHIP IN SUSTAINABLE DESIGN

Luigi Ferrara
MRAIC, OAA, Hon. ACID O, ICSID Senator,
Director, School of Design, Faculty of Business, Arts and Design, George Brown College—Toronto

It might seem unlikely that a country endowed with an excess of resources and a seemingly unlimited land mass for its relatively tiny population could become known around the world as a leader and innovator in the emerging field of sustainable design. Despite Canada's lack of visible design history and culture, it does have a significant tradition of environmental design in the sectors of transport, telecommunication and building. Strength in developing technology has positioned Canada to take a lead in building sustainably.

Historically, Canada has relied on exploiting its natural resources. From the time of the fur trade to the mid-20th century when the country was dominated by mining, agriculture and fishing, Canada has had its share of negative experiences and harsh lessons with regards to resource over-utilization leading to environmental degradation. Throughout its history the country has also had to develop solutions to deal with climate, terrain and resource extraction. The issue of extracting resources to assist with survival in a harsh climate is not only part of modern Canadian history but a central feature of the identity and philosophy of the First Nations communities that occupied the country prior to the industrial era. It also continues to be a central feature of the psyche of the many waves of immigrants who helped to expand human settlement of the land.

From early in the nation's history, people understood that while the resource base was potentially vast, its extraction and distribution was hampered by climatic hardship, travel over great distances and dispersed population centres. In the agrarian era the very real limits of available arable land and its capacity to sustain ongoing community growth was experienced by pioneering settlers.

Out of this hardship grew the foundation of character that would make Canada a fertile ground for acceptance of the principles and approaches that characterize sustainable living. The traditions of our aboriginal peoples reflect this bias for sustainable thinking. Those in the Canadian territory of

The Evolution of Sustainability

While the idea of environmentalism is as ancient as culture itself, there is a development of environmental philosophy which can be seen more clearly in the context of key moments in history. The following timeline and accompanying flow chart indicate how thought on environmental issues is developing at a rapid pace, but also builds on past achievements.

Compiled by Emily Visser

References

McGraw Hill Construction, New York
NY SmartMarket Reports

Canada Green Builidng Council, *Report: A Business Case for Green Builidngs in Canada*, presented to Industry Canada, lead author Mark Lucuik
Morrisson Herschfield, Ottawa, ON

Green Building Alliance

1961

The Death and Life of Great American Cities by Jane Jacobs

Responsible for new ideas about urban planning and the importance of local, sustainable economies

1962

Silent Spring by Rachel Carson

Advocates for conservation and protection of the environment from human intervention

1968 to 1972 +

The Whole Earth Catalogues

Instrumental in disseminating ideas about the environment

ENVIRONMENTAL

1960

Nunavut call it "avativut", which describes a healthy and balanced environment. First Nations cultures see the linking of one generation to the next as part of a continuum, and emphasize planning for seven generations of children so as to ensure the future of their peoples. This penchant for systems thinking as a strategic tool, which society can use to guide its life design, is typical of Canadian culture and characterizes the bias of governments, businesses and the public alike.

While Canada's land mass might appear to be unlimited, charting in as the second largest country in the world after Russia, the habitable areas of the country, if shaded in, give the appearance of a long thin country approximately the size of Chile. Unfortunately, Canada's length runs latitudinally across the planet instead of longitudinally, giving the nation much less climatic variety. In truth, the Canadian climate is one of the harshest and most severe climates on the planet in terms of cold, heat and temperature fluctuation. This has consistently posed a challenge to its inhabitants who have relied on ingenuity, migration and modification of the environment to sustain communities in these hostile conditions. It could be argued that without technical innovation around building design it probably would not be possible to sustain the type of permanent dwellings that are typical in the country today.

If one looks at Toronto, the country's current leading economic centre, it was not initially a centre of permanent inhabitation, but rather a place of confluence for aboriginal tribes to exchange, share and meet for the short yearly intervals that allowed for human habitation. The city, a metropolis with a population of over three million, is presently occupied year round, however the tradition of 'meeting place' has been carried forward. It is now a place of convergence for immigrants from over 172 nations who have settled together to collaborate quite harmoniously. The city aims to sustain prosperity for all of its citizens. It fosters cultural diversity, equity and access, and nature is nurtured within its boundaries.

1970
First Earth Day

1972
UN Conference on the Human Environment, Stockholm

1972
The Club of Rome published the report
The Limits to Growth
This document asserts that economic growth is restricted by the limited availability of natural resources, particularly oil

1973-1974
OPEC Oil Embargo

1979
Three Mile Island nuclear power plant in the US suffered a partial core meltdown, contributing to public fears around nuclear power

ECONOMIC

It is essentially "a city within a park" as its slogan attests. These same words could be used to describe Montreal and Vancouver, Canada's other great cities. Despite their unique features these cities share many of the same characteristics as Toronto and honour the same values and principles.

As a citizen, one constantly marvels at how settlement took root in this difficult country and how it produced the current urban landscape. Through a gradual process of evolution, communities learned to cohabit by mutual agreement. They set up tiny centres of gravity that were open to each other and yet spaced far enough apart to evolve naturally in relationship to a larger economic, political, social and cultural accord guided by compromise, tolerance and acceptance. In this way, Canada has grown a set of global villages and with each village is an authentic global soul aware of the needs of the larger planet and open to discussion and deliberation on the matters that are at the core of sustainable development – environmental, economic, social and cultural continuity and evolution.

It is no coincidence that the Club of Rome, which first brought to the public's attention environmental issues that over time would lead to the evolution of the sustainability platform, was founded by a Canadian, Maurice Strong. Throughout his exceptional career Mr. Strong has tried to balance the complex bottom line that links economy, social development, cultural and environmental preservation. This was something he instinctively understood as a boy growing up on the Canadian prairie. John Peters Humphrey, another Canadian, was the principal drafter of the Universal Declaration of Human Rights. The systemic operating platform that underpins the current sustainability movement and its emphasis on access and equity is evident at the very root of Canadian society. In opposition to generations of strategy for conflict resolution based on war, former Prime Minister Lester B. Pearson developed the concept of peacekeeping to safeguard the planet against the threat posed by the atomic era. These contributions by Canada to the international debate on the future of the planet provide a cultural

1986

Chernobyl in Ukraine is considered the world's worst nuclear accident

1987

Bruntland Report
Oxford University Press

The Brundtland Commission (convened by the United Nations) issued this report dealing with sustainable development and the associated political changes it required.

1989

Exxon Valdez Oil Spill (EVOS) off Alaska

1989

The Montreal Protocol on Substances That Deplete the Ozone Layer is an international treaty signed to protect the ozone layer by phasing out the production of a number of substances responsible for ozone depletion

SOCIAL

ECONOMIC
ENVIRONMENTAL

1980

ground which informs the contemporary framework of ideas that in turn fuels the movement for sustainable design within our country and around the world.

Brilliant Canadian historians and communication theorists such as Harold Innis and Marshall McLuhan reveal an understanding of ecological systems in their studies. This example of holistic thought still guides Canada's leaders in sustainable design. Canada's historic participation in the creation of global standards is best exemplified by Sir Sandford Fleming's invention of standard time. Canada has participated globally from Rio through to the Kyoto Accord with innovative practice that defines the trajectory of sustainable policy development. The results of this policy are now visible in the building design community where architects, landscape architects, industrial designers, interior designers, planners, engineers, constructors and developers are looking at new ways of doing things. They are re-imagining the principles by which we build to meet the challenges that face our country in the 21st century.

This publication collects examples of Canadian innovation in sustainable building from practitioners across the country at the dawn of the 21st century. It captures how Canada innovates in sustainable building and design. It includes essays that cover the history of sustainable design, the best practices of leading practitioners, projects on the drawing boards and examples of the most unique projects in community planning, residential building, commercial construction, educational facilities and institutional patronage. A product and consultant list along with other sustainable resources are also found in this publication. The information compiled in this volume provides a picture of our contemporary cultural evolution as manifested in the buildings we create for our environments.

1990

British Research Establishment Environmental Assessment Methodology (BREEAM), the UK green building rating system, is launched

1992

Energy Star was introduced by the US Environmental Protection Agency (EPA) as a voluntary labeling program that identifies and promotes energy-efficient products

1992

United Nations Conference on Environment and Development (UNCED), in Rio de Janeiro, leads to the adoption of Agenda 21: a blueprint for global sustainable development

1993

The United States Green Building Council (USGBC) is founded

1997

The Kyoto Protocol—The United Nations Framework Convention on Climate Change—is opened for signature

Leadership in Energy and Environmental Design (LEED®) rating system is developed by the US Green Building Council (USGBC)

1998

Japan Green Building Council is founded

1998

The Triple Bottom Line

Includes consideration of environment, social and financial responsibility, an idea coined by John Elkington of SustainAbility in his 1998 book *Cannibals with Forks: the Triple Bottom Line of 21st Century Business*

1999

World Green Building Council is founded

Sustainable Design: Beyond Modernism

The most serious threat to modernism's continued ideological control of architectural design is the emerging movement embracing sustainable design and the holistic values that drive it. In its most radical "deep green" expression, the sustainability movement calls for a regression to a pre-industrial lifestyle that abandons industrial means of production and returns us to an organic agrarian society. At its most benign, the deep green movement accepts high-tech communication as an enabler of the return to the land and a facilitator of a dispersed knowledge-based society living in harmony with a preserved natural environment untouched by humans. The movement has the potential to return us to pre-industrial norms on social, political, economic and religious fronts; It could forseeably lead to globalized central planning and a strong spiritual movement that would cross religion and state in ways unseen in hundreds of years.

Fortunately for us all, most sustainable design ideology falls within a more moderate and evolutionary direction, building a new post-industrial world from our industrialized foundations. Often sustainability is based on incremental adaptation and improvements on current systems. Our efforts to develop new best practices in an ongoing cycle of innovation and our effort to use our resources more efficiently, regenerate polluted environments and improve quality of life will allow us to pass on a better world to our children.

While sustainability grew out of a concern for balancing the utilization of diminishing resources within a fragile environmental system, it has increasingly become a more complex moral ideology that attempts to create balance between natural ecosystems and the human built environment. It addresses issues of equity in our society by creating an inclusive system with equitable distribution of wealth and it provides visibility and acceptance of biological and cultural diversity.

The "abundance" economy of the industrial era and the "scarcity" economy of the agrarian era are being superceded by the vision of a "balanced" society where environmental preservation, economy equity, cultural diversity and social

---

2002
Green Globes green building performance tool is released in Canada and the US

2002
The Canada Green Building Council (CaGBC) is founded

2002
Sustainable Building Conference in Oslo, Norway

2004
Establishment of the National Australian Building Environmental Rating System Project (NABERS)

2004
LEED® Canada is established

2005
The Green Building Alliance is established in Canada

2005
The Kyoto Protocol to United Framework Convention on Climate Change
Aiming to reduce greenhouse gasses, this international agreement came into force on February 16

2006
George Brown College, School of Design begins the World House Project in its Institute without Boundaries putting Massive Change into action

2006
As of April 163 countries have signed the Kyoto Accord

The inuit symbol for *avativut* which describes a healthy and balanced environment, used by the Green Building Alliance in Canada

CULTURAL

BALANCE

SOCIAL
ECONOMIC
ENVIRONMENTAL

inclusion are viewed as a complex and interrelated set of systems that need to be planned for, nurtured, developed and sustained.

This may not seem that different from the modernist ideology that fostered scientific, technological and design innovation as core drivers for an improved lifestyle that could be empirically measured. In fact the new sustainable ethos expands the criteria for what we consider successful living to look at our own needs as well as the needs of the system as a whole, determining the long term impact of our actions on the systems that govern our lives.

It is remarkable how far the evolution of sustainable thinking in design has progressed in just a few years. In doing our historic research for this book it was clear that there was a strong environmental bias in early green building. The retro-craft nature of those buildings, the special relationship of building to site and the use of renewable and recyclable building materials typified this approach. As knowledge and time progressed, a more technological system-centred sustainable design evolved based on building performance, life cycle costs, energy use and materials selection featuring embodied energy. As sustainability has gained momentum,

▾ Structure of the Development Process
Diagram: Monica Contreras

Management
Post-construction, Occupancy, Economic Return

Assessment	Service
User Input	Pro-Forma
Publishing/Awards	Operational/Inventory
Final Approvals/LC/Bond	Schedule
Site Cleaning	As-build Documents

Due Diligence
Planning, Pre-design, All-risk Investment

Strategic Planning	Financing
Market Analysis	Pro-Forma
Needs Assessment	Design Brief
Approvals	Contracts
Site Investigation	Consultants
Project Structure	

PRODUCT DEFINITION

PRODUCT IDENTIFICATION

PRODUCT ASSIMILATION

Implementation
Pro-forma Management, Construction, Economic Risk

Design Implementation	Insurance Policies
Sales/Lease Terms	Pro-Forma
Tender/Contracts	Budget
Inspection/Testing	Schedule
Safety Policies	Documents/Information

Pre-Development
Pro-forma Management, Design Development, Economic Investment

Schematic Design	Budget
User Input	Schedule
Design Strategy	Documents
Approvals	
Site Preparation	
Marketing/Advertising	
Pro-Forma	

PRODUCT SOLUTION

▾ Collaborative Process in Building Construction.
This diagram explores the development stages and
overlays degrees of collaborative discussion, overlapping
responsibilities of all the stakeholders and maps out all of
the restrictions, opportunities, concerns, etc.
Diagram: Monica Contreras

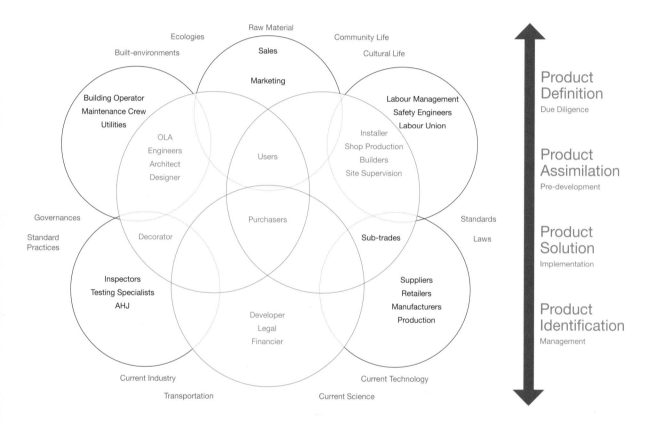

issues of cultural appropriateness, social inclusion, healthy living and rural and urban regeneration have come to the fore. These have coalesced into a complex and holistic definition of sustainable building design that forms a coherent alternative to the neo-modernism and neo-historicism prevailing in architectural circles during the 1980s and 1990s.

It is inspiring to see a new sustainable design aesthetic emerging in these new "holistically" conceived buildings. What is even more remarkable is that while the sustainable design aesthetic has a consistent imprint, the buildings are visually diverse and regionally sensitive.

My most profound personal experience of the imprint found in the highest quality sustainable projects was quite literal in its manifestation as a sensory experience. It was a veritable smell and touch reaction to these buildings. On a tour of York University's Information Technology Building, (designed by Busby, Perkins+Will and Architects Alliance) I understood how a building could be designed through its massing and organization to create an organism that breathed, exchanged air, and biologically supported its inhabitants. On the site visit I toured through an exit stairwell that had been intentionally built to unsustainable building standards by the designers—the usual modernist exit stairwell. Upon entering this space I was struck by how terrible it smelled and how unappetizing it was in relation to the rest of the building. It was then explained to me that the stairwell

was built to typical standards to contrast with the rest of the building and that the awful smell I was experiencing was the common smell of most off-gassing materials found throughout modernist buildings.

It was clear to me at that moment that sustainably designed buildings are not only designed and built differently but most importantly they smell and feel different. They smell better, just like a world without second hand smoke. Sustainable buildings feel palpably healthier than your typical building. They work to give you a "just right" feeling found in many older buildings that use traditional building techniques. Whether you are walking through the halls of the Gladstone Hotel, sitting in an office space at the Electronic Arts Headquarters or shopping at a Mountain Equipment Co-op store, you can sense the difference. You can feel it. You can smell it. It is this difference that is the point of sustainable design, which detail by detail, building by building is part of an ongoing dialogue that helps to balance, restore and regenerate the planet we occupy.

Modernism was built on the idea that if each of us did our own specialized task we could improve productivity. Sustainability counts on each of us thinking of the system as a whole and impacting it through our interventions. If we practice this new axiom not only will our future will be secured, but it will smell much better in the process.

THE LEGACY OF CANADIAN INDIGENOUS ARCHITECTURE

Emily Visser
BA, AOCA
Editor, Canada Innovates: Sustainable Building

Canadians have a rich legacy of knowledge acquired over time by First Nation Peoples. With over 144 different tribes, they have developed a great number of innovative shelter designs. Born out of an intimate understanding of the environment, designs such as the long house, pit shelters, plank houses, teepees and igloos are the original sustainable Canadian buildings.

The knowledge generated by thousands of years of vernacular architecture serves as a pool of expertise increasingly valued for its sustainable attributes. Designers are exploring the cooling properties of the earth long exploited by builders of pit-shelters. The insulation advantages of roofs planted with greenery, and the flexibility offered by the portable shelters of nomadic cultures are being integrated into current design on an unprecedented scale. Site-specific attributes are increasingly explored in an effort to maximize energy efficiency, bringing us back to lessons learned in the development of vernacular shelter designs.

It is important to note that while sustainable architecture has finally entered the realm of the media in a big way, there is a simultaneous and parallel interest in sustainable construction at a grass-roots level. A return to the knowledge of our ancestors has enabled local communities to build community-serving structures on a small scale. This is in turn growing into a powerful drive for sustainability in which increasing numbers of people from all walks of life are invested. One important example of this grass-roots interest in sustainable design is happening in public parks. As examples of urban public spaces, which are increasingly thriving centres for community activity, park groups are beginning to build their own shelters. One cutting edge and forward thinking example of this initiative is the new cob structure in Dufferin Grove Park in Toronto.

The Dufferin Grove Park community boasts numerous awards as a trend-setting example of what can be done with urban public space. Recognized with a Public Space Award

Indigenous North American Housing

References

Ministry of Indian and Northern Affairs Canada
http://www.greatdreams.com/native/nativehsg.htm
Wikipedia.com

Chickee

Native to the Seminole tribe of the Everglades, the chickee is a thatch-covered log frame structure developed as a disposable shelter

Chukka

Native to the Choctaw, these are mud-and-bark cabins with thatched roofs

Earth Mounds

Prehistoric, Mississipian

Hogan

Native to the Navaho, the Hogan resembles a pyramid with five, six, or eight triangular faces and is built from a framework of logs, the spaces are filled with earth

◀ Cob Structure
▼ Mixing the Cob
 Photos: Emily Visser

in Chicago in 2001, it has been the subject of study by scholars around the world. The summer of 2005 marked a particularly cutting edge event in the park. Georgie Donais together with an estimated 400 volunteers from the community and across the city have constructed a cob structure.

Gathering recycled materials and volunteer labour via their biweekly newsletter and thriving listserv, the project has been constructed as an answer to new legislation requiring food carts to have access to hand-washing facilities. Through an organic approach to the design process, the project has expanded to include not only the mandatory sinks, but also a diaper-changing station, a fireplace for cooking community meals, and even a puppet theatre window for children.

Sponsored by a city grant, the construction is made from cob, a form of adobe construction popular in areas of the world as diverse as England, Kenya, and Australia. Mud and clay are mixed together with hay to form a sturdy building material applied to a wooden frame. This is then sealed with a cement-based plaster. The storage portion of the structure is covered by a green roof planted with native species. The sustainability of this structure includes the fact that in time it will naturally return to the earth and be indistinguishable from the rest of the landscape. On the level of cultural sustainability, the creation of this structure has contributed to the growth and strength of the community. Not only have the volunteers been inspired by the project to work hard over many months, they have also simultaneously been educated in the benefits of sustainability and have learned many aspects of the art of building an environmentally responsible shelter. The construction process has been cross-cultural, intergenerational, and democratic, with children, seniors and adults from a wide variety of backgrounds mixing the mud and straw with their feet, and helping to apply mosaics of their own design to the walls.

Projects such as the cob house at Dufferin Grove Park are leveraging the growing interest in sustainability at a grass-roots level; this growing movement is critical to the quest for sustainability on a larger scale.

Igloo/iglu

The igloo is constructed from carved blocks of snow. With the flexibility to be multiple room dwellings and form extensible camps, igloos are now commonly temporary structures used for hunting expeditions.

Jacal

Starting with a framework of close-set thin poles, the jacal is filled out with mud, clay and grasses

Long House

Long houses include the buildings of Ontario's Iroquois as well as the Haida in British Columbia. Called longhouses because they are longer than they are wide, they are built of logs and have door openings at both ends. During the winter, these openings are covered with skins.

Pit House/Pit Shelter/ Keekwillie/ Quiggly

Common in forested areas, the pit house is dug down below grade, which provides natural cooling and insulation by the earth

Plank House

Built on a framework of posts and beams, these dwellings were covered with detachable planks for the walls and roofs and were commonly found on the West Coast

◀ Cob Structure
▼ Fireplace
▼ Decoration Detail
  Photos: Emily Visser

Pueblo

Built from adobe, these buildings are traditional housing of the Pueblo communities of the Southwest United States of America

Sweat Lodge

A ceremonial sauna in various styles ranging from oblong huts to a hole dug in the ground covered with planks or tree trunks used by First Nations or Native Americans

Tipi (teepee)

Originally a conical tent of bound poles covered with bark, mats or skins, the tipi is native to the plains and lake regions

Wikiup (Wickiup)

These dome-shaped buildings are similar to the wigwam, but native to the west and southwest regions as opposed to those of the northeast of America

Wigwam

Constructed from a frame of arched wooden poles, wigwams are covered with grass, brush, bark, rushes, mats, reeds, or cloth, and are often temporary dwellings.

MOVING TOWARDS GREEN:
A BRIEF HISTORY OF THE BEGINNINGS
OF SUSTAINABLE DESIGN IN CANADA

Terri Meyer Boake
B.E.S. B.Arch. M.Arch. LEED® AP, Associate Professor, Associate Director, Undergraduate Academic Officer
School of Architecture, University of Waterloo

Real change does not just "happen". It requires either a catalyst or a series of events to effect evolution. Lasting change requires both success and commitment. Sustainable design is no exception. The directed evolution of green building, from its inception in the mid 1960s to its current state in the year 2006, is the result of a series of publications, key events, legislative encouragement and significant buildings. Commercial and institutional building are slow on the uptake, but progress is evident.

It wasn't always called "green building" and it wasn't even always about building. It started in the 60's with the publication of Rachel Carson's book *Silent Spring* that dealt with the effects of pesticides and herbicides on the environment. Carson's book was followed very closely by two important works that brought environmental concerns to the field of architecture: *Design with Climate* by Victor Olgyay, published in 1963, and *Design with Nature* by Ian McHarg, published in 1969. Olgyay's book initiated a different approach to thinking about building. Its premise, that buildings should be designed to accommodate regional climatic differences based on vernacular models, ran completely counter to the more popular ideas behind modern architecture.

Olgyay pioneered a way of thinking that favoured solar control and natural ventilation in buildings. This trend in thinking, of course, went counter to the creation of the hermetically sealed glass boxes that were springing up all over Europe and North America during the post-war building boom. Needless to say, this revolutionary idea of using architectural devices (operable windows, shading devices, building orientation, planting) to modify the interior environment, rather than handing over the job to one's mechanical engineer, proved to be very unpopular with the majority of architects.

The new "solar" buildings looked so remarkably different from mainstream modern architecture that by-and-large they were rejected as a viable alternative for designing commercial and institutional buildings. Most of the "environmentally designed" buildings that were developed during this period were houses or smaller community type projects, taken on by

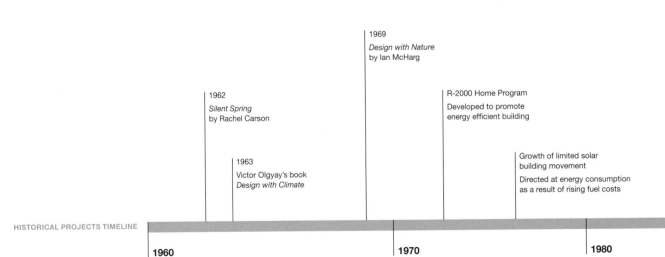

1969
Design with Nature
by Ian McHarg

1962
Silent Spring
by Rachel Carson

R-2000 Home Program

Developed to promote
energy efficient building

1963
Victor Olgyay's book
Design with Climate

Growth of limited solar
building movement

Directed at energy consumption
as a result of rising fuel costs

HISTORICAL PROJECTS TIMELINE

1960   1970   1980

◄ CMHC Healthy House
Close up view of PV screen
suspended from balcony railing
▼ Healthy House Waterloo Biofilter unit in a closet
Photo: www.architecture.uwaterloo.ca/
faculty_projects/terri/cmhc.html

1993

C-2000 Program

Developed to promote
energy efficient building in
commercial buildings

1993

The Body Shop Canada Headquarters

Don Mills ON,
Keen Engineering,
Colborne Architectural Group

Uses the Living Machine site waste water
treatment system, designed by Dr. John Todd,
which uses biological processes to clean
domestic sewage water

1991

Toronto City Council established
the Toronto Atmospheric Fund
(TAF) to finance local initiatives
to combat global warming and
improve air quality in Toronto

1991

Healthy House
Competition

Developed to promote
energy efficient building

1992

CMHC Healthy House

Toronto, Ontario
Martin Liefhebber Architect

(See Above)

1990

daring clients. These unique clients were interested in working with the innovative ideas and building systems presented by environmentally designed buildings, and were less concerned with "high design appearance."

The 1970s saw the growth of a limited solar building movement that was directed at reducing the energy consumption in buildings as a result of rising fuel costs. In Canada, winter conditions governed design choices. Window strategies were developed to maximize sunlight penetration for passive heating. Insulation levels were increased and buildings were tightly sealed to cut down on leakage. When people began to suffer the ill effects of buildings that were too tight, fresh air requirements were examined and standards modified to include indoor air quality as a consideration. These concerns resulted in a return to operable windows which began to come back into "vogue", but in limited application on commercial and institutional buildings.

Throughout the 1970s and 1980s such concerns remained "residential" in their influence. Larger buildings continued to follow traditional modernist principles of design. Many of the early solar buildings were quite unattractive and strange looking. In some cases excessive amounts of unprotected south facing glass resulted in extreme overheating as wood frame construction lacked the thermal mass required to store this free energy. In Canada, the R-2000 Home Program was developed during the 1970s to promote more energy efficient building. Canada Mortgage and Housing Corporation announced the "Healthy House Competition" in 1991. In 1993 the C-2000 program for commercial buildings was introduced. Energy efficiency remained the primary focus for early "green" buildings.

Architectural design has never been about willfully creating buildings whose primary concern is aesthetics. Commercial buildings need to be viable. Tenants want smart looking buildings. Institutional buildings must answer to the public. The public also wants "accountable" architecture that is fiscally responsible. The 1980s experienced numerous stylistic changes in architectural design: post-modernism, high-tech,

1994

Low Cost Dwellings
for the Environmentally Hypersensitive

Barrhaven, Ottawa, ON
Phillip Sharp Architect Limited

Integrated into a conventional suburban neighbourhood, this project acts as a catalyst for social and environmental responsibility. It allows many people who would otherwise be institutionalised to live in the community at large.

1994

Renfrew Library

Vancouver, BC
Hughes Condon Marler: Architects

Features include a reflecting pool on the roof and durable local building materials such as glulams, local brick and concrete

neo-rationalism, deconstructivism. Environmentalism was not a major part of these approaches. Environmental design required scientific calculations to make it credible. It required a lot of work. Only the hardcore environmentalists were committed to that degree of effort.

The World Commission on Environment and Development, Our Common Future, 1987, defined sustainable development as meeting the needs of the present generation without compromising the ability of future generations to meet their own needs. The boundary conditions had changed from concern about the mere consumption of increasingly expensive fossil fuels, to global issues of environmental stability. Statistics regarding dwindling supplies of natural resources required to create and maintain our lifestyle caught the attention of many. It was becoming increasingly obvious to architectural educators as well as a wider body of practicing architects that the problems posed by the sustainable design question were pressing. Architectural curricula began to develop and expand courses in "environmental building design".

The new definition of sustainable design was increasingly holistic in its approach to building, expanding the definition of "energy efficient" architecture to include energy and atmosphere, materials and resources, indoor environmental quality, site design and water efficiency.

It is difficult to pinpoint an exact "event" that changed the game, however, in 1992 the German corporation of Commerzbank announced a competition for a radically innovative skyscraper. It was to be the first and tallest ecological building. The programmatic requirements included: reduction in energy use, a specialized skin that would allow natural ventilation (unheard of in high rise construction), high levels of daylighting for occupant comfort, skygardens, and recycled greywater systems as well as care at ground level to integrate the building into the community surroundings. The winner of this limited competition was Sir Norman Foster and Associates—an acknowledged design superstar. The sustainable building game had just changed.

1995

401 Richmond Street

Toronto, ON
UrbanSpace Property Group

Established 10 years ago, the building's café/bistro, roof garden, quarterly newsletter and community bulletin boards promote a sense of community and cultural space. 401 Richmond received a surprisingly high rating by an environmental audit for a heritage building.

1996

The Conservation Co-op

Ottawa, ON
Cole and Associates

This 84 unit, four-storey apartment building committed to "housing that won't cost the earth" stays within stringent Ontario Ministry of Housing budget limits

Still, the majority of green buildings that were constructed in Canada during the 1990s remained small in scale, limited in budget and purposefully experimental in nature. The intention of the YMCA Environmental Learning Centre in St. Clements, Ontario, and the Boyne Conservation Centre, in Shelburne, Ontario, was to provide visitors with the experience of living with sustainable and natural systems. The more systems used the better. The motive in these buildings was public education.

The YMCA and Boyne sites include buildings that are dependent on passive ventilation, solar heating, daylighting, and feature specialized greywater treatment systems. They also use a new architectural language of sustainable materials that was not easily incorporated into mainstream practice at that time.

Slowly throughout the 1990s the green building movement started to gather steam. An increasing number of higher profile Canadian architectural firms took interest in the movement and began working with clients and engineering consultants to create more sustainable commercial and institutional projects.

The Green Building Challenge, an international gathering and competition for quality sustainable buildings, has provided a key opportunity to show off and learn about varying strategies and solutions to sustainable building issues from around the globe. The Challenge started in 1998, and has been running approximately every two years since. In 1998 the first three Canadian buildings submitted at the initial Vancouver based conference were: Revenue Canada Taxation Centre, Surrey, BC, Busby + Associates; Horton Secondary School, Nova Scotia; and the Conservation Co-op in Ottawa. They were chosen to identify environmental building solutions from a variety of building types. Where the exterior solar shades of Revenue Canada would signal a higher level of environmental concern to the public, both Horton and the Conservation Co-op maintained a normative appearance.

The 2000 Green Building Council (GBC) submissions included: the Angus Technopole, Montreal; the renovation

1996

Niagara Parks Butterfly Conservatory

Niagara, ON
Baird Sampson Neuert Architects

Includes a large tropical environment as well as an orientation theatre and interactive displays. Its integrated design includes a sophisticated computer control system which exploits natural thermo-cycling and evaporative cooling.

1996

YMCA Environmental Learning Centre

Kitchener-Waterloo, ON
Charles Simon Architect + Planner

Uses the Living Machine site waste water treatment system, designed by the Canadian Dr. John Todd, which uses biological processes to clean domestic sewage water

1996

BREEAM Canada and
BREEAM/Green Leaf™

Introduced by ECD Energy
and Environment Canada

to the William Farrell Telus Building, Vancouver, by Busby + Associates; and the York University Computer Science Building by Busby + Associates with Van Nostrand di Castri Architects. Both Angus and Telus were unique in that they involved significant reuse of existing buildings. This reflected a changed position about the environmental potential in the existing building stock and increased awareness about issues of limited natural resources and embodied energy in buildings and their components.

The York Computer Science building replaced a similar structure that was only ten years old. The planning of the new building was done to recognize the likelihood for significant planimetric changes in this type of building—so flexibility in the partition layout was a key sustainable notion in the design. Add to that the selection of buildings for the GBC "Poster Projects", including the Terasan Gas Operations Centre and Liu Centre for Asian Studies, and we begin to have a wide range of building uses and scales as well as high profile architectural and environmental engineering firms involved in promoting green building. A cursory look at the complexity of the projects and materials development, as well as the architectural "style" of the buildings, is quite telling. There has been a fast paced evolution of green buildings in a mere 5 to 10 years. Human comfort, occupant health, fresh air and environmental accountability in general, are becoming routine considerations in contemporary buildings. Sustainable "style" has entered mainstream architecture in a significant way.

The Kyoto Accord of 1997 focused the discussion of sustainable design on the production of greenhouses gases (mainly CO_2). The developed notion of sustainable building design expanded the area of concern in building design to include greenhouse gas emissions as a result of the burning of fuels associated with the heating and cooling of buildings; emissions from the production of building materials, their embodied energy, in addition to transportation costs, and resource depletion with respect to deforestation were also areas of concern. Canada has recently backed out of ratification of this agreement, which seeks to reduce greenhouse

1997
Boyne River Ecology Centre
Shelburne, ON
Sustainable Edge Ltd.

This renowned educational facility at the Toronto Board of Education's natural sciences school on the Niagara Escarpment features a 100% renewable energy supply and a sod roof

1997
Model National Energy Code of Canada for Houses and Model National Energy Code of Canada for Buildings are established

1997
Kyoto Accord

1997
The Commercial Building Incentive Program (CBIP) is created by Natural Resources Canada's Office of Energy Efficiency encouraging energy efficiency in the design of commercial and institutional buildings

1998
Offices for Revenue Canada Taxation
Surrey, BC
Busby Perkins+Will

This modern office building blends into the streetscape. A staggered floor plan maximizes natural lighting. Large and column-free floor plates allow for flexibility. The building envelope is designed with a continuous air-barrier, according to rain-screen principles.

gas emissions from 1990 levels by 7% from the period 2008 to 2012. Both the United States and Russia have still not signed the agreement.

During the mid 1990s the US Green Building Council was formed. A means to evaluate the relative "greenness" of buildings was sought. The British counterpart, BREEAM, had been developed, but did not suit American standards and codes. The LEED® assessment tool, launched in 1998, post Kyoto, was developed to: establish a common standard of measurement for green buildings; promote integrated, whole building design processes; stimulate environmental building and competition; make consumers more aware of the benefits; and, transform the building market. By awarding buildings bronze, silver, gold and platinum medals, based on their sustainable design qualifications, the tool was designed to respond to commercial marketing strategies.

This is not to say that all good sustainable buildings are LEED® medal driven. A number of highly successful Canadian examples have been motivated by the same principles that ground LEED®, but did not go the certification route. The ideals include a responsible attitude towards energy and resource use, natural ventilation strategies, sustainable site design, the benefits of daylighting as it connects to both indoor environmental quality as well as reduction in electrical consumption. The newest buildings featured on the coming pages show some of the main strategies that are now being used in commercial and institutional construction. They are outstanding mainstream architectural projects.

1999

Condominium at 77 Governors Road

Dundas, ON
Enermodal Engineering Ltd.

Focus is on high-quality construction and design, better ventilation, and is only 6 storeys high

2000

Locoshop
Angus, QC
Aedifica

A 2.5 hectare business park in east central Montreal.

Transformation of an historic industrial complex into a two-story high-tech industrial office mall

2000

Liu Centre for the Study
of Global Issues
University of British Columbia

Vancouver, BC
Stantec

An international policy and research centre, in a dramatic wooded site on the UBC campus.

First use of EcoSmart™
high volume ash concrete.

2000
Mountain Equipment Co-op Head Office

Vancouver, BC
Proscenium Architecture and Interiors Inc.

Incorporates a series of grass-roof
shifts in traditional building practices;
recycled building on a brownfield site;
materials were recycled throughout the
demolition and construction

2005
The Green Building Alliance
is established in Canada

2005
Project Green is launched
by the Government of
Canada, Moving forward
on Climate Change:
A Plan for Honouring our
Kyoto Commitment

2005
Stratus Vineyards becomes
the first LEED® certified project
in Ontario and the
first LEED® Canada project
to be certified

FUTURE DIRECTIONS AND NEEDS

Ian Chodikoff
OAA, MRAIC
Editor, *Canadian Architect Magazine*

Without a doubt, the architecture profession in Canada is aggressively pursuing projects that are environmentally sustainable. It is becoming increasingly commonplace to learn of projects that achieve sustainability benchmarks of excellence established by such programs as LEED-Canada. In the coming years, we can expect to find that our current preoccupation with producing architecture that is based on a checklist of basic sustainable design features will be replaced with a more holistic approach to sustainable thinking. Canada's architects have the potential to increase their momentum by approaching sustainable design that integrates a larger number of criteria resulting in greater improvements to the health of a given community through urban design and not only by individual works of architecture.

A decade ago, a handful of firms addressed issues of sustainability head-on. Today, expertise on sustainable architecture is nearly commonplace. Architects must now learn to become active brokers and broaden their thinking and scope of services when designing sustainable communities by increasing their ability to collaborate with allied design professionals such as scientific, legal and financial experts. They must also investigate opportunities to incorporate critical players that may include landscape architects, biologists and chemists directly into their practice. Including these specialists in the process of design will demonstrate that architects are not merely paying lip service to sustainable design but are preventing clichéd responses to good environmental practices. The result is a higher propensity to produce design excellence. By continuing to modify their practice's approach to extend beyond object-based and sculptural buildings, architects can tackle greater opportunities associated with buildings that are integrated within a sustainable community.

The next generation of work produced by Canada's best practitioners will reflect an increased proficiency in collaborating with lawyers, businessmen and politicians to overcome legal, financial and political roadblocks associated with producing architecture that is competitive in a global market. Architects must learn to assert themselves in the development process so that issues like technical and policy reforms, brownfield remediation, development charges, tax incentives

The Acqua and the Vento

Calgary, AB
Windmill Development Group

These projects are part of an innovative plan to form the Bridges Redevelopment Masterplanned Community on the site of an old hospital and laundry facility

Boreal Centre for Birds

Lesser Lake, AB
Manasc Isaac Architects

Without access to potable water, a sewer system and a gas supply, this project will feature a reduced dependency on traditional infrastructure

The Currents

Ottawa, ON
Windmill Development Group

Featuring clean green power usage, the Currents will also use innovative water, air, energy and waste management, and 'smart' building technologies

▾ Douglas Border Crossing Featuring
Geothermal Pump and Photovoltaics
Watercolour: Ron Love

Douglas Border Crossing

Surrey, BC
Bunting Coady

Features a geothermal
pump and building-integrated
photovoltaics which improve
the efficiency of the
mechanical system

(see above)

The Element Condo Building

Toronto, ON
Tridel

Featuring the innovative Deep
Lake Water Cooling system,
The Element Condo will draw
from a natural reservoir of
cool water in Lake Ontario,
reducing energy consumption

Government of Canada
Office Building

Charlettetown, PEI
Urbana and HOK

Hamilton Firehall

Richmond, BC
Johnston Davidson
Architecture and Planning Inc.

Powered by a geothermal
energy loop, the Hamilton
Firehall will save on municipal
costs for years to come

(see next spread)

The Living City Centre
The Living City Campus

9550 Pine Valley Dr
Woodbridge, ON

Edward Russell Architect

The Kortright Living City
Centre is currently being
expanded to serve as the
new sustainable centre for
the Toronto Region
Conservation Authority

and innovative financial instruments can overcome potential obstacles affecting the realization of a high-quality project. Effective planning on the part of architects requires that they collaborate with other specialists and consultants to improve the sustainability quotient of new developments that must remain attractive to politicians and developers—not to mention the interests of the public good. Without a doubt, this will result in not only a better quality of life for Canadians, but also in better planned communities with a higher quality of architecture.

Is this a tall order for architects? No. Sustainable design initiatives offer architects tremendous opportunities through successful collaborative efforts. One such firm is the Vancouver office of Busby Perkins+Will. These architects are aggressively developing intelligent and holistic strategies associated with broadening the practice of sustainable design through projects like The Acqua and The Vento in Calgary or the Dockside Lands development in Victoria. The Dockside Lands is a particularly strong example of how an architecture team can take a multi-pronged approach toward a sustainable program that is attractive to the developer, municipality and general public.

Designed to be a gateway community to downtown Victoria, Dockside is an 11.6 acre brownfield site located adjacent to the Upper Harbour and downtown, between the Johnson and Bay Street bridges. The site is currently owned by the City of Victoria. The design consortium is formed by Windmill Developments, VanCity, terence williams architect inc., Busby Perkins+Will, Keen Engineering, Aqua-Tex Scientific Consulting Ltd., BuildGreen Consulting and PWL Partnership Landscape Architects.

In October 2004, the City of Victoria issued a Request for Proposals (RFP) to redevelop the site with a range of stakeholders that would include one million square feet of mixed use and environmentally-sustainable developed buildings on a remediated site. Using the "Triple Bottom Line," Dockside addresses a series of concerns relating to ecological, social and economic performance guidelines designed to attract the interest and involvement of many public and private stakeholders. The financial backers for Dockside

Library and Classroom Building
Langara College

Vancouver, BC
Teeple Architects

Features natural stack ventilation

Morningside Heights
Public School

Scarborough, ON
BSN Architects

Maximizes green space with a courtyard system

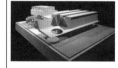

NRC Institute
for Fuel Cell Innovation

Vancouver, BC
Bunting Coady

The first of seven nodes in the Hydrogen Highway™ and includes an innovative use of fuel cell systems

Operations Centre, Gulf Islands
National Park Reserve

Sidney, BC
Larry McFarland Architects Ltd.

Minimizing dependence on outside sources of energy and services, ocean water will be circulated through floor tubing to cool the building in the summer, and existing materials and plantings will be incorporated into the new building and landscaping

◄ Hamilton Firehall Façade
▼ Firehall South Elevation

Pierre Elliot Trudeau
Federal Justice Building

Ottawa, ON
NORR architects and engineers,
Envision, the Hough Group

Through the integration of a
'green citizen program', the new
Federal Justice Building will promote
awareness of how occupants, visitors
and users can participate in the
success of its sustainable features

Poirier Aquatic Facility

Coquitlam, BC
Hughes Condon
Marler Architects

Innovative use of pool water
to reduce potable water
consumption for landscape
irrigation is one of the
sustainable features

The Residence

Guelph, ON
Skinner and Skinner
Architects Inc.

This will be the first project in
Canada built of autoclaved aerated
concrete, replacing typical wood
frame assembly with no waste,
non-polluting production

The Shaw House
for Seniors

Toronto, ON
Breathe Architects in joint
venture with Ian Trites Arcthitect

Sponsored by the Toronto
Atmospheric Fund (TAF),
this addition and renovation
aims to reduce greenhouse
gas emissions

are the Windmill Development Group out of Victoria and VanCity, a Vancouver-based credit union. As a developer, Windmill is recognized as a leader in green building design. VanCity has a strong reputation in British Columbia for its community efforts.

What makes Dockside unique is its integrative approach to sustainable design. Economic, environmental and social objectives overlap to form a holistic approach to development that will not only attempt to achieve its architectural goals, but contribute to a mixed-use community. This is attractive to consumers while benefitting the local community through job creation and economic diversification. The Integrated Design Process (IDP) allows each of the collaborators to flex their respective professional muscle to achieve a sustainable community that incorporates design excellence.

Collaboration is critical in an ambitious program like Dockside. With IDP, the client's role in the design process is increased and the architect becomes a team leader. The engineers and specialized consultants such as an energy specialist and a bio-climatic engineer will enter the process earlier than usual. With this methodology, the overall long-term operating costs are reduced and the design process is conducted much more efficiently. Daniel Pearl[1], an expert on the IDP process, notes that changes to the design are "relatively easy to make at the beginning of the process, but become increasingly difficult, expensive and even disruptive as the process unfolds."

According to the Dockside Lands website[2], the architecture firm of Busby Perkins+Will will attempt to use the IDP process for the whole site in order to develop "a holistic approach as the only way to enhance synergies between building systems, building scales and façades, landscapes, surrounding communities, activities and amenities, community health and well-being, transportation, economy, and relationship building." Using the IDP for the design of the entire site is critical for this project given the challenges associated with remediation, meeting the community's needs, and achieving the necessary density to make the project financially viable.

St. Joseph's Oratory

Montreal, QC
Jodoin Lamarre Pratte

Uses passive sustainable strategies such as green roofs and geothermal energy

Toronto Region Conservation Authority

Toronto, ON
Montgomery Sisam

Features include composting toilets and waterless urinals. Orientation and insulation will eliminate need for air-conditioning.

Vaughan Civic Centre

Toronto, ON
Kuwabara Payne McKenna Blumberg Architects

The new Vaughn Civic Centre will feature a green roof and an accompanying storm water retention system

The Water Centre

Calgary, AB
Manasc Isaac Architects Ltd.

The Water Centre will transform an industrial area into a livable part of the city

Whistler Public Library

Whistler, BC
Hughes Condon Marler Architects

This project features an innovative roof design made of local Hemlock wood

The development is demarcated by a series of ponds and natural water treatment systems that run through the middle of the site, connecting all of these diverse areas and providing outdoor green spaces. Dockside Village, located at the southernmost portion of the site will include a boutique hotel and residential, commercial, retail and live-work spaces. There will also be some light industrial spaces. The precinct will be anchored by a central plaza.

Small-scale marine industrial activity will continue to exist and be incorporated into the new development. To displace these functions would be counterproductive to the local economy and community fabric. The process of designing for sustainable communities must include issues such as job creation programs along with the health of local businesses. The project will also attempt to source local products and materials wherever possible. The nearer the manufacturer is to Docklands, the less amount of energy is required to transport the material to the job site. Thinking about urban design and local economic growth simultaneously will also allow the area to densify and permit infrastructure to efficiently service the development while reducing vehicle dependency. The density is targeted at two times ground coverage which is low relative to other cities in Canada.

Surrounding the Dockside Village, the architect team will design a series of townhouses with minimal setback to the street. Known as the Tyee Uplands Neighbourhood, this residential neighbourhood will consist of streets and courtyards with views through the site. One section of the development will step down across the garden apartments and face an internal greenway.

Dockside Wharf comprises the northernmost section of the site and will include a wharf with public access to the water, a small-scale retail plaza and waterfront developments. As a northern entry point to the site, the development will encourage access to the existing Galloping Goose Trail and a proposed Harbour Ferry Dock.

When designing a sustainable building, it is important to think about how stakeholders arrive at the site. Carpools, bicycles, and public transportation along with pedestrian access and ferries all factor into the Dockside development. Innovative alternative transportation strategies include a car share program with bio-diesel Smart Cars and Neighbourhood Electric Vehicles (NEV), as well as a mini-transit system. Where and how people work, shop and park their cars is increasingly relevant in planning sustainable communities.

Locating the architecture within the landscape is a high priority at Docklands and suggests an ecosystem as much as it suggests green architecture. The design team is developing on-site treatment of storm water runoff through bioswales while rainwater will be harvested for re-use. Since Victoria's raw sewage gets dumped into the Pacific Ocean, the architect team intends on treating 100% of all sewage produced onsite. Green roofs and rooftop green trellises, standard at Dockside, are emerging as a best practice as architects incorporate this strategy when designing for their "architectural ecosystem."

In addition to becoming increasingly proactive in formulating sustainable developments, architects are understanding the value of educating the public with good environmental practices. By communicating with the public, architects can shift market demands so that developers respond by increasing their ability to include sustainable design in their projects. Architects and their collaborators can learn a lot from the Dockside Lands. It remains to be seen how this development will evolve from thought to reality. Nevertheless, it is important to utilize the merits of an integrative design process that incorporates the skills of as many specialists as possible. Planning sustainable communities through a holistic and integrated design and development approach provides a tremendous opportunity for architects to emerge as team leaders and deliver design excellence as Canada's urban environment matures.

[1] see Daniel Pearl's article entitled "An Integrated Design Process (IDP)" in *Canadian Architect*, *vol. 49*, *no. 6*, June 2004, pp. 32-35.
[2] please visit the Dockside Lands site at http://www.docksidegreen.ca/sustainable_initiatives/

SUSTAINABLE BUILDING: A PRACTITIONER'S PERSPECTIVE ON FUTURE BEST PRACTICES

Peter Busby
FRAIC, MAIBC, AAA, OAA, AIA, LEED® A.P., BCID

Sustainable design is founded upon the recognition of the importance of meeting current needs without compromising the ability of future generations to meet their own needs. Rather than following conventional methodology, or simply addressing isolated environmental phenomena, to practice in a truly sustainable manner requires a holistic approach—careful consideration and analysis of all the environmental, social, and economic impact of alternative design solutions, and of their effects over the course of a building's life. The sustainable practitioner must be adept at identifying synergistic opportunities between natural processes and building design, and must work with an eye to the future, to ensure flexibility and adaptability to future uses and technologies.

Though sustainable design does take advantage of a number of cutting-edge technologies, it is fundamentally based on a series of simple, common sense principles. Many of these principles are predicated on maximizing a building's ability to take advantage of naturally occurring resources (solar energy, natural ventilation patterns, rainwater, and so on) while minimizing the amount of energy that must be expended in opposition to natural processes.

Sustainable design requires the cooperation and coordination of all the inherent disciplines, reliant upon the integration of a sustainable mandate early in the development process. While a truly sustainable design is, by definition, based on a unique and tailor-made approach, it is nonetheless possible to identify a number of criteria that are integral to ensuring that a project adheres to the triple bottom line of environmental, social and economic responsibility.

▾ Centre for Interactive
Research on Sustainability (CIRS)
Sample Floor Plan
Diagram: Busby Perkins+Will

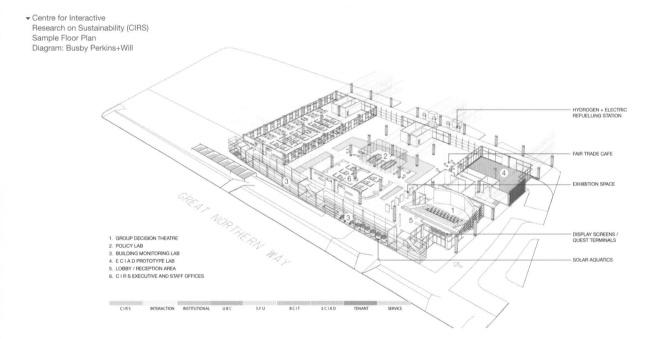

HYDROGEN + ELECTRIC
REFUELLING STATION

FAIR TRADE CAFE

EXHIBITION SPACE

DISPLAY SCREENS /
QUEST TERMINALS

SOLAR AQUATICS

1. GROUP DECISION THEATRE
2. POLICY LAB
3. BUILDING MONITORING LAB
4. E C I A D PROTOTYPE LAB
5. LOBBY / RECEPTION AREA
6. C I R S EXECUTIVE AND STAFF OFFICES

GREAT NORTHERN WAY

CIRS   INTERACTION   INSTITUTIONAL   UBC   SFU   BCIT   ECIAD   TENANT   SERVICE

1. The CIRS site is a remediated brownfield.

2. Adjacent industrial areas under redevelopment

3. Great Northern Way Campus (shared by UBC, SFU, BCIT, ECIAD)

4. Science World – public education and outreach

5. High density residential community

6. Live/work community

7. Industrial area under redevelopment to house South East False Creek Sustainable Neighbourhood and 2010 Olympic Athletes' Village

8. Transportation infrastructure: roadways (solid); future roadways (dashed); and Skytrain (dotted)

Diagram: Busby Perkins+Will

Criteria for Adherance to the Triple Bottom Line

Envelope Performance
Issues relating to optimal energy performance and interior/exterior exchange with the building envelope; incorporates design elements such as glazing selection, operable window orientation and passive solar shading; R30/R40 for walls and roofs in coastal zones and R40/R60 in more severe zones.

Building Orientation and Shaping
Building façades are treated individually according to the specific solar orientation, sunpath, prevailing wind directions and other climatic conditions of the site. Solar, shading and massing studies are conducted to determine the most appropriate building design and orientation for the site.

Natural Ventilation
Strategies to optimize natural systems for cooling and ventilating the building; these strategies are capable of minimizing or eliminating the need for mechanical systems including air conditioning, fans and ducts. Up to 30% of total energy savings come from effective natural ventilation strategies such as operable windows and atrium or skylight stack effects.

Thermal Massing
Strategies to optimize energy performance and thermal comfort while reducing the load on other energy systems. For example, a typical concrete building has sufficient thermal mass to release heat in winter or to absorb heat in summer. This principle requires the concrete structure to be exposed where possible, reducing interior finishes and avoiding suspended ceilings.

Technology Bridges
Advanced technology solutions that link two or more larger strategies to produce even greater energy benefits. These include features such as raised floor systems which are efficient for ventilation distribution and can be combined with thermal massing strategies. Other examples of sophisticated technological solutions include thermal chimneys and heat recovery ventilators.

Renewable Energy Technologies
High-tech strategies and technologies for on-site net energy production including wind turbines, photovoltaic panels, solar hot water and air systems, building integrated photovoltaics, biomass co-generation, and hydrogen fuel cells. These technologies are integrated into the site and building design, and used to generate energy on-location.

Cost Benefit Analyses
Individual building elements are analyzed and optimized for energy efficiency and capital investment. Cost is balanced against long-term performance to achieve state-of-the-art systems that have reasonable returns. This is not only applicable to large strategies but also includes the selection of high efficiency lighting fixtures and low energy LED screens.

Energy Budgeting
A method for programming and organizing the building in relation to performance and orientation criteria. It shapes the way the internal functions of the building are programmed to capture inherent efficiencies. For example, placing laboratories on the north face of a building allows for wasted radiant energy to create a heat buffer during cooler winter months.

Energy Modelling
A method for determining the overall energy consumption of the proposed building design. Preliminary energy modeling enables the team to compare and contrast systems and technologies, resulting in high performance and energy efficient building design.

Life-cycle Assessment of Building Material Assemblies
A process of examining the building material assemblies and comparing their up and down stream impacts on the environment with regard to emissions to air and water, solid waste generation, embodied energy, and primary energy use.

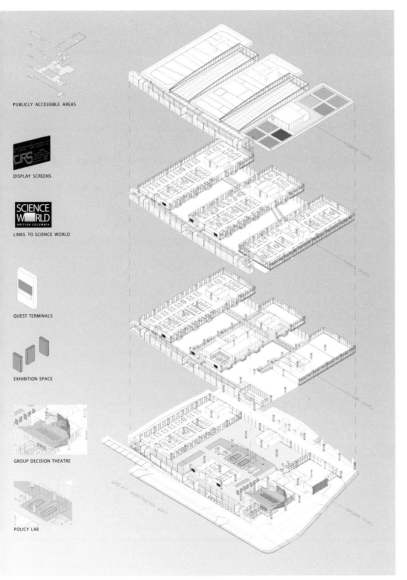

PUBLICLY ACCESSIBLE AREAS

DISPLAY SCREENS

LINKS TO SCIENCE WORLD

QUEST TERMINALS

EXHIBITION SPACE

GROUP DECISION THEATRE

POLICY LAB

▲ CIRS Entrance View
  Graphic: Busby Perkins+Will

◀ Floorplan Showing Public Outreach Initiatives
  Graphic: Busby Perkins+Will

These criteria offer an oversight of how the development of sustainable design has been applied to building projects in Canada. One particular project, the multi-institutional Centre for Interactive Research on Sustainability (CIRS), offers a glimpse of what lies ahead for the sustainable design movement in Canada. The project is destined to become one of, if not the most, sustainable structures in North America— encouraging and accelerating the adoption of sustainable building technologies and urban development practices.

Located on a former brownfield site in downtown Vancouver, the Busby Perkins+Will designed CIRS is aspiring to perfect the aforementioned systems and technologies; a definitive example of innovation and high performance green building in North America. The CIRS project is designed to function as a state-of-the-art 'living-lab' in which researchers from leading academic institutions can perform interactive research on, and assessment of, current and future building systems and technologies. Partners from private and public sectors will share the facility, working with CIRS researchers to ensure that the conducted research is connected to real world needs of the community, industry and policy makers—bringing together satellite campuses from the University of British Columbia, Simon Fraser University, the Emily Carr Institute of Design, and the British Columbia Institute of Technology. The

outcome of research, product and policy development manifested by CIRS will play a fundamental role in accelerating the path to sustainability in Canada and around the globe.

This exciting project is a culmination of the early efforts of pioneering organizations in the fields of architecture, engineering, education and various levels of government. These organizations have played a significant role in producing a portfolio of high performance buildings in Canada. With the creation of the Canada Green Building Council (CGBC), a formalized movement and industry has spawned, bringing the green design agenda to the forefront of building design.

Federal and provincial commitments are gaining momentum while municipalities and educational bodies are leading the cause with the construction of green building facilities and the development of green building and procurement guidelines. The Canadian green building movement has attained sufficient critical mass to move the industry from the fringe into mainstream practice, allowing for significant progress in the development of green buildings and sustainable design.

Sustainable projects, like CIRS, integrate and intertwine economic, environmental, and social objectives into one holistic objective, providing payback to developers, the environment, and end users for decades to come.

POLICY LAB

◄ Atrium featuring bridges
  and lightshelves
  Graphic: Busby Perkins+Will

▼ CIRS will be a holistic building,
  using feedback from each
  of the building's systems to
  improve overall performance
  Graphics: Busby Perkins+Will

FEATURED
PROJECTS

COMMERCIAL
COMMUNITY PLANNING
EDUCATIONAL
INSTITUTIONAL
RESIDENTIAL

CDP CAPITAL CENTRE
E'TERRA INN
ELECTRONIC ARTS
FREYBE GOURMET FOODS
THE GLADSTONE HOTEL
JACKSON-TRIGGS NIAGARA ESTATE WINERY
THE ROBERTSON BUILDING
MICROSOFT CANADA HEADQUARTERS
MOUNTAIN EQUIPMENT CO-OP STORE
SMITH CARTER OFFICE SC3
THE TERRACE BUILDING
TOHU: CHAPITEAU DES ARTS DU CIRQUE

TORONTO WATERFRONT REVITALIZATION
ALLOWAY RECEPTION CENTRE
COMMUNITY HEALTH AND WELLNESS CAMPUS
DOCKSIDE GREEN
DOWNSVIEW PARK MASTERPLAN
GREEN ENERGY BENNY FARM
HUMBER BAY SHORES WATERFRONT PARK
LASALLE PARK
REFORD GARDENS VISITOR CENTRE
REGENT PARK
TORONTO BOTANICAL GARDEN
UNIVERSITY OF ONTARIO INSTITUTE OF TECHNOLOGY

TERRENCE DONNELLY CENTRE FOR CELLULAR AND BIOMOLECULAR RESEARCH
BEAMISH-MUNRO HALL INTEGRATED LEARNING CENTRE
BURNABY MOUNTAIN SECONDARY SCHOOL
NICOLA VALLEY INSTITUTE OF TECHNOLOGY
RED RIVER COLLEGE PRINCESS STREET CAMPUS
SIR SANDFORD FLEMING COLLEGE
UNIVERSITY OF BRITISH COLUMBIA LIFE SCIENCES CENTRE
UNIVERSITY OF GUELPH-HUMBER
UNIVERSITÉ DU QUÉBEC À MONTRÉAL BIOLOGICAL SCIENCES PAVILION
YORK UNIVERSITY COMPUTER SCIENCE BUILDING

BC CANCER RESEARCH CENTRE
CANMORE CIVIC CENTRE
ENERGY CENTRE BEDFORD INSTITUTE OF OCEANOGRAPHY
YMCA ENVIRONMENTAL LEARNING CENTRE
GLENEAGLES COMMUNITY CENTRE
HAR-EL SYNAGOGUE
RICHMOND CITY HALL
SPRING CREEK FIREHALL
ST. JOHN AMBULANCE PROVINCIAL HEADQUARTERS
THUNDER BAY REGIONAL HEALTH SCIENCES CENTRE
TORONTO MILITARY FAMILY RESOURCE CENTRE

SUSTAINABLE CONDO
328 EUCLID AVENUE
GASPER HOUSE
ISLAND HOUSE
PORT PERRY HOUSE
QUAST STRAW BALE HOME
R40 STRAW BALE HOUSE
SUMMER HOUSE
THE MILL
UNIVERSITY OF TORONTO AT MISSISSAUGA ERINDALE HALL
WILSON HOUSE

COMMERCIAL
CASE STUDY AND FEATURED PROJECTS

During the 1970s and 1980s Canada was recognized for its leadership in addressing energy-saving and building performance issues through the R2000 and C2000 construction programs. The economic recession that dampened the real estate market, however, also dampened innovation during the 1990s. The period after the Millennium (2000-2005) is characterized by a renewed commitment to sustainability by business.

Over the last five years, landmark retail, office and entertainment projects have been built across the country creating a "tipping point" in the commercial buildings sector.

All of the buildings featured on the following pages have been driven by visionary leadership. The case study project of the CDP Capital Centre in downtown Montreal is a tour de force of sustainable design practice, revitalizing a whole "quartier" in downtown Montreal. The city's torn urban fabric has been repaired and the area has undergone a cultural and economic renaissance.

Mountain Equipment Co-op has systematically lived up to sustainability principles in their Montréal, Winnipeg, Toronto, Ottawa and Vancouver locations. They have used sustainable design as a strategic differentiation for the company.

Similarly, head offices for Microsoft and Electronic Arts attract and retain highly skilled and specialized staff in a competitive hiring marketplace through sustainable building.

Smaller projects such as the Freybe Gourmet Foods, E'Terra Inn, The Robertson Building and Gladstone Hotel demonstrate a personal commitment by some of the country's leading entrepreneurs to incorporate sustainable design features in their projects. These projects use a holistic approach to create humane developments. The Gladstone Hotel, for example, has incorporated the energy of the local arts community, transforming a dilapidated building into a sustainably designed boutique hotel.

Social innovation can also be found in the Tohu project, a landmark redevelopment spearheaded by the Cirque du Soleil. This former brownfield site has had its ecosystem restored and has been integrated into the economy of the local suburban region of Montreal.

Sustainable design in commercial building has the potential to generate and foster long-term economic benefit for communities and businesses. These projects allow us to imagine a time when growth and development will become re-associated with positive values.

◄◄ CDP Capital Building
Fritted Glass Detail
Photo: Alain Laforest

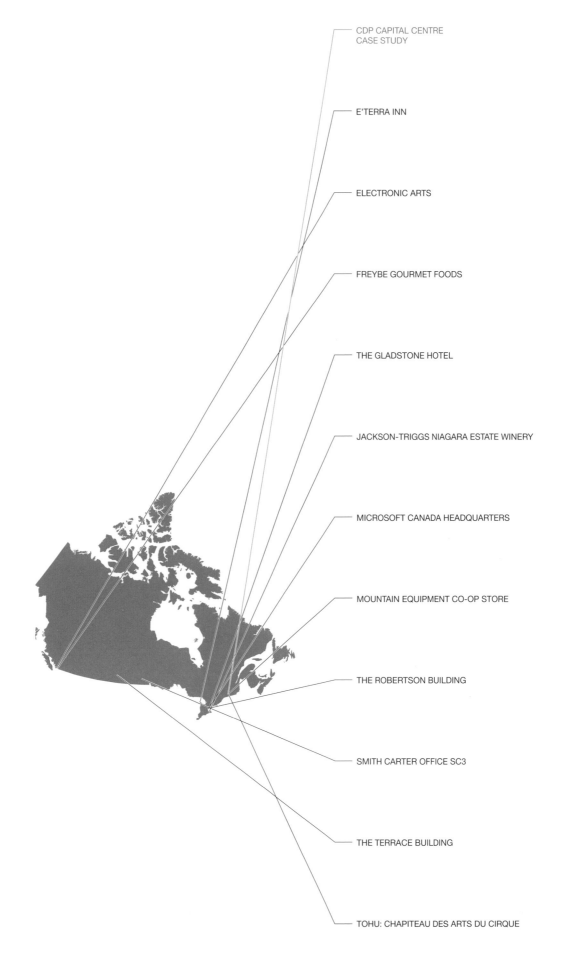

CDP CAPITAL CENTRE
CASE STUDY

E'TERRA INN

ELECTRONIC ARTS

FREYBE GOURMET FOODS

THE GLADSTONE HOTEL

JACKSON-TRIGGS NIAGARA ESTATE WINERY

MICROSOFT CANADA HEADQUARTERS

MOUNTAIN EQUIPMENT CO-OP STORE

THE ROBERTSON BUILDING

SMITH CARTER OFFICE SC3

THE TERRACE BUILDING

TOHU: CHAPITEAU DES ARTS DU CIRQUE

CLIENT Société immobilière Camont / SITQ ARCHITECTURAL Le consortium Gauthier, Daoust Lestage inc., Faucher Aubertin Brodeur Gauthier - Lemay et Associés STRUCTURAL Le consortium Pasquin St-Jean - Saia Deslauriers Kadanoff - Consultants S.M. MECHANICAL/ELECTRICAL Le consortium Bouthillette Parizeau et Associés inc., Dupras Ledoux ingénieurs, Groupe HBA BUILDER Décarel-Verreault co-entreprise

COMMERCIAL CASE STUDY

CDP CAPITAL CENTRE

MONTREAL, QUEBEC, 2003

Located in the heart of the Quartier International de Montréal, the CDP Capital Centre is part of a major urban renewal operation. Home to the fund managers Caisse de Dépôt et Placement du Québec, it brings together all of the company's Montreal personnel. Built for the most part directly above a sunken expressway and a subway line, this horizontal sky-scraper successfully meets the technical challenge of weaving back the urban fabric and provides 726,000 sq. ft. of office and commercial space.

The building encompasses two city blocks connected by a multi-story atrium underneath which traffic still flows. Called the Parquet, the atrium is an immense gathering place. The CDP Capital Centre showcases numerous innovations in the fields of bio-climatic and energy efficiency, which put it in the forefront of new sustainable building.

Highlights

■ A conventional curtain wall system with an independent second layer of glazing on the exterior serves as a neutralizing wall. The space between these two layers is mechanically ventilated with warm or cool air. Motorized shades installed in the cavity control solar gains. ■ Vent units are integrated into the building's double skin. When a window is opened by the user, a signal is sent to the control system that interrupts the mechanical ventilation in the room to let natural ventilation take over. ■ Shades are pulled up or down automatically by a photometric sensor that detects the intensity of daylight for each elevation. The user can bypass this automated system to adjust the shade to their need. ■ Heat gains are recuperated by mechanical transfer and serve as the main heating source. ■ Office partitions are reusable, creating greater flexibility thereby reducing demolition waste. ■ Natural light penetration is allowed by narrower floor plates, interior atriums with skylights, glass office partitions and open work stations.

The Site

Before anything could be built above it, a 30-metre stretch of the sunken expressway had to be covered. Within the limited height available, U-shaped pre-stressed concrete beams span over the five lanes and meet all the requirements of extreme durability, fire-rating and insulation while providing a technical crawl space for the restaurant above.

The choice of a steel structure for the entire building was based on weight comparison. The lighter weight of steel is comparable to the original 12 metre deep backfill that was removed from the top of the underground expressway's shell to create the basement floors.

To carry the weight of the new building erected above the sunken expressway off to the sides, oversize transfer beams were made up of WWF steel members. Each one weighs 55 metric tons. The spacing of these 5.4 metre high and 30 metre long joists is wide enough to allow appropriate use of that space. Their installation was done at night and required the closing of the expressway.

Powerful ventilation equipment was required to exhaust the carbon monoxide generated by the expressway and the toxic fumes from a potential fire. A 300,000 CFM fan has been installed in the building and brings the polluted air all the way out at the roof level, eleven stories above ground.

The Parquet

To support the roof of the main common area known as the Parquet, unique and gigantic tree-like structures were created out of tubular steel members with cast iron connections, a first in Canada. They also carry the weight and the wind-loads of a 9-story tall curtain wall that runs east-west across the building and along the sun-filled Parquet.

▲ Sectional Drawing
Drawing: Le consortium Gauthier,
Daoust Lestage inc. - Faucher
Aubertin Brodeur Gauthier - Lemay
et Associés

◀ Fritted Glass
Photo: Alain Laforest

"When I am working on a problem I never think about beauty. I only think about how to solve the problem. But when I have finished, if the solution is not beautiful, I know it is wrong."
BUCKMINSTER FULLER

▾ Trading Room
▾ Site Overview
Photos: Alain Laforest

To help regulate the indoor temperature of this magnificent space, fritted glass was used and the values that govern the management of the Caisse were inscribed on the glass to create an unusual fritting pattern. Its higher shading coefficient prevents overheating caused by excessive sunlight penetration without blocking the view towards Old Montréal.

The Building's Skin

Installed for the first time in Quebec, the neutralizing wall is innovative not only in its principle but also in its composition. It is made up of a conventional curtain wall system doubled with an independent second layer of glazing on the exterior. The space between these two layers is mechanically ventilated with warm or cool air. Motorized shades installed in the cavity control solar gains.

These shades are pulled up or down automatically by a photometric sensor that detects the intensity of daylight for each elevation. The user retains the ability to bypass this automated system to adjust the shade to his or her need. The goal to provide individual control to the user over his or her direct environment, be it lighting, heating or air conditioning is also reflected in the closed offices' motorized shades and vent windows. The shades also contribute to controlling glare.

The most important innovation lies in the integration of vent units into the building's double skin. When a window is opened by the user, a signal is sent to the control system that interrupts the mechanical ventilation in the room to let natural ventilation take over.

This system's higher energy efficiency allows a higher percentage of fenestration, which in turn increases the potential penetration of natural light in the building and the visual contact with the exterior.

Ventilation

The building's main heating source is the recuperation of its own internal heat gains generated by lighting equipment, computers, electrical equipment and the occupants. The excess heat in one location is transferred mechanically to cooler areas of the building. Furthermore, the atriums can be used to funnel out excessive warm air during the summer months or retain it in the winter. The raised floors conceal the electrical components throughout the building and the adjustable openings provide a more efficient way to distribute fresh air in office space. This system, along with the reusable partitions, allows greater flexibility in office layout reconfiguration, therefore producing less demolition waste.

Lighting

Increased natural light penetration throughout the building was also facilitated by narrower floor plates that never exceeded 15m in depth and by the creation of interior atriums with skylights. As opposed to a traditional office floor layout, 65% of the work stations are open and defined by low partitions, while the remaining 35% are closed offices with mostly glass partitions that do not prevent natural light from reaching the core of the floor plates. This configuration also has the advantage of allowing views to the exterior for all employees. This optimal use of natural light reduces the direct costs in energy consumption associated with artificial lighting. The first two peripheral rows of light fixtures on each floor are turned on or off by a photometric sensor that detects the intensity of exterior light.

Overall, this office building integrates technological and architectural innovations that respond to the site conditions but that are also oriented towards the comfort of the occupants (i.e. visual, acoustical, functional and psychological comfort), therefore improving productivity and creating a healthier environment. The thermal simulations done by the engineers have demonstrated that the integration of these innovative features considerably reduces the energy demand of the office building.

The bioclimatic approach to user comfort goes beyond the construction techniques of the building to encompass environmental aspects such as an emphasis on sustainable development, a renewed landscape structure and the creation of major networks of urban connections, linking the building to its surroundings.

Awards

2004

■ Laureate: Prix Orange – Aménagement by Sauvons Montréal, Quartier international de Montréal ■ Laureate: Award for Excellence, Canadian Institute of Steel Construction – Category Coup de cœur du jury (for CDP Capital Centre Atrium) ■ Laureate: Montreal Award – Institute of Design Montreal – Architecture Category ■ Laureate: Grand prize – Quebec Consulting Engineering Association – Building Category

2003

■ Gold Award: National Post Design Exchange – Category Interiors ■ Technical Innovation Award, The Royal Architectural Institute of Canada (RAIC)

▾ Entrance Upon Arrival
▸ Looking out onto Georgian Bay
▸ Mechanical Room Components
  Photo: Rob Cotton

E'TERRA INN
TOBERMORY, ONTARIO, 2005

Built directly into the Niagara escarpment on Georgian Bay, this 750m² "eco-lodge" offers first class luxury through a holistic design approach. The owner, Laurie Adams, was personally committed to achieving a high level of sustainability in every detail of the project, with a goal of promoting health and well-being through the benefits of the earth.

Featuring six guest rooms, of which four have lofts, the Inn is also equipped with a small boardroom for executive meetings, library, sauna, natural spa and a wine cellar, which is built into the bedrock to keep it naturally cool. An indoor waterfall is a dominant feature and flows down a six-foot by twelve-foot block of limestone. The design features a high-performance envelope, radiant heating, natural cooling, concrete "earth tube" technology to temper make-up air, rainwater harvesting and on-site waste-water bio-filtration. Local materials were selected, and suppliers were chosen who were committed to issues of sustainability. Domestic hot water is heated by a 20m² roof-mounted solar heating system and supplemented by the high efficiency space heating boilers. No permanent irrigation system was installed, but rather drought resistant, native and adapted vegetation was utilized for landscaping. The intelligent, energy-efficient lighting design comprises fluorescent, compact fluorescent and LED fixtures. Renewable technologies were also included in the plans. These consist of the solar water heating system and a number of high efficiency wood burning devices. The building has no need for air conditioning.

Highlights

■ Low VOC products help to promote a healthy indoor environment. ■ Insulation is provided by high R-value wall and roof assemblies and high performance double-glazed windows with a low-e coating and argon gas fill. ■ Temperature is controlled by radiant heating and high efficiency wood burning equipment. Natural cooling rather than air conditioning is enforced with high efficiency ceiling fans. Kitchen make-up air is drawn through concrete earth tubes to normalize supply temperature. ■ Energy efficient lighting design uses fluorescent and LED fixtures. Lighting Power Density is less than 10W/m². ■ Hot water is provided by a solar-thermal domestic hot water heater with high-efficiency propane back-up. A non-potable system is in place for toilets, clothes washing and heat rejection from water-cooled kitchen appliances. ■ Drought resistant vegetation for landscaping eliminates the need for irrigation. ■ LEED® Gold, certified by the CaGBC

Team

OWNER Laurie Adams INITIAL DESIGN Levit Goodman Architects FINAL DESIGN/CONSTRUCTION Grant Diemert Architects STRUCTURAL Frank St. Clair Engineering MECHANICAL/ELECTRICAL Enermodal Engineering SUSTAINABLE & LEED CONSULTANT Enermodal Engineering CIVIL Conestoga Rovers & Associates BUILDER Bruce Mallard Contractors GENERAL CONTRACTOR Laurie Adams

▾ Interior Light Shelf
▸ Exterior Light Shelf
Photos: Nic Lehoux

ELECTRONIC ARTS

BURNABY, BRITISH COLUMBIA, 2005

Musson Cattell Mackey Partnership designed the Electronic Arts headquarters building in Burnaby, BC in 1999 and Phase I has been occupied for about five years. Phases II and III have been advanced and Phase II is in construction. All of these facilities incorporate many state-of-the-art green building features. Phase I has an access floor throughout, high ceilings and deep daylight penetration with external shading devices. Phase II will have radiant cooling with associated high performance energy efficient mechanical systems. It also incorporates storm water management that comprises detention on site and a constructed wetland. Additionally, the Phase II studio and Motion Capture buildings will have green roofs with extensive and intensive planting. Phase II and III both are targeting LEED® Silver levels of environmental performance.

Electronic Arts' soccer field—popular with employees—was replaced atop a massive underground parking structure (644 stalls) using artificial turf. The studio has an outdoor staff area on the roof with trees, shrubs and seating areas; the Motion Capture Studio (a separate building) has an extensive green roof with low maintenance planting. Arrangements are underway for a monitoring program with BCIT to advance green roof technology.

Highlights

■ Reduced heat island effect has been achieved by placing 50% of parking underground, and utilizing extensive and intensive green roofs. ■ Reduced light pollution includes no direct beam illumination leaving the site. ■ Storm water management includes detention and treatment in constructed wetland, and is limited to 50% of the two year existing runoff. ■ A massive detention tank and a constructed wetland area supports indigenous flora and fauna in a buffer zone between the development and the street. ■ There is a 50% reduction in potable water use through water efficient fixtures and landscaping. ■ A high-performance building envelope and mechanical system achieve more than 25% reduction from Model National Energy Code. ■ External shading devices, light shelves and use of daylighting reduce energy consumption. Daylight reaches 90% of occupied spaces. ■ Over 90% construction waste is diverted from landfill. This is achieved through recycled content materials and maximum use of local/regional materials. ■ Indoor environmental quality is achieved through low VOC limits for adhesives, sealants, paints, carpet, wood and agrifibre products.

Team

CLIENT Electronic Arts (Canada) Inc.
ARCHITECTS Musson Cattell Mackey Partnership

▶ Water Management
  Diagram: Cedric Burgers

▼ Interior Cleaning
▼ South West Exterior
  Photos: Nic Lehoux

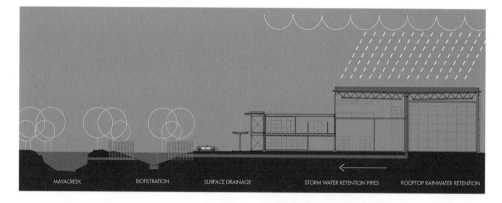

MAYACREEK   BIOFILTRATION   SURFACE DRAINAGE   STORM WATER RETENTION PIPES   ROOFTOP RAINWATER RETENTION

FREYBE GOURMET FOODS
LANGLEY, BRITISH COLUMBIA, 2001

Freybe required a larger, more efficient facility to meet increased consumer demands for their internationally award winning gourmet foods. Open to developing an innovative approach to design and construction, Freybe recognized that conventional methods did not address quality and environmental issues. The most significant benefit of the design process is that the project was built despite the Township of Langley's apprehension towards meat processing facilities. By proving that the facility could set a precedent for low environmental impact, the Township was won over.

The client's objectives and mission statement, centred on the motto "people, nature, tradition, technology", had to fit the budgetary constraints, but more importantly, it had to fit the primary objectives. These consisted of environmental sustainability, flexibility of structure, product safety and compliance with the Canadian Food Inspection Agency regulations.

The sustainability objectives were executed for the benefit of the environment and the community. Employees are very appreciative of the care and attention that went into the design and execution of the project created to enhance their work environment. There has been a significant positive improvement in morale, efficiency employee happiness and retention.

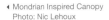
◄ Mondrian Inspired Canopy
Photo: Nic Lehoux

"Always design a thing by considering it in its next larger context—a chair in a room, a room in a house, a house in an environment, an environment in a city plan."

ELIEL SAARINEN

Highlights

■ Smoke generated for product enhancement is based upon technology that does not release any contaminant or odour into the atmosphere. ■ Organic materials are separated from wastewater, treated and used as a component for fertilizers. ■ A framework of structural steel for columns and beams was developed to address flexibility for future expansion and recycling. ■ A considerably more costly ammonia based system was chosen over the alternative Freon system for its greater energy efficiency and human and environmental safety. ■ The property borders a salmon-bearing creek: an extensive biofiltration system slowly releases storm water into the creek. ■ Smoke generated from the production process is recycled, eliminating all odour and the use of after burners. ■ The layout, energy systems, equipment and use of water are constantly being adjusted to ensure maximum efficiency. This process is made possible by the open plan and flexible construction.

Team

CLIENT Freybe Gourmet Foods Ltd.
ARCHITECT Robert Burgers Architects Inc.
INTERIORS MBI Interiors STRUCTURAL C.A. Boom Engineering Ltd. MECHANICAL Benlen Engineering Ltd. ELECTRICAL Mahanti/Chu Engineering Ltd. LANDSCAPE Moriarty Condon Landscape Architects
GEOTECHNICAL Golder & Associates
ENVIRONMENTAL Golder & Associates
CIVIL Hub Engineering

‣ Exterior Circa 1900
▾ Exterior Circa 1950
‣ Room 314
‣ Gargoyle
‣ Room 404
‣ Room 314
   Photos: Cat O'Neil

THE GLADSTONE HOTEL

TORONTO, ONTARIO, 2005

The Gladstone Hotel is the oldest continuously operating hotel in Toronto. Architect George Miller built the Gladstone in 1889. Owned by the Zeidler family, the important role that the building plays in the Parkdale neighbourhood and artistic life is reflective of their feeling of responsibility to the community.

The Gladstone has 51 hotel rooms and three bars: The Melody Bar, The Art Bar and The Gladstone Ballroom. From cabaret performances to film screenings, book launches to wedding parties, the Gladstone Hotel hosts events for a vast range of artists and community groups.

The Gladstone renovations respect the architectural history of the building, and include an application of the principles of sustainability, eco-restoration and heritage preservation. An extensive green roof, photovoltaics, eco-efficient lighting and water use technology are merely a few of the elements that are incorporated in the retrofit.

"Old ideas can sometimes
use new buildings.
New ideas must use
old buildings."
JANE JACOBS

Highlights

■ Eco-restorative features include efficient HVAC systems, photo-sensitive light fixtures, low flow water features, and compact florescent lights. ■ Historically replicated windows are equipped with new thermal panes. ■ Sunshades are used to control passive solar gain on the south and west sides of the hotel and all windows are operable to promote cross breezes in the summer.

■ An extensive green roof is planned for part of the Gladstone roof in 2006. ■ A green procurement policy serves to direct purchases for cleaning agents used throughout the bar and hotel, administrative supplies, and washroom supplies. ■ A new line of biodegradable take-out food containers and cutlery is being used at the Gladstone Hotel kitchen.

Team

CLIENT Zeidler ARCHITECTS Zeidler Partnership Architects MECHANICAL E.C.E. Group ELECTRICAL E.C.E. Group STRUCTURAL Jiri Tichy Design Ltd. CONSTRUCTION MANAGEMENT Maher Construction Inc.

◄ South Elevation
  Photo: Eduard Hueber, Arch Photo New York
▼ Fermentation Cellar
  Photo: Peter Sellar, KLIK

JACKSON-TRIGGS NIAGARA ESTATE WINERY

NIAGARA-ON-THE-LAKE, ONTARIO, 2001

Nestled in the bucolic Niagara wine region of southern Ontario, the Jackson-Triggs Niagara Estate Winery is situated to maximize the arable vineyard area and to benefit from the dense greenery on the Two Mile Creek edge. The extended horizontal form is sited parallel to the Niagara Escarpment. The raison d'etre for wine making in the region, is essentially the flow of mild air from Lake Ontario recirculating off the Escarpment and back towards the lake. The building footprint is minimized by locating barrel cellars, storage and warehouse facilities in the basement level. Mechanical systems use one cooling plant that provides both air-conditioning and process cooling to respond to varying seasonal requirements.

The linear plan is intersected by a large, double-height Great Hall, which acts as both the link and the buffer between public and production areas. The north and south openings of the Great Hall are equipped with industrial sliding doors to create a convertible open space that can open up to the vineyard to take advantage of the relatively temperate Niagara climate. The production spaces are organized to use gravity flow in the winemaking process. Storage spaces are located in the cave-like basement, where the heat sink effect of the surrounding earth maintains a stable, cool and humid environment.

▼ Barrel Cellar
Photo: Peter Sellar, KLIK

Highlights

■ A design charette was conducted to weigh green design versus business issues and to establish an integrated design process. ■ An east/west oriented building with a five to one floor plate ratio maximizes south facing passive solar gain and a five metre roof overhang on the south-west and east façades minimizes direct solar heat gain. ■ Natural ventilation is maximized with operable windows and large sliding doors, reducing reliance on building heating and cooling systems. ■ Maximum use of equipment for dual purposes minimizes the use of embodied energy; e.g. dual use of refrigeration equipment for process cooling of wine storage tanks and for chilled water for HVAC equipment. ■ Radiant floor heating uses concrete mass for storage thermal flywheel effect, and air-to-air heat exchangers pre-heat fresh air for the building. ■ Source separation of sanitary waste streams minimizes the amount of treatment of wine effluent. A storm water collection system discharges to "soak away" pits. ■ Use of recycled and natural materials as exterior cladding includes cement board siding, and overburden Owen Sound strata stone in rubble walls.

Team

CLIENT Vincor International Inc. ARCHITECTS Kuwabara Payne McKenna Blumberg Architects STRUCTURAL Blackwell Engineering MECHANICAL Keen Engineering ELECTRICAL Carinci Burt Rogers LANDSCAPE Janet Rosenberg & Associates CONTRACTOR Merit Contractors of Niagara

▸ Front Exterior
▸ Rooftop Garden
  Photo: Courtesy
  of Urbanspace
  Property Group

THE ROBERTSON BUILDING

TORONTO, ONTARIO, 2002

Built in the early 1900s, The Robertson building was designed by the local firm Denison and Stephenson architects, and served as a factory/warehouse in downtown Toronto selling plumbing fittings and fixtures. Restored by Zeidler Partnership Architects in 2002, it is now home to a community of businesses, entrepreneurs and non-governmental organizations. It is also the home of The 215 Centre for Social Innovation, a group of 15 organizations that work to catalyze, inform and support innovations that advance the social, cultural, environmental and economic well-being of Canadians.

An innovative example of eco-sustainable restoration, this project features a 26 metre biowall (green plant wall) designed by Alan Darlington of Air Quality Solutions, which graces the lobby while removing polluted air from the indoor environment. A glassed atrium and wooden roof deck provide access to a fabulous city skyline view and overlook a 4,000 sq. ft. extensive green roof. Perennial native Ontario species have been planted in the garden which add biodiversity to the urban environment.

Highlights

■ The biowall is a vertical hydroponic green wall containing a full range of plants that were specifically selected for use in this system. The biowall improves the quality of the indoor environment, reduces the energy demand of the building and improves the well-being of the occupants. ■ The 4,000 sq. ft. green roof is supported by over 20 native Ontario perennial species. Improving the longevity of the roof membrane, it also improves building energy and storm water performance, and reduces urban heat island effect and air pollution. ■ Access to the glass atrium and wooden viewing deck provides the tenants with added social recreational amenity space where peaceful views of green plants and the city skyline can be enjoyed both day and night. ■ It is predicted that the environmental benefits of the building renovations will translate into tenant satisfaction and transfer into lengthy leasing tenures.

Team

CLIENT Zeidler DEVELOPERS Urban Space Property Group ARCHITECTS Zeidler Partnership Architects MECHANICAL E.C.E. Group-division of CRA Ltd. ELECTRICAL E. C.E. Group STRUCTURAL RWB Engineering Ltd. CONSTRUCTION MANAGEMENT Dalton Construction GREEN ROOF Perennial Gardens, Toronto

▾ Sunshades on Southeast Façade
▸ Lobby Reception Area
▸ Hallway
  Photos: Ben Rahn - Design Archive

MICROSOFT CANADA HEADQUARTERS

MISSISSAUGA, ONTARIO, 2002

The Microsoft Canada Headquarters in Mississauga incorporates state-of-the-art technology and workplace design and includes a fitness centre and landscaped courtyard. The facility was designed specifically to suit the unique requirements of Microsoft Canada, with the primary vision of creating a preferred workplace environment for its employees at a comparable cost to standard market office buildings.

This project was conceived to accommodate growth and corporate consolidation within a single signature building. The design brief for the new national headquarters emphasizes a practical approach to the creation of a building that expresses an elegant and humane technological image within the surrounding context. It is an office building approached as a series of integrated systems; a flexible machine, which can act as a supportive stage for the changing requirements of the contemporary workspace. The resulting building is light and airy, with unusually high ceilings, enhanced views and more natural light than conventional office buildings. Its simple modern approach achieves distinctiveness through the clarity of elements and the elegant expression of functional needs.

Highlights

■ Sunshades on the exterior southeast façade reduce glare and heat gain during summer months. ■ The exterior envelope produces minimum glare for computer screens and employees while maximizing energy efficiency. Interior light shelves and perimeter daylighting control are combined with floor to ceiling exterior glazing. ■ Operating costs are approximately 50% of those of a typical commercial office building due in part to such features as 'free cooling' controlled by an advanced Web-controlled building automation system. ■ A raised floor technology platform supports state-of-the-art mechanical, electrical and data systems—allowing individuals to adjust their working environment to their own requirements. ■ Exposed reflective concrete ceilings work together with non-glare indirect lighting, exterior sunshades and interior light shelves to provide a glare-free environment full of natural light. ■ The building creates quality pedestrian scale spaces around its edges by recessing the ground floor. This provides pedestrian comfort to visitors and occupants in all seasons. ■ Artificial lighting is automatically switched off when natural light levels permit.

Team

CLIENT Microsoft Canada DESIGN ARCHITECTS Sweeny Sterling Finlayson & Company Architects Inc. (project completed under Dermot J. Sweeny Architects Inc.) PRODUCTION ARCHITECTS Adamson Associates Architects MECHANICAL ENGINEERING The Mitchell Partnership Inc. ELECTRICAL ENGINEERS Mulvey + Banani International INTERIOR ARCHITECTURE Sweeny Sterling Finlayson & Co. Architects Inc. INTERIOR MECHANICAL ENGINEERING Stantec (formerly Keen Engineering) INTERIOR ELECTRICAL ENGINEERING Stantec (formerly Carinci Burt Rogers)

▸ Angled Light and Air Shaft Projections
▾ Entrance to Store and Café
   Photos: Van Royko

"The human brain now holds the key to our future. We have to recall the image of the planet from outer space: a single entity in which air, water, and continents are interconnected. That is our home."

DAVID SUZUKI

MOUNTAIN EQUIPMENT CO-OP STORE

MONTREAL, QUEBEC, 2005

The MEC store used an integrated design process involving the owner, construction manager and design professionals. This process benefits from the positive synergies of the various participants and promotes integrated design solutions.

The building forms and materiality create a unique presence on the site and a dramatic interior effect of rugged spaciousness perfectly compatible with the store's identity. Its popularity makes it a key player in the promotion of green buildings in Quebec. Incorporating geothermal energy, radiant heating and cooling, and a natural ventilation system, the store uses at least 65% less energy than a similar reference building. The various water conservation strategies result in

a 50% reduction of potable water use compared to a typical baseline case. The use of an 'ecological' concrete mix reduced the CO_2 emissions associated with Portland cement manufacturing. The annual estimated reduction of carbon dioxide emissions from the use of geothermal energy instead of fossil fuel is 400 tonnes.

The store was the first C-2000 compliant commercial building in Quebec and was selected as one of three projects to represent Canada at the International Sustainable Buildings Conference (SB05) in Tokyo in 2005. It has won numerous awards and recognitions for the quality of its design and its environmental achievements.

▾ Second Floor of Store Interior
Photo: Van Royko

Highlights

■ The building is heated and cooled using hydronic radiant slabs and geothermal energy. Solar panels pre-heat the domestic hot water. ■ Building system controls retrieve weather forecasts via the Internet sufficiently in advance to accommodate the reaction time of the thermal mass of the structure. ■ Window sizing and location was determined using computer simulations to optimize natural lighting and control thermal heat gain. ■ Fresh air is drawn through filtered intakes along underground tunnels (which provides free pre-cooling/pre-heating), distributed by vertical ventilation shafts across the building via horizontal displacement and finally exhausted, using a stack effect, by motorized dampers. ■ Parking lot storm water is filtered and returned to the water table. Roof storm water is collected in an underground cistern and then used to flush toilets and to irrigate the landscaping. ■ A green roof, accessible to staff, was installed by the store entrance. Indigenous, drought resistant planting was used. ■ Healthy, local, recycled and salvaged materials were used in the project. A waste management strategy diverted construction waste from dump sites.

Team

CLIENT (MEC Project Manager) Corin Flood (presently working for reSource rethinking building) ARCHITECTS The consortium MTF architects (Studio MMA (Mamfredis Miners Architects), Lyse M. Tremblay Architect and (Duschenes & Fish Architects) MECHANICAL/ELECTRICAL Pageau Morel and Associates, Inc. STRUCTURAL Saia Deslauriers Kadanoff Leconte Brisebois Blais CIVIL Vinci Consultants LANDSCAPE Williams Asselin Ackaoui and Associates Inc. CONSTRUCTION MANAGER Broccolini Construction Inc. WASTE MANAGEMENT CONSULTANT Jacques Whitford

▸ Geothermal Heat Pump
▸ Studio
  Photos: Gerry Kopelow

SMITH CARTER OFFICE SC3

WINNIPEG, MANITOBA, 2004

SC3 is a new office building for Smith Carter Architects and Engineers Incorporated.

Smith Carter's new offices include sustainability concepts for site, building and workplace. An integrated design process was employed achieving a building where waste was minimized.

Smith Carter is a multidisciplinary consulting firm and staff is encouraged to work collaboratively. Status and corporate class definition have been eliminated within a completely open work station environment. The building systems allow workstation configuration and air/light systems to be individually personalized.

Site features include preservation of existing mature trees, storm water detention pond, walking paths and restoration of native planting and local bird habitat. The building features exercise areas, low flush faucets/toilets, waterless urinals, geothermal heating/cooling, use of natural day-lighting, a displacement ventilation system, and operable windows. Exterior/interior finishes are primarily natural materials and rapidly renewable regional products.

SC3 presents an opportunity for the firm to experiment with leading-edge materials, technologies, and spatial and office organizational concepts. SC3 has applied for LEED® Gold certification.

◀ Exterior with Storm Water
Detention Pond
Photo: Gerry Kopelow

Highlights

■ The site preserves 150 mature spruce trees and restores 1.4 acres to native prairie grassland, promoting biodiversity. ■ Water is conserved through xeriscape landscaping, low-flow dual-flush toilets, waterless urinals, battery operated touchless taps recharged by the flowing water, as well as low-flow faucets, showerheads and appliances. ■ Raised flooring is used, providing an easy access route for data and electrical wiring, and doubling as an air plenum for an Underfloor Air Distribution (UFAD) system. ■ Air intake is on the tree side of the building, so that fresh air is scrubbed by the spruce forest before entering the building. ■ A solar-shading wall at the south end of the building reduces cooling requirements. ■ All appliances are 'Energy Star' rated, the most energy efficient rating available. Copiers, fax machines and other office equipment have been selected to minimize process loads. ■ Exterior lighting has been designed to virtually eliminate light spill from the site. ■ Regionally produced strawboard and sunflower seed board are used. These are rapidly renewable materials that regenerate in less than 10 years.

Team

CLIENT Smith Carter Architects and Engineers Incorporated ARCHITECTURE/ ENGINEERING Smith Carter Architects and Engineers Incorporated CONSTRUCTION MANAGER M.D. Steele Construction Ltd.

▸ Cantilevered Helical Stair
from Top Floor
▾ Exterior View from South
Photos: Redleaf Studios

THE TERRACE BUILDING

REGINA, SASKATCHEWAN, 2003

The Terrace Building is the first building at the new Regina Research Park. This facility is operated by the government-run Innovation Place, which supports the growth and success of the Saskatchewan technology sector. A 130,000 sq. ft. information technology facility, The Terrace Building was designed with the intent of providing the standard for all future construction at the Park. It also acts as a symbol for the client, the Saskatchewan Opportunities Corporation. Housing multiple tenants on three floors, a unique central rotunda extends almost four stories in height to a round skylight ten metres in diameter. This rotunda also acts as a chimney, regulating air temperature. Constructed with a high speed LAN and access to the Internet via state-of-the-art hardware and fibre optics, this infrastructure is designed to support information technology clusters. Located next to the University of Regina, this 78 acre site is already home to knowledge clusters in areas such as information technology, petroleum, and environmental sciences research. The Terrace Building is the recipient of a Canada Energy Efficiency Award.

◀ Rotunda Skylight from Base
of Helical Stair
Photo: Redleaf Studios

Highlights

■ Building massing was developed after examining sun orientation through the seasons, prevailing winds and other environmental impacts. ■ The energy budget for lighting is one watt per square foot, with an average illumination level of approximately 500 lux. ■ The 10 metre skylight in the central rotunda is the heat stack for the building. ■ Recyclable building elements which can be dismantled or have manufacturer's certificate for take back were used. Material selection was based on life-cycle analysis. ■ Local materials such as composite metal cladding, manufactured into panels in Calgary, were used.

Optimum modular size was researched to produce a minimum of material waste during manufacturing. ■ Four-pipe fan-coil zone heating & cooling system units are used, and are complete with multi-speed fans, which operate at the lowest fan speed possible. ■ When the outside temperature drops below approximately -12°C, the building produces its own chilled water for cooling via coils in the exterior make-up air ventilation units. ■ Variable frequency drives were provided for all of the major mechanical fan systems and pumps.

Team

CLIENT Saskatchewan Opportunities Corporation ARCHITECTS/PRIME CONSULTANTS P³ Architecture Ltd. STRUCTURAL Cochrane Engineering Ltd. MECHANICAL MacPherson Engineering Inc. ELECTRICAL Ritenburg and Associates Ltd.

◄ Gallery
▼ Exterior 1
▼ Exterior 2
Photos: Alex Legault

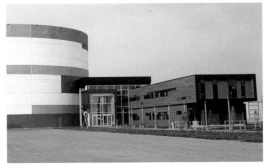

TOHU: CHAPITEAU DES ARTS DU CIRQUE

MONTREAL, QUEBEC, 2004

In 1997, Cirque du Soleil elected to build its production studio near a disused dumping site on the periphery of the city of Montréal. Just as travelling entertainers set up their big top on the edge of town, Cirque's creators endeavoured to revitalize this abandoned industrial site. Since then, the École nationale du cirque—a circus arts school—and other performance groups have joined them in establishing the Cité des arts du cirque, a space for producing and promoting the circus arts. The Cité des arts du cirque, otherwise known as TOHU, also invites reflection on environmental issues by serving as the gateway to the Complexe environnemental de Saint-Michel, a vast urban park being developed on the old dumping site.

In this context, the Chapiteau des arts project is structured along two developmental axes: that of culture, embodied by the circus arts, and that of environmental quality and recycling. Thus, it aims to reflect both aspects of the TOHU mission by integrating in a single construction a performance space—or permanent big top—with a seating capacity for 1,000 spectators, and a recycling research and interpretive centre.

▼ Interior Staircase and Entrance
Photo: Alex Legault

Highlights

■ Site conservation includes a non-excavated basement level and a minimum of excavated material removed from the site. ■ All surface and building runoff water is retained on-site in open basins, which harness the natural filtering abilities of aquatic plants to treat the surface water before its absorption into the soil. ■ Through an agreement with the local company Gazmont, biogas from an excavation site at the Saint-Michel environmental Complex is converted into energy used in the heating system. ■ TOHU uses passive geothermics and an 'ice tray' that visitors can observe through a window in the floor of the reception area. ■ A natural/hybrid ventilation system uses the funnel effect of the theatre to diffuse the air with a low velocity system. ■ A natural basin bordering the administrative sector of the building receives and retains rainwater, which gradually flows into the Ville de Montréal rain sewers. ■ The grand stairway is adorned with recycled pieces from old La Ronde bumper cars that have been transformed into a ramp. Recycled metal beams from Angus factories are integrated into the structure of the pavilion.

Team

ARCHITECTS Schème consultants - L'architecte Jacques Plante - Jodoin Lamarre Pratte et associés architectes in consortium STRUCTURAL Martoni, Cyr et associés inc. MECHANICAL M. Martin Roy SCENOGRAPHERS Trizart alliance CONSTRUCTION MANAGEMENT Construction Vergo inc.

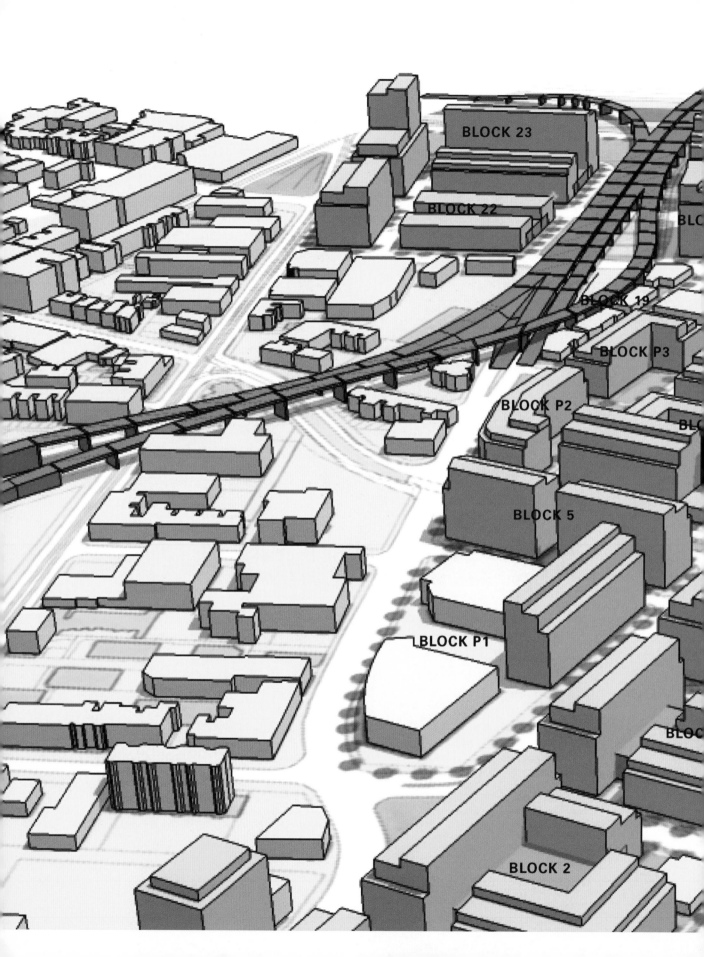

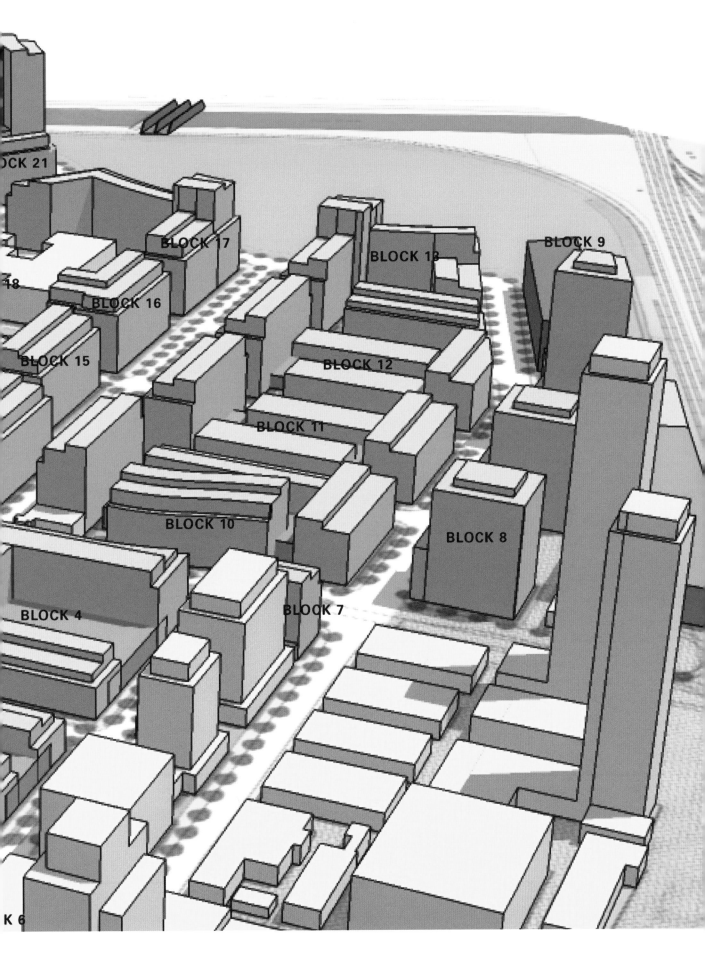

COMMUNITY PLANNING

CASE STUDY AND FEATURED PROJECTS

Many of the projects in the community planning section are yet to be realised and will unfold over an extended period of time. They are cutting edge, and predict a new urban landscape where the environment, commerce, culture and social opportunity are integrated into the lives of residents of urban communities.

Often these projects are the result of an integrated design process that involves communities, local stakeholder groups, inter-disciplinary consulting teams, authorities with jurisdiction and federal, provincial and municipal agencies. Because many of the plans call for Canadian LEED® certification as a requisite for planning approval, the projects anticipate the development of new standards such as LEED® certification for community planning in addition to certification for building design.

The planning of mixed-use facilities and envisioning of complex, integrated design projects is part of an increasing sophistication in the awareness of what sustainable objec-

tives and practice means to society as a whole. Community planning offers the ideal venue to foster sustainable development. In this regard the projects for Toronto's Waterfront Redevelopment Agency, Downsview Park, and Dockside Green in Victoria reflect an enormous potential to develop substantial pieces of a city using alternate planning models. The case study of Toronto's waterfront plan belies the enormous potential for international demonstrations of best practices should forces be mobilized to deliver and implement the recommendations of the plan.

On a more incremental scale, projects such as Benny Farm in Montreal demonstrate more "invisible" sustainable approaches to design that respond to and respect community needs for redevelopment through interventions that are barely noticeable. The result is improved living standards in the community while maintaining continuity of tenure and empowering local community groups.

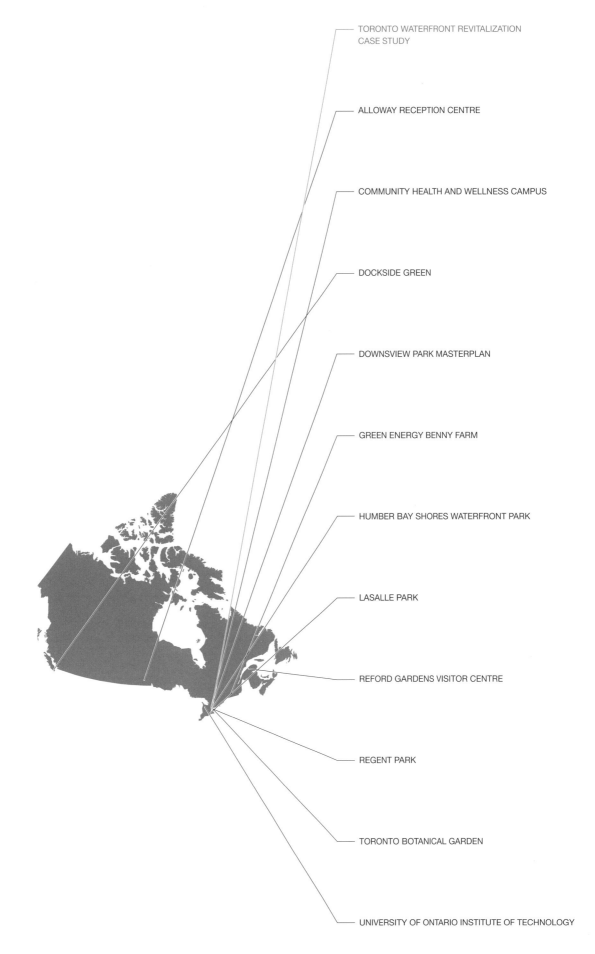

TORONTO WATERFRONT REVITALIZATION
CASE STUDY

ALLOWAY RECEPTION CENTRE

COMMUNITY HEALTH AND WELLNESS CAMPUS

DOCKSIDE GREEN

DOWNSVIEW PARK MASTERPLAN

GREEN ENERGY BENNY FARM

HUMBER BAY SHORES WATERFRONT PARK

LASALLE PARK

REFORD GARDENS VISITOR CENTRE

REGENT PARK

TORONTO BOTANICAL GARDEN

UNIVERSITY OF ONTARIO INSTITUTE OF TECHNOLOGY

CLIENT Toronto Waterfront Revitalization Corporation (TWRC) ENGINEERS Halsall Associates Ltd. SUSTAINABILITY FRAMEWORK DOCUMENT CH2M Hill

COMMUNITY PLANNING CASE STUDY

TORONTO WATERFRONT REVITALIZATION

TORONTO, ONTARIO, 2005

The revitalization plan for the Toronto waterfront is intended to position the city as a world leader in creating sustainable communities. This is a key part of a bigger plan to re-establish Toronto's reputation as a city that other municipalities aspire to imitate: attractive places in which to live, work and do business. Halsall was retained to transform the Toronto Waterfront Revitalization Corporation's (TWRC) goals for sustainability into a performance standard for application at the level of individual buildings.

This project is significant because it integrates the experiences of green building experts, the successes other municipalities have had implementing green building performance requirements, and the opportunities and constraints faced by local developers. The result is the establishment of stretch goals for developers—aggressive, but economically viable. These goals will influence development across this 90 acre site where 6,000 housing units and support services are to be built.

Committed to remediated brownfields, reduced energy consumption, the construction of green buildings, improved air and water quality, expanded public transit and diverse, vibrant downtown communities, the TWRC sees sustainable development as the key driving concept behind the revitalization of Toronto's waterfront.

Highlights

■ Buildings will be placed to allow for the installation of productive solar electric and solar thermal systems. ■ For optimal performance, all building walls will be configured to suit their solar orientation. ■ The collection, storage, and use of storm water is planned to occur at different elevations, minimizing the need for pumping. ■ This site is adjacent to a rail yard and line, and to a major freeway. Planning has assumed these uses will continue, and conditions are included to address the current and envisioned noise and emissions. ■ 10% of energy consumed will be provided through on-site renewables. ■ The maximum annual potable water consumption per person will be 260 litres residential, 80 litres commercial.

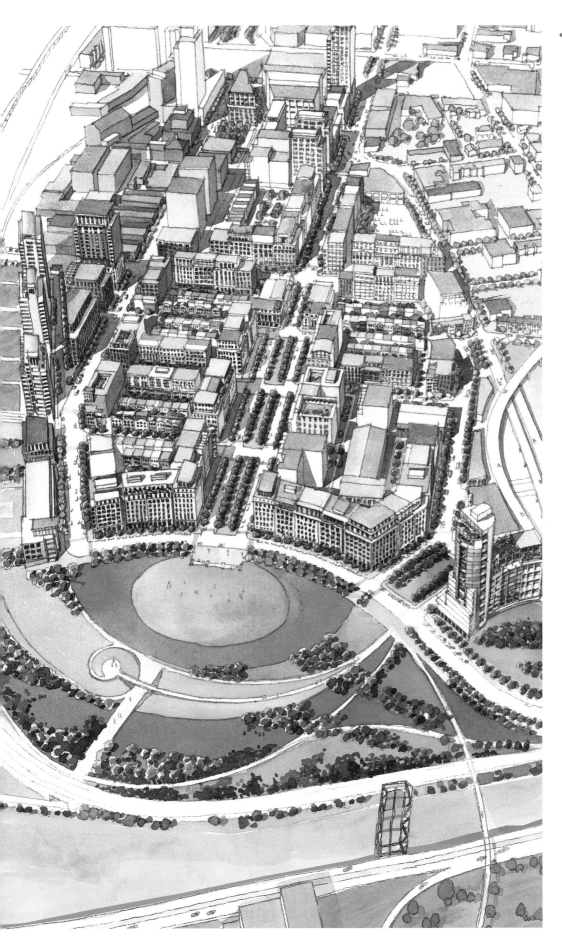

▾ Site Plan

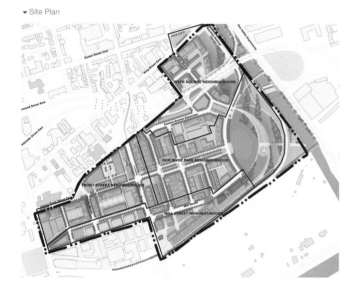

"Neighborhood gives identity.
Frontiers snatch it away."

MARSHALL MCLUHAN

▲ Front Street East

Green Building Performance Standard

The TWRC's global goals for sustainability, as defined in the Framework, were transformed into a Performance Standard for application at the level of individual buildings: ■ To ensure that the standard would represent leadership at an international level, information on other municipal programs was collected. ■ To determine an appropriate energy performance target for this first phase of work, published energy performance data for multi-unit residential buildings was reviewed. ■ Published data was reviewed regarding incremental costs for green building to use in considering appropriate incentives and penalties for exemplary performance or non-compliance. ■ Discussions were held with leading Toronto developers about what they saw as obstacles and opportunities associated with developing green buildings.

Precinct Planning Support

In the standard development process of moving from land acquisition, to community onsite planning, to building design—sustainable thinking has typically been 'added on' at the building design phase. Green buildings, although not yet the norm, are increasingly common, while entire green communities are still rare.

Planners strive to create communities that are enduring, and appealing to the public. Building performance considerations were incorporated into the planning process early enough to result in decisions that are consistent with achieving long life, loose fit, low energy buildings.

One of the fundamental shifts in thinking on this project results from the client's desire to plan for a 500-year life of the main building structures. In Toronto this may seem unreasonable, but many European centres include buildings that are already several hundred years old. History has shown that this target is achievable.

As one example, the waterfront has been envisioned as part of a future where car ownership and usage patterns are substantially altered from the current state. This vision was made more compelling when the

TWRC team was considering parking levels. Compliance with current City requirements for minimum parking levels for residential buildings would require in the order of 7 spaces for every 10 suites. However, it was pointed out that in New York City, residential developers are prohibited from providing more than 2 spaces for every 10 suites, and no minimum levels are required. In planning for the envisioned future at the West Don Lands, parking will only be required to meet minimum market demands, with mandatory structural capacities and floor to floor heights in parking garages that allow for adaptive re-use.

Cultural expectations can have an impact on the desire for long service life. West Don Lands includes plans for townhouses that face and are set close to the street. The building massing plans allow a step up from street level to the ground floors of the residences since homeowners prefer to have their windows elevated above the street. This, however, makes them less desirable if converted to commercial spaces in the future. Planning for easily movable/removable floors is being considered to facilitate re-use.

▼ Park
▼ Front Street

"Our hopes are high. Our faith
in the people is great. Our courage
is strong. And our dreams for this
beautiful country will never die."
PIERRE TRUDEAU

◀ Interior Hall
   Photo: Henry Kalen

▾ Exterior South Side
   Photo: Henry Kalen

ALLOWAY RECEPTION CENTRE
WINNIPEG, MANITOBA, 2000

The Fort Whyte Centre in Winnipeg is a public, environmental education facility overlaid on a post-industrial landscape. A series of quarries, left over from the production of cement and filled with water by extreme flood events, have been allowed to regenerate into major waterfowl staging lakes.

On the edge of one of these lakes, the Alloway Reception Centre is designed to control access to the site and to provide visitor services such as a café, meeting room, washrooms, gift shop and a multipurpose hall.

The building is a hypersensitive response to its environment, both in terms of architectural form and in the selection of building systems. Sustainable design strategies include passive solar heating and shading, a high performance thermal envelope, rainwater collection and distribution, onsite wastewater treatment, the use of recycled building materials and an HVAC system fueled by heat pumps that extract energy from the lake.

A stone wall rises from the prairie clay and its funnelesque shape draws visitors into the centre. Inside, dynamic soil pressures have pushed the piles out of the ground causing the roof planes to shift and walls to tilt. By the time visitors happen upon the building, the structure has achieved stasis.

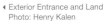
◂ Exterior Entrance and Land
Photo: Henry Kalen

Highlights

■ The layout of the site uses the landscape to gently control access to the facility while optimizing the solar harvest. ■ The landscape around the building is designed to be self-sustaining through the use of indigenous plants. ■ The site and roof drainage patterns encourage self-irrigation. ■ The long east-west form facilitates passive solar heating and passive ventilation by being highly transparent on the south and largely solid on the north. Louvered overhangs prevent overheating on the south side. ■ The post and beam structural system utilizes resource-efficient PSL timbers. ■ The roof deck is fabricated from resource-efficient TSL panels.

Team

CLIENT Fort Whyte Centre ARCHITECTS Syverson Monteyne Architecture Inc., Carl Nelson Jr. STRUCTURAL ENGINEERING Glenville and Associates MECHANICAL ENGINEERING SMS Engineering ELECTRICAL ENGINEERING SMS Engineering

▼ Massing Diagram
Diagram: Montgomery Sisam Architects Inc.

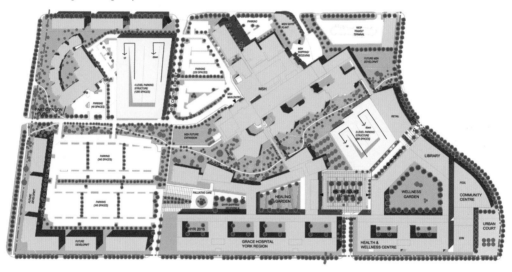

COMMUNITY HEALTH AND WELLNESS CAMPUS

MARKHAM, ONTARIO, 2005

The original Markham Stouffville Hospital (MSH) was completed in 1990 amid open farm fields. In the following decade the new urbanist community of Cornell was built to the north of the hospital. This growing community will shortly envelop the hospital site. A Masterplan for the site has been completed involving a partnership between MSH, the Grace Hospital York Region (GHYR) and the town of Markham. The site development includes additions to the 210 bed MSH, a new 309 bed GHYR for rehabilitation, complex continuing care, geriatric and palliative care services, a Health and Wellness Centre shared by the two hospitals and a community centre and library. With an emphasis on sustainable planning with regards to both the structures and the community, the development supports the 'walkable community' concepts of Cornell by reinforcing street edges and creating a series of courts within the block. A publicly accessible landscaped trail traverses the site. It has recently been announced that provincial investment has been approved and construction on this project will commence in 2009.

Highlights

■ A new York Region Transit Terminal with improved service will reduce the current reliance on cars and decrease the amount of surface parking currently required. ■ The Masterplan has been developed to maximize day lighting conditions for the new buildings through the use of shallower floor plates, landscaped courts and skylights. ■ A central heating and cooling plant incorporating cogeneration will provide reduced emissions and fuel consumption while ensuring reliability and long equipment life.

Cogeneration will significantly lower utility operating costs for the hospital. ■ Application of the Cognos business intelligence solution drives time and cost savings throughout the organization and empowers Hospital staff to use data effectively to improve patient care and service. ■ Intention is to purchase certified green power for a minimum of 50% of the electricity consumed by the building. ■ Cross contamination of regularly occupied areas by chemical pollutants, including housekeeping areas is minimized.

Team

CLIENT Markham Stouffville Hospital, Toronto Grace Hospital ARCHITECTS Architects Zeidler Partnership + Montgomery Sisam Architects in Joint Venture MASTER PROGRAMMING RPG - Resource Planning Group Inc. PLANNING AND URBAN DESIGN Urban Strategies Inc. COMMUNITY CENTRE PROGRAMMING dma Planning & Management Services LANDSCAPE Vertechs Design Inc. WELLNESS CONSULTANT Anchor Health Properties MECHANICAL/ELECTRICAL/CIVIL H.H. Angus & Associates Limited STRUCTURAL Carruthers & Wallace Consultants Ltd.

"It is a wholesome and necessary thing for us to turn again to the earth and in the contemplation of her beauties to know of wonder and humility."
RACHEL CARSON

▾ Aerial Perspective.
 Photo: Busby, Perkins+Will

DOCKSIDE GREEN

VICTORIA, BRITISH COLUMBIA, 2005

Dockside Green is a mixed-use urban community to be constructed on a 15-acre brownfield in Victoria, BC. This largely vacant site, comprised of contaminated landfill and remnants of its industrial past, is being transformed over the next five to ten years into a mixed-use waterfront development, a town within a city comprising 26 buildings and totalling over one million square feet. The City of Victoria requested proposals to develop the site, calling for a triple bottom line of social, economic and environmental performance.

Dockside Green moves beyond energy conservation to a sustainable energy creation model, with a greenhouse gas neutral commitment to be achieved through a mix of renewable energy sources and carbon offsets. Innovative financing tools including green loans, marketing of climate benefits, and micro-utility investment opportunities are being developed and implemented to support this goal.

Dockside Green also creates positive social and economic dividends for the community. The Victoria Sustainability Centre will house local social and environmental non-profit groups and private firms working towards sustainability and will be a focal point for their collaboration and community activity. Citizens, involved at every stage of the project, will continue to guide Dockside Green's development through a Community Liaison Group. The City of Victoria gains jobs, an increased tax base, and lower ongoing municipal costs due to the project's small environmental footprint.

Highlights

■ New urbanism concepts guided site planning and design, with pedestrian-friendly neighbourhoods that encourage social interaction. ■ The project provides a mix of uses and housing types, and attention to accessibility stimulates a diverse community. ■ Municipal costs for investment in infrastructure will be reduced through the creation of significant new public spaces such as parks and plazas. ■ A wood gasification plant will produce energy and heat for the development; solar and other renewable energy sources will provide complementary energy. ■ All sewage will be treated on site and resulting water will be used in landscaping features, which support native species and reduce harmful runoff. ■ Existing local transit is integrated with a car-share co-op (smart cars/low emission vehicles), biodiesel powered and NEV shuttles, and extensive bicycle and pedestrian features. ■ Public art is used from local and native artists. ■ The developers are targeting a minimum LEED® Platinum rating for each building: there is an associated penalty of $1 per square foot, to a maximum of $1,000,000, if this rating is not achieved.

Team

PROJECT DEVELOPMENT Windmill Development Group, VanCity Enterprises Ltd. ARCHITECTS Busby Perkins+Will, Terence Williams Architects Inc. LANDSCAPE PWL Partnership ENGINEERING Stantec ENVIRONMENTAL ENGINEERING Quantum Environmental Inc., BuildGreen Consulting, Aqua-Tex Scientific Consulting

▾ Site Plan
  Graphic: Bruce Mau Design Inc.
▸ Terraces
  Rendering: Bruce Mau Design Inc.

DOWNSVIEW PARK MASTERPLAN

DOWNSVIEW, ONTARIO, 2005

The Downsview Park Masterplan takes one of Toronto's most remarkable assets—the Downsview lands—and transforms it into one of the nation's greatest civic amenities. Driven by the principles of ecological, social, and economic sustainability, it is an investment at every level in the health of our society, and a chance to demonstrate a whole new understanding of urban life.

With a vision to grow the park incrementally over time, the design will become a 218-acre matrix of planted and programmed clusters separated by open areas. This phased approach will gradually change the appearance of the former Canadian Forces Base into a lush, recreational green space. Standing in contrast to the classical park of previous eras, it is not a rigid and formal design, but rather a series of operational strategies that respond to the evolution of the park, the community and society.

The interdisciplinary team of international and local talents creating the park includes architects, designers, ecologists, landscape architects, urban planners and environmental engineers. Ultimately, Downsview Park will connect the city's parklands to form a green infrastructure for the Greater Toronto Area.

▾ Water Purification Facility
Rendering: Bruce Mau Design Inc.

Highlights

■ The park provides a diverse range of open and accessible activities, encouraging intergenerational and cross-cultural use. Visitors are removed from the stresses of the city and reconnected with the natural cycles of life. ■ Working within the carrying capacity of the park and supporting biodiversity and ecosystem health, the Tree City design encourages park growth while minimizing demand for maintenance. ■ The design strives to encourage a critical mass to take leadership roles in sustainability. Business ventures within the park aspire to apply sustainable practices, thus actively minimizing their ecological footprint. ■ Wastewater is minimized through the maintenance, treatment and reuse of water on site. ■ Recycled materials are used wherever possible, as are sustainable materials and renewable resources.

Team

CLIENT Parc Downsview Park Inc.
LEAD DESIGNER Bruce Mau Design Inc.
LANDSCAPE ARCHITECT PMA Landscape Architects ENGINEERING SNC Lavalin
ARCHITECTS Oleson Worland Architects

▸ Energy Services
▸ Water Services
▸ Comparison
▸ Masterplan
  Diagrams: l'OEUF

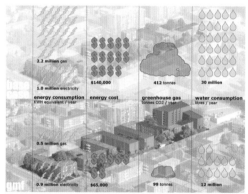

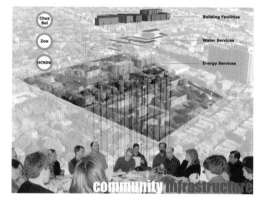

GREEN ENERGY BENNY FARM

MONTREAL, QUEBEC, 2005

The Benny Farm property was developed in 1947 to provide housing for WWII veterans and their families. The redevelopment plan is designed to support the socio-cultural heritage of the site. This project's core innovation is the unique integration of building, sustainable systems and community process in a sector—low-cost housing—that does not usually support such innovation.

Sustainable design knowledge and technology are applied at all scales, from the urban human community and community infrastructure to the finest-grain details within each housing project. They are seamlessly integrated into the community, social and economic patterns that are evolving at the Benny Farm site.

In addition to the sustainable construction and renovation of 187 units on four properties, each unit is linked with a shared green infrastructure. A non-profit, community-run utility company oversees the ownership, management and continual re-investment in sustainable construction for this common energy, water and waste infrastructure. This new model for collectively driven sustainable construction was developed by the many stakeholders, private and public, from grassroots groups to the City of Montreal and the Federation of Canadian Municipalities (FCM). All groups have collaborated to move the Benny Farm redevelopment forward for over a decade.

Highlights

■ By reducing the operating costs of 187 housing units, the project is made more affordable in the long term and cushions the residents against rising energy costs by incorporating on-site renewable energy production for 50% of the heating loads. ■ The project is committed to the hiring of local workers as well as non-skilled labour. ■ The geothermal systems implemented in the project have the lowest life-cycle cost and the lowest impact on the environment. The projects are heated by efficient water-based radiant systems. ■ The infrastructure provides for the treatment of grey water from showers, bathroom sinks and laundry. Storm water discharge at grade is addressed through the reduction of impervious surfaces in the landscaping, allowing the slow percolation of water back into the water table. ■ Conserving the embodied energy of the existing buildings through renovation achieves sustainable construction practices and significant greenhouse gas reductions. ■ A major goal for this project is the long-term financial viability of the green infrastructure. Green Energy Benny Farm, the non-profit utility company created by the project, will manage itself autonomously over the long term.

Team

CLIENT Z.O.O., Chez Soi, HCNDG/SHDM, ÉVBF (GEBF) ARCHITECTS L'OEUF (L'Office de l'eclectisme urbain et fonctionnel) Pearl Poddubiuk et associé architectes BIO-CLIMATIC ENGINEERING Martin Roy et associés Groupe Conseil inc. CIVIL AND WATER ENGINEERS Teknika HBA, SDKLBB VENDOR Canada Lands Company

▾ Waterfront Trail
▸ Home Garden
　Photos: Gera Dillon

HUMBER BAY SHORES WATERFRONT PARK

TORONTO, ONTARIO, 2004

Located on the Lake Ontario waterfront by the mouth of the Humber River, work on the masterplan for this significant, controversial waterfront began in 1996. Integrating ecology with mixed-use urban landfill, the concept behind the creation of this urban waterfront ecological park is based on the interrelationship between the urban community and the natural realm. The park includes spaces for community events and serves as a public gathering place. It also has fish and wildlife habitat areas which include a storm water management system. The Beaches area offers walking and cycling trails and lookouts for wildlife observation.

The site's ecology was further enhanced in 2002 with the Humber Bay Butterfly Habitat, providing specific plant communities and habitat for native butterfly species. Volunteers, through the City of Toronto's Parkland Naturalization Program, installed 90% of the plant material, contributing to this phase of work earning a CSLA Regional Award of Merit in 2003. Naturalization efforts were later extended to the eastern edge of the site towards the mouth of the Humber River.

Highlights

■ This integration of ecology with mixed-use urban intensification is constructed almost entirely on lake fill. ■ Ecological conservation includes shoreline protection, aquatic habitat creation and extensive naturalization. ■ Water management includes a storm water management facility and a final polishing wetland area. ■ A publicly accessible pontoon boardwalk across the lagoon provides opportunities for education and interpretation. ■ The Humber Bay Butterfly Habitat provides specific plant communities and habitat for native butterfly species. ■ Wetland emergent plants provide natural habitat for fish and are also critical for other wildlife including many birds, reptiles and amphibians.

Team

CLIENTS The City of Toronto, Toronto Regional Conservation Authority
ARCHITECTS ENVision - The Hough Group

◄ Boardwalk
▾ Shoreline
   Photos: Ian Dance

LASALLE PARK

HAMILTON, ONTARIO, 2005

The LaSalle Park fish and wildlife restoration project forms a significant and integral part of the Hamilton Harbour Remedial Action Plan. ENVision, in association with a team of coastal engineers and aquatic biologists, worked with the Remedial Action Committee, the Hamilton Harbour Commissioners, the City of Hamilton, and the City of Burlington to prepare a series of site plan concepts, a detailed masterplan, and contract documents for the one-kilometre shoreline area at LaSalle Park.

The LaSalle site was initially identified in the study of the harbour as a primary location for creating an intensive series of fish habitat enhancement initiatives, as well as an area for restoring shoreline wildlife habitats. The new shoreline edge is based on a naturally vegetated edge concept, and an intensive planting program has been detailed to create this environment. Integrated with the shoreline planting is a diverse range of fish enhancement structures, which include log shelters, log fans, root complexes, wetland zones, and culvert shelters. Recreational demands on the site are also addressed in an extensive shoreline trail system, including a series of scenic lookout points.

Highlights

■ Amphibian crossings have been reconnected between shoreline and backshore wetlands and pools. ■ Coastal habitats are created in the shoreline reconstruction. These include fish shelters, spawning areas and cobble beaches. ■ The project has included the reforestation of coastal lands, as well as protection of wetland zones along the shoreline. ■ Shorebird habitats have been created out of newly built coastal islands, while protection has been ensured of existing sensitive habitats. This includes the restoration of beach zones for amphibian migration and habitats. ■ Pedestrian trails are elevated over sensitive ecological zones to enforce their protection.

Team

ARCHITECTS ENVision - the Hough group
COASTAL ENGINEERS Mar-Land Engineering

▾ Exterior Deck
Photo: Alain Laforest

REFORD GARDENS VISITOR CENTRE

GRAND MÉTIS, QUEBEC, 2003

The Reford Gardens/Jardins de Métis are located on the shores of the St. Lawrence and Mitis rivers in eastern Québec. The Gardens are a national historic site created by Elsie Reford over a period of 30 years, and are a testimony to her passion for gardening and plants. Over 3000 species and varieties of native and exotic plants that she collected are on display.

The masterplan for the historical Reford Gardens includes an innovative International Garden Festival, a new visitor centre, and revised pedestrian and vehicular circulation in and around the site. It is articulated around the notions of perception, movement and temporality. Visitors enter the

Reford Gardens after driving for several hours across a regional landscape at high speed. Through the creation of three 'filters' implanted along disused roads located before the entrance to the grounds, the project helps the guests decelerate to reach a state of mind more appropriate for the contemplation of the gardens. One of these 'green screens' is formed by the reception centre, its rose garden and a linear garden containing herbs and spices, which fill the air with their scent. This project achieved the Regional Merit Award from the Canadian Society of Landscape Architecture in 2004 and one of the Governor General's Medals in Architecture in 2006.

- In Vitro, 2001. Garden: NIP Paysage (Mathieu Casavant, France Cormier, Josée Labelle, Michel Langevin, Mélanie Mignault,) Photo: Michel Laverdière
- The You are Here Garden, 2002. Garden: Christopher Bruce Matthews, Taco Iwashima Photo: Michel Laverdière
- Coloured Reflections: Wrapping and Framing Savage Nature, 2003. Garden: Hal Ingberg, Photo: Hal Ingberg
- Sous la pelouse, le jardin 2001. Garden: Sophie Beaudoin, Marie-Ève Cardinal, Michèle Gauthier, Photo: Michel Laverdière
- Summer-dry, 2003. Garden: Maria Goula, Anna Zahonero, Alexandre Campello, Andrew Harris, Claudia Illanes, Photo: Les Jardins de Métis
- Shushu, 2004. Garden: SE BUSCA (Michele Adrian, Paula Meijerink,) Photo: Robert Baronet
- Layers, 2002. Garden: Christopher Bradley-Hole, Photo: Les Jardins de Métis
- O Hendiya, 2003. Garden: Siham Ben Sari, Photo: Robert Baronet
- La Source, 2004. Garden: BGL (Jasmin Bilodeau, Sébastien Giguère, Nicolas Laverdière,) Photo: Robert Baronet

Highlights

■ Innovative demonstrations of sustainability are created by leading designers from Canada and abroad each season as part of the International Garden Festival. ■ The Jardins de Métis serves as a community catalyst, offering culinary and cultural events such as tastings, literary teas, concerts, performances, and lectures. ■ Over 3000 species and varieties of native and exotic plants are maintained on the property. ■ A series of 'green screens' enables visitors to better ready themselves for appreciation of the gardens. ■ The yearly International Garden Festival includes educational activities for visitors including workshops, lectures and exhibitions. ■ The Festival serves as a laboratory for innovative ideas, and a showcase for avant-garde design.

Team

CLIENT Les Amis des Jardins de Métis ARCHITECTS Atelier in Situ LANDSCAPE Vlan Paysages GRAPHIC DESIGN Uniform STRUCTURE Nicolet Chartrand Knoll MECHANICAL/ ELECTRICAL/CIVIL BPR PROJECT MANAGER Lauréat Pépin inc. MAIN SUB-CONTRACTORS Charpenterie & Menuiserie Petchedetz, Construction GHM

▼ Site Plan Diagram
▸ Dundas and Parliament
▸ Major Park
Images: Markson
Borooah Architects

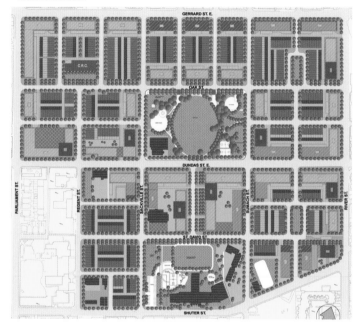

REGENT PARK

TORONTO, ONTARIO, 2004

The Toronto Community Housing Corporation (TCHC) is pursuing a fully integrated sustainability agenda with the redevelopment of Regent Park. Regent Park today houses 7,500 people in 2083 subsidized apartments on 28-hectares. The revitalized neighbourhood will include the rebuilding of all the units while adding 5,000 private sector dwellings with a goal to achieve an estimated population of 12,500.

Originally designed in the 1950's, this downtown Toronto subsidized housing community was first conceived as a 'garden city' where parks and houses are integrated but set apart from the city fabric. The new plan will reintegrate the Regent Park area with the surrounding district while preserving the spirit of community that thrives there. The revitalization of Regent Park will include commercial and community amenities such as retail and large new parks, cultural and education facilities as well as a range of apartment buildings and townhouses. Recommendations encompass fully integrated sustainable community design guidelines, energy reduction targets, and efficient, local cogeneration to reduce greenhouse gases by 80% and achieve a significant reduction in the ecological footprint for Regent Park. These savings achieve highly sustainable design while supporting the business plan, which relies on higher densities and lower operating costs to finance redevelopment.

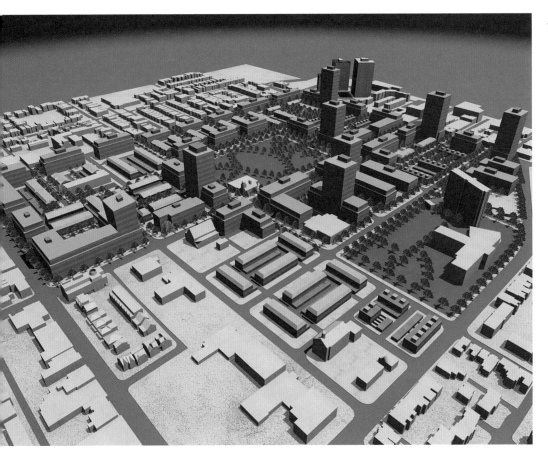

◄ Isometric Site Plan
Images: Markson
Borooah Architects

Highlights

■ Social sustainability considerations included a process of extensive community engagement. Over 2000 residents, consultants and designers contributed to the action plan. ■ 76% reduction in energy use and 80% reduction in green house gas emissions will be achieved in residential units. ■ Apartments include solar shading, reduced thermal breaks, increased insulation levels, high performance window frames and glazing. ■ Radiant in-ceiling heating and cooling systems utilize hot and chilled water supplied by the district energy system. Domestic hot water is also supplied by district energy with efficiency enhanced by greywater heat recovery. ■ Per capita water use will be reduced by 35% and storm water run-off will be reduced by 20%. 84% of suspended particulates will be removed from storm water. ■ A green bin program is planned for townhouses, a three-chute system for multi-unit buildings and a yellow bag program for small commercial establishments. ■ Requirements include reduced parking facilities, provision of bike parking, external bike lockers and change facilities, provision of transit shelters, support for carpooling and provision of autoshare programs.

Team

CLIENT Toronto Community Housing Corporation SUSTAINABLE BUILDING DESIGN GUIDELINES Young + Wright Architects with Sustainable EDGE URBAN DESIGN Markson Borooah Architects and Ken Greenberg SUSTAINABLE SITE SERVICING/INFRASTRUCTURE STRATEGIES/SUSTAINABLE COMMUNITY DESIGN FACILITATION Dillon Consulting LANDSCAPE/ PUBLIC REALM DESIGN ENVision SOLID WASTE MANAGEMENT RIS International CONSTRUCTION WASTE MANAGEMENT Renova Consulting GREEN ROOFS Athena Institute LEGAL Goodmans PROJECT MANAGEMENT GHK International

▼ Site Plan
  Diagram: PMA Landscape Architects Ltd.
▼ Building Court View
  Watercolour: Guanghao Qian

TORONTO BOTANICAL GARDEN

TORONTO, ONTARIO, 2005

The Toronto Botanical Garden located in Edwards Gardens is a charitable organization offering educational programs, garden tours, meeting places and an extensive horticultural library for public use. This building project expands on two existing linked buildings originally designed by Raymond Moriyama and Jerome Markson. Renovations and an addition to the existing buildings include an expanded library, a new store and a children's centre, providing access to the latest in educational tools year-round, with both indoor and outdoor classrooms.

The benefits of this project are far-reaching, from helping to educate our children, to driving tourism, to preserving our native landscapes and habitats. A pavilion of fritted glass forms the addition and is positioned to create a series of garden courts directly related to interior public spaces. The pavilion has a sloping green roof visible from one of the courtyards which draws people in and enlightens them about environmental sustainability, sensitivity and responsibility. It encourages visitors to help Toronto become a healthy, green space for all of its citizens. Landscaping enhances the educational experience by providing demonstration gardens and hands-on learning areas for thousands of students.

Highlights

■ The Toronto Botanical Garden adds four acres of garden space to the city of Toronto, converting hardscaping to softscaping. ■ A green roof reduces water run-off, and reduces the heat island effect. ■ Non-developed area on the site maintains the natural habitat. ■ There is ready access to public transport, and secure bicycle spaces and change/shower rooms are provided. ■ Waterless urinals, ultra-low flow faucets, showers and toilets help to conserve water. ■ Locally manufactured materials and salvaged material are used as well as recycled mineral wool insulation, drywall, steel and carpet. ■ Implementation of a waste management plan includes diversion of 75% of the project's construction waste. ■ Operable windows and personal environmental controls are in place, and there is daylight access for occupants to most of the occupied space. ■ Green building education in the form of public outreach and displays informs the public on how to green their properties and contribute to the city's vision.

Team

CLIENT Toronto Botanical Garden, City of Toronto ARCHITECTS Montgomery Sisam Architects Inc. LANDSCAPE PMA Landscape Architects Ltd. STRUCTURAL Blackwell Bowick Partnership Ltd. MECHANICAL/ELECTRICAL Rybka Smith & Ginsler Ltd. ENVIRONMENTAL Enermodal Engineering Limited PROJECT/CONSTRUCTION MANAGEMENT Dalton Engineering and Construction Ltd.

▸ View of Campus from
  Storm Water
  Management Pond
  Photo: Steven Evans

▸ Academic Building
  Atrium Section
  Diagram: Cicada Design

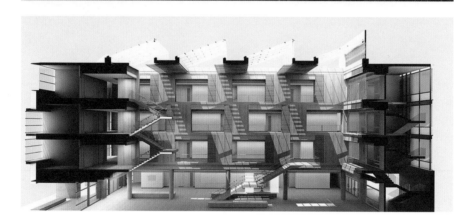

UNIVERSITY OF ONTARIO
INSTITUTE OF TECHNOLOGY

OSHAWA, ONTARIO, 2005

The new University of Ontario Institute of Technology is an example of a comprehensive strategy to employ integrated sustainable building and site practices on a large scale.

The opportunity to design the first new University campus in Ontario in 35 years from first principles presented the team with the responsibility to ensure that every effort was made to mitigate the negative effects on the environment, and to be innovative in the creation of a model sustainable academic educational community. The project consists of nine new buildings and infrastructure to accommodate 6,000 students.

The heart of the campus is a landscaped commons, which is surrounded by five academic buildings and the new library. The Commons is entirely pedestrian and is a place for reflection, relaxation and gathering. Linked by walkways with the valley lands, the connection between nature, education and research is reinforced. The masterplan includes six state-of-the-art academic buildings, a student services building, an automotive research facility and a four-storey library, with a two-storey fireplace reading room.

◀ Business and Information
Technology Building
Photo: Steven Evans

Highlights

■ Located beneath the heart of the campus Commons is a Borehole Thermal Energy Storage System (BTESS) that provides 2000 tonnes of energy efficient sustainable heating and cooling. ■ The building designs incorporate high performance building envelopes and atriums (daylight harvesting, heat recovery, displacement ventilation). ■ Water consumption is reduced through the implementation of greywater re-use in buildings and irrigation and the use of drought resistant native species in the campus landscape design. ■ Storm water management integrates environmental technologies with public outdoor open spaces. This protects the adjacent environmentally sensitive watershed while beautifying the campus and making the filtration process transparent to the campus community.

Team

CLIENT University of Ontario Institute of Technology, Durham College ARCHITECTS Diamond and Schmitt Architects MASTERPLAN Phil Weinstein and Brad Johnston STRUCTURAL Yolles Partnership Inc. LANDSCAPE DuToit Allsopp Hillier MECHANICAL Keen Engineering Company Ltd., Beatty & Associates, Groundheat Systems International Inc. ELECTRICAL Carinci Burt Rogers Engineering Inc. CIVIL Toten Sims Hubicki Associates

EDUCATIONAL

CASE STUDY AND FEATURED PROJECTS

Educational institutions have taken the lead on the Canadian scene in pioneering sustainable buildings. A result of the commitment of academic faculties and administration to the research and practice of sustainability, these buildings incorporate breakthrough ideas and test and evaluate them in practice. Often the buildings have complex evaluation and monitoring components as part of their briefs.

Examples of sustainable building in the Canadian educational sector are so vast in number as to have merited their own category. From public schools to community colleges and universities, institutes of learning across Canada are the true early adopters of sustainable building techniques.

The selected case study, the Terrence Donnelly Centre for Cellular and Biomolecular Research, places the University of Toronto as one of the front-runners in sustainable design for educational buildings. In this project, local and international practitioners combined their talents to create a building that is as state-of-the-art as the research being conducted there.

Smaller projects such as the Nicola Valley Training Centre combine aboriginal history and practices to create a uniquely local version of sustainable design. York University has pursued a green design agenda with the Computer Science Building project, monitoring and evaluating its performance as part of a commitment to sustainability. The Beamish Munro Hall project follows suit, allowing its systems to be monitored and accessible online and building a sense of community around the sustainable objectives of the project shared by faculty, students and administrators. Features such as the living wall at Guelph-Humber and the integration of school and forest at University Hill speak of an ambition to balance society, nature and development—themes at the heart of the sustainability debate.

◄◄ University of Toronto Terrence Donnelly
Centre for Cellular and Biomolecular Research
Double-Skinned Exterior Providing Maximum Transparency
Photo: Ben Rahn/A-Frame Inc.

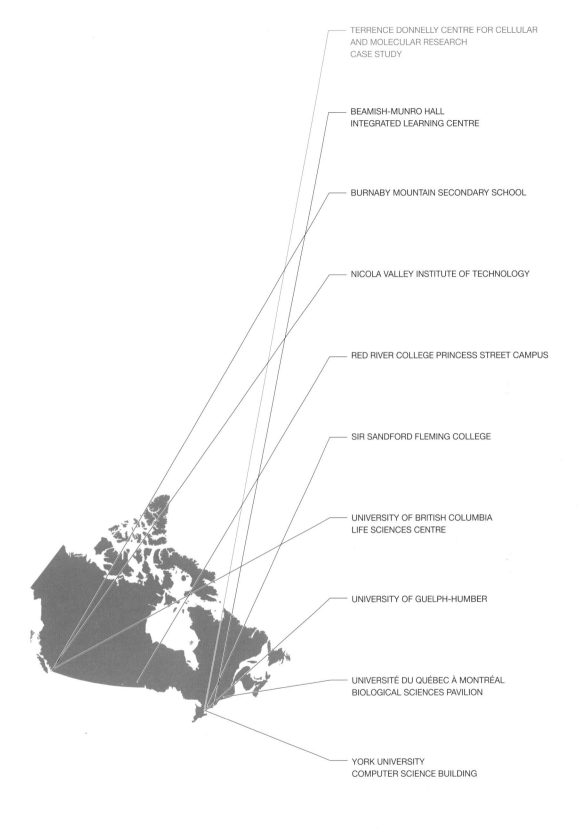

TERRENCE DONNELLY CENTRE FOR CELLULAR
AND MOLECULAR RESEARCH
CASE STUDY

BEAMISH-MUNRO HALL
INTEGRATED LEARNING CENTRE

BURNABY MOUNTAIN SECONDARY SCHOOL

NICOLA VALLEY INSTITUTE OF TECHNOLOGY

RED RIVER COLLEGE PRINCESS STREET CAMPUS

SIR SANDFORD FLEMING COLLEGE

UNIVERSITY OF BRITISH COLUMBIA
LIFE SCIENCES CENTRE

UNIVERSITY OF GUELPH-HUMBER

UNIVERSITÉ DU QUÉBEC À MONTRÉAL
BIOLOGICAL SCIENCES PAVILION

YORK UNIVERSITY
COMPUTER SCIENCE BUILDING

CLIENT University of Toronto ARCHITECTS architectsAlliance, Behnisch Architekten ENGINEER Yolles Group, H.H. Angus and Associates LANDSCAPE Diana Gerrard Landscape Architecture CONSTRUCTION PCL Constructors, Vanbots Construction

EDUCATIONAL CASE STUDY

UNIVERSITY OF TORONTO TERRENCE DONNELLY CENTRE FOR CELLULAR AND BIOMOLECULAR RESEARCH (TDCCBR)

TORONTO, ONTARIO, 2005

The University of Toronto commissioned architectsAlliance and Behnisch Architekten to create this 20,750 m² facility on the University's St. George Campus. The TDCCBR consolidates the University's strengths in biomolecular medicine, genetics and engineering, within an advanced research facility that reflects the University's status as a world leader in the field of genome research.

Bringing together investigators from the Faculty of Medicine, the Leslie Dan Faculty of Pharmacy and the Faculty of Applied Science and Engineering, TDCCBR encourages new ways of approaching biological problems by stimulating unconventional interactions among disciplines. An advanced sustainable environment contributes to this process.

Highlights

■ Each face of the building has its own unique design and configuration, enabling the TDCCBR to respond to its orientation (north, east, south or west), so as to maximize daylighting and reduce radiant thermal loads. ■ The south elevation has a Twin-Face façade, comprised of a conventional curtain or massive wall system with an outer skin of single glazing. The double-skinned building incorporates a range of integrated sunshading, natural ventilation, and thermal insulation devices and strategies. ■ Glazed floors in the double-skinned façade permit the highest level of transparency and allow the greatest amount of natural light to enter the building. ■ Building management systems automatically control operable windows to help ventilate spaces. ■ Cisterns on the roof collect rainwater for irrigation of gardens throughout the building.

◁ South Façade and
Landscaped Forecourt
Photo: Ben Rahn/
A-Frame Inc.

TERRENCE DONNELLY
CENTRE FOR CELLULAR
AND BIOMOLECULAR
RESEARCH

▸ Multi-Storey
Winter Garden
Photo: Tom Arban

The Site

The TDCCBR is located at the University of Toronto's downtown campus, on a tight infill site—a closed street right-of-way—between two historic buildings. A new forecourt and a highly permeable ground floor provide access to the building and a gateway into the campus precinct. The ground plane mediates a full level grade change from sidewalk, through forecourt, new entry, atrium and cafeteria to meet the grade level of the Medical Sciences Building beyond. A free form plan is articulated by gentle grade changes, an atrium garden, and a series of floating lecture halls.

"Sustainable development
is development that meets the
needs of the present without
compromising the ability
of future generations to meet
their own needs."
BRUNDTLAND REPORT

◄ Sketch Model
Photo: Behnisch Architekten

◄ South Façade Detail
Photo: architectsAlliance

116
Canada Innovates: Sustainable Building
Educational Projects
TERRENCE DONNELLY
CENTRE FOR CELLULAR
AND BIOMOLECULAR
RESEARCH

▼ Staff Lounge on
Lab Floor
Photo: Ben Rahn/
A-Frame Inc.

▼ 'Winter Garden' is
Visible from Lab Floors
Photos: Tom Arban

Interior Spaces

Above grade, a series of repetitive lab floors are housed in a simple, elegant glass tower, punctuated by mechanical floors. Each floor contains open lab space with a generous corridor to the west and offices facing the forecourt. A loft approach to lab floors—rigorous functional zoning, simple open plans, exposed structure and systems—creates tremendous flexibility over time.

Recognizing that many significant breakthroughs actually occur in casual conversation outside the laboratory, a number of social spaces have been integrated to promote in-formal, cross-disciplinary contact. Each floor has an informal lounge area, while a series of multi-storey gardens interspersed on the lab floors and linked by staircases further promote contact between researchers.

A series of sustainable design initiatives—internal gardens, naturally ventilated office/admin areas and corridors, double glass façade for research offices, fritted west façade and dramatic reduction in air changes per hour in labs—enhance amenity and reduce energy costs.

▲ Ground Floor Walkway with Lecture Hall, Office Space and 'Winter Garden' Photo: Tom Arban

▾ Living Wall, a Three-storey
  Bio-filter Vertical Garden
▸ Terraced Atrium Teaching Laboratories
  Photos: Richard Johnson

BEAMISH-MUNRO HALL
INTEGRATED LEARNING CENTRE

KINGSTON, ONTARIO, 2004

Beamish-Munro Hall Integrated Learning Centre brings together leading-edge technology and curriculum aimed at removing barriers between disciplines and between university and community. Sandwiched between two existing buildings on the Queen's University Campus, the three-storey, 100,000 sq. ft. space for six faculties of engineering takes the form of a terraced central atrium flanked on three sides by innovative learning environments designed specifically for Queen's project-based learning curriculum.

The building is unusual in exemplifying good practice in energy saving and other aspects of sustainable technol-ogy, but also provides education in those technologies to undergraduates. It teaches by example. From the client's point of view, sustainable innovation is particularly important at the intersection of the 'green building' approach (where the client and architect consciously sought to make the building as good an example of sustainable design as possible) and a 'live building' approach (to make all aspects of the building design and operation available for learning). By making people at Queen's aware of the environmental issues, there is the potential to influence the extent to which these concerns are given consideration in future Queen's buildings.

Highlights

■ Internal saw-toothed section and light scoops and slots were configured to allow light into both the existing buildings and the new building, which has only two elevations on the east and west sides. ■ Beamish-Munro Hall is a student-oriented building, designed in collaboration with students. ■ The facility is instrumented as a working laboratory so students can see structural elements of the building that are usually hidden, and monitor air quality, heating, lighting and cooling systems using specially designed software. ■ Students understand the opportunities and limitations of environmental technology and building systems since this data is available for analysis. ■ Inside the front doors a green wall filters particles from the air before it is distributed throughout the building.

Team

CLIENT Beamish-Munro Hall, Queen's University ARCHITECT Bregman + Hamann Architects STRUCTURAL Halsall Associates Ltd. MECHANICAL Smith and Andersen Consulting Engineering ELECTRICAL Crossey Engineering Ltd. ENVIRONMENTAL Allen Kani Associates LANDSCAPE Janet Rosenberg + Associates

▸ Sand Based Sportsfield
▸ Commons
▾ Tessler

BURNABY MOUNTAIN SECONDARY SCHOOL

BURNABY, BRITISH COLUMBIA, 2000

This 15,000m², three-storey facility is able to accommodate approximately 1500 students. Sited within an existing highway right-of-way, it is also adjacent to an environmentally sensitive watershed. An integrated management approach to the design process involved arriving at solutions through group meetings with all of the consultants involved. This process led to the project's success and reduced costs.

The geothermal system saves energy and lowers costs, while enhancing the local fish habitat of Stoney Creek.

Other contributing elements to the energy saving strategy include a heat pump which saves 126,000kg of CO_2. Use of t-8 fluorescents together with multi-level switching provides user control. Heating needs are reduced through the use of high efficiency boilers and heat recovery chillers. Natural landscaping and life-cycle assessment strategies were incorporated as was an analysis of the building envelope.

Highlights

■ An integrated technology supports the extended day, multi-site and distributed collaborative running aspects of educational delivery. ■ The GSHP (ground source heat pump) extracts heat from, and rejects heat to the ground through 24 km of pipe below the playing field. The heat pump allows excess heat in one part of the building to be pumped to where it is needed. ■ In winter, high efficiency heat recovery chillers boost the temperature of the extracted ground energy. On the coldest days, high efficiency condensing boilers give supplementary heat. ■ Rainwater run-off is designed to flow through the geothermal trenches to increase GSHP efficiencies and reduce water consumption. ■ Use of t-8 fluorescents and metal halides allows energy density below 1.2 watts. Multi-level switching allows user control and energy savings. ■ The site is close to Skytrain, which expands transportation options.

Team

CLIENT School District No. 41, Burnaby PROJECT MANAGER BKG Consulting ARCHITECTS Hotson Bakker Boniface Haden Architects + Urbanistes, Cornerstone Associated Architecture CIVIL HUB Engineering MECHANICAL/ELECTRICAL Stantec Consulting Ltd. LANDSCAPE Durante Kreuk Ltd. CONTRACTOR Dominion Company ENVIRONMENTAL ENKON Ltd. GEOTHERMAL CSLM Associates

◄ Column Forest Surrounding Atrium
and Gathering Space
▼ Planted Roof Emerges From
Surrounding Landscape
Photos: Nic Lehoux

NICOLA VALLEY INSTITUTE OF TECHNOLOGY

MERRITT, BRITISH COLUMBIA, 2004

The Nicola Valley Institute of Technology (NVIT) is one of Canada's first post-secondary facilities shared by a native and non-native institute. It is funded by the Province of British Columbia, and located on a 17.5 hectare site on the north side of the City of Merritt in the BC interior. This first building on the new campus is designed to reflect the cultural characteristics of aboriginal students, and provide state-of-the-art learning spaces as required by University College of the Cariboo (UCC). The 4,519m² building includes classrooms, faculty offices, social spaces, labs, bookstore, cafeteria and a library. Functional spaces were intentionally organized to eliminate any sense of hierarchy.

The masterplan is based on a circular geometry, chosen due to its significance as a cultural symbol to the five nations occupying this land. The design process involved intensive user group interaction and numerous tours of the site. The design of NVIT respects the historical native dwellings which were on this site, and recognizes their advantages by including elements in the design of the new building. The aboriginal elders played a major role in this process and ensured ideas such as the circle and the cardinal points were incorporated into the design of the building.

"It is wonderful to feel the grandness of Canada
in the raw, not because she is Canada but because
she's something sublime that you were born into,
some great rugged power that you are a part of."
EMILY CARR

▾ Building Geometry References
Aboriginal Symbolism
Photo: Nic Lehoux

Highlights

■ The building is located below the elevation of natural water pressure to avoid pumping water uphill. Pit-house structures were historically located near underground streams where the inhabitants could tap into the water supply. ■ The envelope is a wood frame rainscreen wall, clad with yellow cedar. Yellow cedar was chosen for its durability, insect resistance, and having no need for a chemical preservative treatment. ■ A glazed clerestory on the roof, reflective of the extended teepee, provides natural ventilation and daylighting to the interior street. ■ The lower section of the roof is planted with kinnikinic, an indigenous, low-level creeping plant. ■ At the heart of the building is a fireplace providing a warm greeting to students and visitors and providing preheating for the ventilation atrium. ■ The primary energy saving strategies of thermal mass and natural ventilation draw from the pit-house and the extended tepee used in the past by the local native people. ■ Classrooms on the second floor are located directly across from faculty offices to remove barriers between teacher and student and to promote dialogue.

Team

ARCHITECTS Busby Perkins+Will Architects CLIENT Nicola Valley Institute of Technology with the University College of the Cariboo STRUCTURAL Equilibrium Consulting Inc. MECHANICAL Keen Engineering ELECTRICAL Earth Tech Canada CIVIL/LANDSCAPE True Engineering

▾ Classroom
▸ Corridor Between Buildings
  Photos: Gerry Kopelow

RED RIVER COLLEGE PRINCESS STREET CAMPUS

WINNIPEG, MANITOBA, 2004

Red River College Princess Street Campus is a state-of-the-art business, multi-media, and information technology learning centre. The new campus is located on one of Canada's National Historic Sites, Winnipeg's Exchange District, a brownfield site in an area suffering from a steady decline in commercial and residential activity. The integration of a 220,000 sq. ft. college facility was seen by many as an opportunity to enhance both the commercial and residential potential of the existing urban community.

The Campus accommodates approximately 2,000 students and 200 staff. Housing the Creative Arts, Electronic Technology, and Business Administration programs, the College represents an aggressive approach to cutting-edge facility design. These programs require the latest in information technology infrastructure, electronic equipment, and contemporary learning environments. The new campus is living proof that old buildings and abandoned sites can be redeveloped for modern functions while maintaining sensitivity to history and existing urban fabric. Municipal and Provincial governments view the campus as a project which has 'raised the bar' for redevelopment in Winnipeg's urban core.

▼ Building Exterior
Photo: Gerry Kopelow

Highlights

■ An extensive green roof is used as the basis for a project monitored by academic researchers in order to establish appropriate species for northern climates. ■ The buildings are rendered with natural colours and textures that are inherent to the material. Extraneous finishes omitted include carpeted floors, wall coverings, and painted surfaces. ■ In some cases historic or reclaimed materials are offset against new ones to assist in functional ways. For example, the building's cores, containing the vertical circulation elements, are constructed of unfinished concrete block, providing clear wayfinding for users. ■ Where new products were specified, preference was given to those having recycled content, those manufactured from renewable resources, or those manufactured locally. ■ Timetabling is computerized to increase classroom utilization.

Team

CLIENT Red River College and the Province of Manitoba ARCHITECTS Corbett Cibinel Architects INTERIOR DESIGN Corbett Cibinel Architects STRUCTURAL Crosier Kilgour & Partners Ltd. MECHANICAL Corbett Cibinel Architects ELECTRICAL PC Engineering Ltd.

▾ Building Entrance
▸ Sunshade Detail
  Photos: Loghman Azar

SIR SANDFORD FLEMING COLLEGE

PETERBOROUGH, ONTARIO, 2003

The new 50,000 sq. ft. wing houses a 150 seat lecture hall, classrooms, faculty offices, meeting rooms, computer centre, engineering, telecommunication and technology labs for high-tech learning. From the start, the client, architect and consultants worked together as an integrated team. As a learning-centred College, the building is designed as an actual learning tool that integrates HVAC with natural ventilation, electrical with daylighting, structural with solar controls, IT with learning, while simultaneously producing an innovative and sustainable energy efficient building.

The Galleria space serves as the main avenue in the new wing and is topped by a glass-vaulted skylight roof to maximize daylighting. The skylight roof rests on a series of steel reinforced wood trusses cantilevered over the existing building without touching it for structural support. These trusses are supported by a single row of restrained lathe-turned and curved formed wood columns instead of double rows. A reference to nature is expressed by alternating wood columns tapered with varying angles to emulate trees in the forest.

◀ Interior of Galleria
Photo: Loghman Azar

Highlights

■ The building has an L-shaped floor plate to reduce the building depth and facilitate natural ventilation and daylighting. ■ The circulation system is interconnected with three thermal chimneys aided by motorized clerestories and operable windows. ■ Mechanical roof top units with economizers and heat exchangers form a multi-zone control mechanism. ■ Air ducts are exposed in the majority of interior spaces eliminating energy loss to ceiling space. ■ A combination of light shelves and sunshades integrated with the structure are installed with specific angles on the south and west façades to redirect daylight and for glare reduction and thermal control. ■ The well insulated building envelope design is based on the rain screen principle and use of high performance windows offers better comfort and lower operating and energy costs. ■ Exterior materials include use of cultured stone—which resembles natural stone but is manufactured with recycled materials, and metal cladding—which can be recycled and re-used in the future.

Team

CLIENT Sir Sandford Fleming College ARCHITECT Loghman Azar LINE Architect Inc. BUILDER Garritano Bros. Ltd. STRUCTURAL Halsall Associates MECHANICAL Keen Engineering ELECTRICAL Mulvey and Banani. QUANTITY SURVEYOR Helyar and Associates ACOUSTICS Valcoustics Ltd. ENERGY SIMULATION Enersys Engineering

▾ Building Exterior, South Canopy
▸ West Building Entry
  Photos: Elizabeth Gyde

UNIVERSITY OF BRITISH COLUMBIA
LIFE SCIENCES CENTRE

VANCOUVER, BRITISH COLUMBIA, 2005

The University of British Columbia Life Sciences Centre is a 565,000 sq. ft. research-academic building providing a variety of teaching and research facilities for the study of life sciences and a new home for the Faculty of Medicine. It is the hub in a network of teaching and research facilities in the Lower Mainland and provides links with distributed-learning facilities at University of Northern British Columbia and University of Victoria. A construction cost approximately 40% less than that of the North American average for this building type was achieved while still retaining the key architectural standards and energy efficient systems. The open plan of the lab area, as well as the provision of exciting social spaces in strategic locations, contribute to an environment of interaction between disciplines. Energy efficiency, a high performance building envelope, a safe and healthy work environment, water conservation and good lighting standards have all been employed in the design and construction of the building. An environmentally responsible remediation process preceded the construction of the building as the site was contaminated with zinc and hydrocarbons. UBC LSC is the largest LEED® Gold certified building in Canada. It is one of only a handful of LEED® Gold laboratory buildings and the only example of its size in North America.

◀ One of Two Atria
between Lab Blocks
Photo: Elizabeth Gyde

Highlights

■ The Integrated Design Process (IDP) was used throughout the project. ■ The site is located in a dense area with existing infrastructure. ■ The brownfield site was contaminated with hydrocarbons and zinc and remediated prior to construction. ■ A site erosion and sedimentation control plan meeting EPA standards was implemented. ■ Planting of native or adapted vegetation restored 50% of the open area. ■ An Indoor Air Quality Plan used during construction followed by a two-week flush out conducted with 100% outside air to remove remaining construction odors. ■ A waste management plan was implemented to recycle/salvage 80% of the construction waste. ■ A consolidated central recycling area to sort and store recyclables is provided. ■ Low flow roof drains are part of a storm water management strategy. ■ Perimeter day lighting with photoelectric sensors minimizes electrical consumption and provides optimum interior conditions. ■ A high-performance building envelope is used and augmented by a Building Management System that dynamically adjusts building systems.

Team

ARCHITECTS Diamond and Schmitt Architects, Bunting Coady Architects STRUCTURAL Read Jones Christoffersen MECHANICAL/ELECTRICAL MCW Consultants CIVIL Aplin and Martin Consultants GEOTECHNICAL Trow Associates LANDSCAPE Phillips Farevaag Smallenberg CONSTRUCTION Ledcor Construction

UNIVERSITY OF GUELPH-HUMBER

TORONTO, ONTARIO, 2004

The University of Guelph-Humber is a 150,000 sq. ft. academic building located at Humber College, North Campus. The building features a range of green design strategies. Most notable are the innovative indoor air quality strategies which impact the building environmentally, mechanically, operationally and aesthetically. Visible from all public floor areas, the central atrium acts as a displacement ventilation chimney with a 1,650 sq. ft. plant wall at the north end, which provides air filtration. This combination offers a potent tool to significantly improve indoor air quality and comfort level. The atrium takes in 70% of the return air for the building. The return air either goes through the plant wall or it can be diverted to the mechanical air return at the top of the atrium. The mechanical system is designed to recirculate the filtered air. The plant wall has the potential to provide 75% to 80% of the building's fresh air intake requirement. The plant wall for bio-filtration is technology that emerged through University of Guelph Plant Agriculture research in affiliation with the International Space Agency. This installation is a prototype and is the largest to date. An advanced computer monitoring system permits a wide range of data gathering for both the mechanical systems and the plant wall to support continued research.

◄ Plant Wall
Photo: Steven Evans

Highlights

■ The building features widespread use of displacement ventilation using the four-storey central atrium as a chimney. The return air is at the top of the atrium and the mechanical penthouse is on the roof. All peripheral rooms have through connections to the atrium via the ceiling plenums allowing return air to use stack effect. ■ The large-scale plant wall features University of Guelph research and is the prototype for the new AQS air quality solutions integrated filtration system. The vertical hydroponic plant wall brings nature inside the building to a location visible from every public space and corridor. It also acts as an indoor air purifier filtering VOC's and other air contaminants. The purified air generated will offset the building air intake load for the heating and cooling season. The system has the potential to cool naturally in summer reducing the need for air conditioning and provide humidification in winter. ■ Tied into a sophisticated building management system, the impact of the plant wall will be monitored for indoor air quality, heating, cooling, and humidification. The controls maintain the building environment at maximum energy efficiency.

Team

ARCHITECTS Diamond and Schmitt Architects, RHL Architects Inc. in joint venture MECHANICAL/ELECTRICAL Crossey Engineering Ltd. STRUCTURAL Yolles Partnership Inc.

◀ Vertical Service Shaft
Photos: Université du
Québec à Montréal

▼ Evans Entry Hall
Photos: Marc Cramer

UNIVERSITÉ DU QUÉBEC À MONTRÉAL (UQAM) BIOLOGICAL SCIENCES PAVILION

MONTRÉAL, QUÉBEC, 2005

The Biological Sciences Pavilion forms part of UQAM's Pierre-Dansereau Science Complex. With an exterior wrapped in a symbolic DNA motif, the building's spiral volumetry seamlessly integrates an intimate campus atmosphere with a broader urban context. Organized around a central court and abundant with natural light, the building rises from four to nine storeys and includes research and teaching labs from three main fields: ecology, biotechnology/molecular biology, and toxicology/environmental health. An evolved laboratory design allows lab modules, arranged around linear service shafts, to be reconfigured with a minimum of disturbance and material waste. Other program elements include classrooms, offices, animal quarters and tenant space. A research

greenhouse forms the western enclosure of the inner court. Within the framework of the LEED® rating system, the design team has been able to collectively formulate, structure and implement many sustainable design strategies that reflect the University's commitment to environmental responsibility and leadership.

From the initial decision to remediate an urban brownfield site to the ecological practices integrated within University operations, green building principles are adopted that promote resource efficiency, occupant health and well-being, and environmental awareness. The project has been selected by the OECD for inclusion in the 3rd Compendium of Exemplary Educational Facilities.

▾ Interior Garden
Photo: Marc Cramer

Highlights

■ Rainwater is collected for use in toilets and landscape irrigation. ■ Waterless urinals and low-flow fixtures reduce potable water use and wastewater volumes. ■ Energy efficiency measures include VAV fume hoods with matching air make-up, closed-loop heat recovery, and variable frequency drives. ■ Construction waste was collected and recycled off-site. ■ A comprehensive 4R recycling program reduces solid waste streams generated. ■ Low VOC materials contribute to improved IAQ and occupant health. ■ Showers and changing facilities are provided for oc-cupants. ■ Landscape vegetation includes indigenous species and plants requiring low maintenance and no winter protection. ■ An ecological housekeeping program integrates green cleaning products, eco-efficient equipment, education and training, and periodic inspections. ■ An educational program is planned integrating instructional signage with descriptive brochures and guided tours. ■ Tenant leases require future build-outs to respect principles of sustainable design. ■ Preferential parking is provided for carpooling and low-emitting and fuel-efficient vehicles.

Team

CLIENT Université du Québec à Montréal (UQAM) ARCHITECTS Tétreault Parent Languedoc et Associés / Saia Barbarese Topouzanov architectes CONSTRUCTION MANAGEMENT Hervé Pomerleau Construction Inc. CIVIL/STRUCTURAL Pasquin St. Jean / Nicolet Chartrand Knoll MECHANICAL/ELECTRICAL Bouthillette Parizeau et Associés Inc. / HBA Experts-Conseils Inc. LANDSCAPE Claude Cormier Architectes-Paysagistes

"No other country is in a better position than Canada to go ahead with the evolution of a national purpose devoted to all that is good and noble and excellent in the human spirit."

LESTER PEARSON

▾ Thermal Chimneys in the West Corridor
▸ Bamboo-Planted Atrium
   Photos: Steven Evans

YORK UNIVERSITY COMPUTER SCIENCE BUILDING

TORONTO, ONTARIO, 2001

The Computer Science Building at York University (CSB) was the first building to be developed under York University's newly created green design agenda, as a joint venture between architectsAlliance, based in Toronto, and Vancouver based Busby Wills + Associates Architects. The CSB houses a 950-seat lecture hall complex, classrooms, labs, and offices for the Faculties of Computer Science and Pure and Applied Sciences.

In order to preserve the surrounding greenfields of the York campus, the structure was built on an infill site between two buildings. The building's footprint area was minimized through stacking, and a green roof compensates for loss of greenery at ground level. The architectural design addresses York's desire to set a new benchmark in sustainability and environmental awareness while providing the flexibility to accommodate long-term changes in technologies and building use. The innovative design of this project has been recognized with two significant awards: the 2002 Governor General's Medal in Architecture, and the World Architecture Magazine 2002 "Green Building of the Year" Award.

Highlights

■ Low-emissivity materials and finishes reduce the need for carpeting and other building elements known for off-gassing, generating dust, and harbouring allergens and contaminants. Suspended ceilings are eliminated entirely. ■ The CSB incorporates recycled brick, steel and aluminum. Recycled copper is used in the wall cladding system. ■ The 50% fly-ash concrete structure is extensively exposed, providing a significant thermal mass to moderate seasonal temperature fluctuations. ■ Aluminum louvres on the south façade control solar gain and glare, while admitting natural light and reducing artificial lighting loads. ■ Storm water is retained through a planted roof, and through above- and in-ground cisterns. ■ The atrium and thermal chimneys create a 'stack effect', drawing fresh air from outdoors through subterranean air plenums that pre-cool the air in summer and pre-warm it in winter.

Team

CLIENT York University
ARCHITECTS architectsAlliance in joint venture with Busby Wills + Associates
STRUCTURAL Yolles Partnership Ltd.
MECHANICAL Keen Engineering Co. Ltd.
ELECTRICAL Carinci Burt Rogers Inc.
LANDSCAPE John Lloyd & Associates

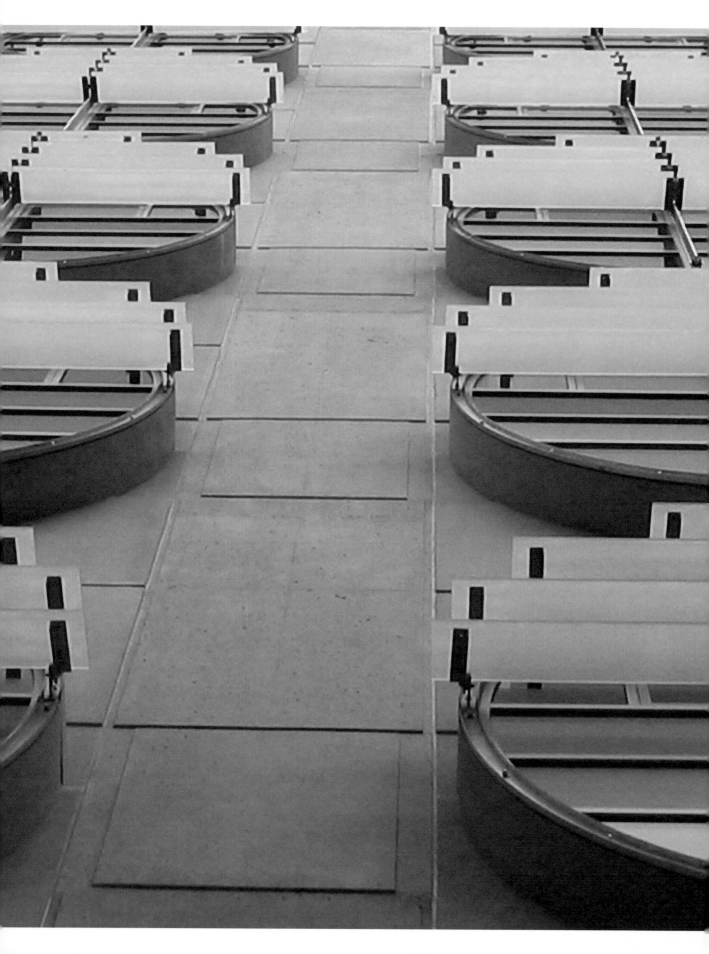

INSTITUTIONAL

CASE STUDY AND FEATURED PROJECTS

Using alternative technologies and materials has required a new breed of designer, engineer and builder: people who are prepared to step forward and experiment with new technologies, learn a whole new set of skills, and take the risk of trying things that are innovative. Increasingly Canadian consulting companies have been taking that step on behalf of their institutional clients.

The projects on the following pages are diverse and reflect the use of sustainable design for cities, community groups, and others—most of which are at least in part government-funded initiatives. The projects included are extremely diverse; among them a library, hospital, research center, fire hall and a community centre. The projects reflect innovation at the municipal level where local communities have attempted to apply sustainable design principles because of the unique and environmentally sensitive locations of the projects. Policy commitments of local councils or non-profit agencies have also driven the sustainability agenda. The sites may vary from large urban centres to rural communities, but the trend is towards a more considerate, humane and accountable public sector design.

When large-scale projects incorporate sustainable technologies and design, these initiatives create a model for other industry players. The BC Cancer Research facility, selected as the case study for this section, has LEED® Gold certification, an impressive achievement for this type of facility. With an innovative integration of research and hospital facilities, it has raised the bar for healthcare design in Canada.

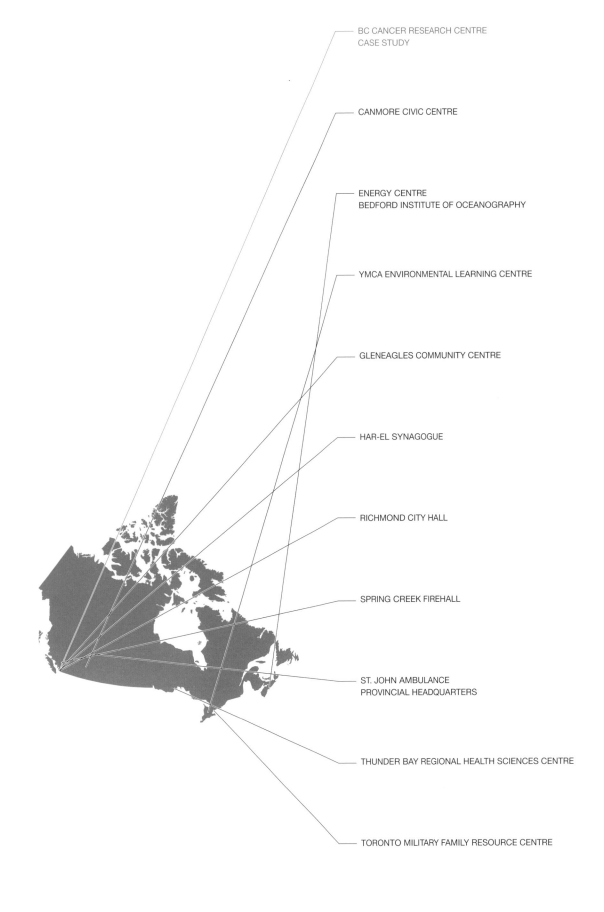

BC CANCER RESEARCH CENTRE
CASE STUDY

CANMORE CIVIC CENTRE

ENERGY CENTRE
BEDFORD INSTITUTE OF OCEANOGRAPHY

YMCA ENVIRONMENTAL LEARNING CENTRE

GLENEAGLES COMMUNITY CENTRE

HAR-EL SYNAGOGUE

RICHMOND CITY HALL

SPRING CREEK FIREHALL

ST. JOHN AMBULANCE
PROVINCIAL HEADQUARTERS

THUNDER BAY REGIONAL HEALTH SCIENCES CENTRE

TORONTO MILITARY FAMILY RESOURCE CENTRE

CLIENT BC Cancer Foundation ARCHITECTS IBI Group / Henriquez Partners, Architects in Joint Venture STRUCTURAL Glotman Simpson PROJECT MANAGEMENT Santec MECHANICAL Stantec ELECTRICAL R.A. Duff & Associates Ltd. GEOTECHNICAL Geopacific Consultants Ltd. LANDSCAPE Durante Kreuk Ltd. INTERIOR DESIGN Juli Hodgson Design

INSTITUTIONAL CASE STUDY

BC CANCER RESEARCH CENTRE

VANCOUVER, BRITISH COLUMBIA, 2005

This 233,000 sq. ft. building, funded through BC Cancer Foundation donors, is the latest fully integrated, state-of-the-art cancer research centre in Canada. Included are facilities for the BC Cancer Agency's Genome Sciences Centre, an agency dedicated to cancer research and the first of its kind in the country.

As part of the design intent for Phase II of this project, a pedestrian bridge, located across the street from the BC Cancer Agency's Vancouver Centre will link the two facilities. This feature will allow bench to bedside research and treatment, resulting in faster absorption and turnaround of information relating to promising new therapies.

The building has six laboratory floors and six interstitial floors, the latter allowing convenient access to the mechanical and electrical systems. Disruption to the research areas as a result off possible reconfiguration is minimized in large part due to this setup. Consisting of 35% office space and 65% laboratory space, the two primary uses each have their own architectural expression.

This is the first health care or laboratory project to earn Gold Certification under LEED® Canada, and an important achievement given the challenges of this building type.

Highlights

■ The roofing membrane is highly reflective. ■ Laboratories and offices have natural ventilation. ■ Variable air volumes supply and exhaust boxes in perimeter zone reduce air volumes during non-peak load times, while low profile fans ensure exhaust air is discharged a safe distance from buildings. ■ A heat recovery system captures heat from exhaust air and condensing units. ■ Office areas have in-slab heating and cooling. ■ Strategic use of glazing allows for deep daylight penetrations within the concrete structure. ■ Dual-flush toilets, waterless urinals and low-flow faucets reduce building water usage. ■ Motorized windows open in the glass clad spiral stairwell eliminating the need for mechanical cooling. ■ 65 fumehoods and 140 bio safety cabinets ensure the safe disposal of toxic chemicals.

◀ Roof Terrace
Photo: Nic Lehoux

"Courage, my friends;
'tis not too late to build
a better world."
TOMMY DOUGLAS

Flexible Workstations

To support the need for flexibility, laboratory modules were developed on a standard grid. These flexible spaces allow for minimal disruptions to adjacent laboratories during future renovations. The ability to change the workstations provides a creative ambiance and serves as a guard against premature obsolescence.

Symbolic Architectural Features

The laboratory block features 15-foot diameter round windows inspired by the form of a Petri dish. The windows communicate that the laboratories are occupied by teams of scientists focused on very specialized research. There are 68 of these windows in total—one for each of the principal investigators. From the inside, the large round windows flood the laboratory space with natural daylight.

Twelve floors of office space look out to ocean and mountain views through multi-coloured strips. This pattern of the vertical, strip-like windows of the office block is an abstraction of a sequence of chromosome six, a subject of study in cancer research. These windows can be opened to encourage natural airflow.

The spiral staircase joining the office floors provides scientists with the opportunity to circulate between floors in an oversized DNA spiral. This provides numerous chance encounters among the scientific community, while enhancing informal interaction and reducing elevator usage. The stair creates another unique architectural element when viewed from the exterior.

◀ Exterior View at Dusk
  Photo: Nic Lehoux
▾ Main Floor Concourse
▾ Spiral Staircase Based on DNA Model
  Photo: Nic Lehoux

▸ South Façade
▸ Theatre
▸ Exterior View into Library
▸ Library
  Photos: Nic Lehoux

Project Facts
BUDGET $95million **FINAL COST** $88milion
COST PER SQUARE FOOT $270
COMPLETED ON SCHEDULE

▲ Typical Lab Module
and Corresponding
Petri-dish Window
Photo: Nic Lehoux.

▾ Sun Screens along South Façade
▸ Exterior View from Town Square
  Photos: Photoganda.ca

CANMORE CIVIC CENTRE

CANMORE, ALBERTA, 2004

The Canmore Civic Centre is part of the urban design initiative for this historic town located in the Rocky Mountains. The facility functions as a meeting area for community groups, encouraging social interaction and political debate. It also promotes public access to local history through the inclusion of the Canmore Centennial Museum. In addition, the building also houses Municipal Offices, a Council Chamber and the Geo-Science Centre. Operating during off-hours as a multipurpose facility providing classrooms, exhibition and meeting spaces for community use, it was conceived as a civic 'hub'—a cultural and administrative heart for this evolving town, rich in railway, mining and mountaineering heritage, and undergoing unprecedented growth and development.

Awarded a LEED® Silver Certification from the USGBC in January 2005, Canmore's Civic Centre has become the first project in Alberta and the fourth in Canada to receive this certification. Environmental stewardship has become a hallmark for Canmore. Their new home represents a pioneering step towards the town's legacy and commitment to sustainable development and preservation of the environment.

Highlights

■ 35% of building materials are composed of recycled content, and 55% of building materials and finishes were procured from local and regional manufacturers. ■ All contractors and subcontractors became a part of the Green Design process, with meetings and seminars held with the trades at regular intervals during construction. ■ The project design promotes the downtown pedestrian core concept, and implements a proactive plan to get staff out of their cars and into alternative transportation. ■ The building consumes 40% less energy than specified in the Model National Energy Code and consumes 55% less water than baseline buildings. ■ There are operable windows in all occupied spaces and narrow floor plates, which connect to a central atrium, utilizing both cross ventilation and stack effect. ■ Access floor displacement ventilation systems are implemented throughout the building. ■ The town's potable water system is used for building cooling, avoiding mechanical refrigeration and the use of harmful CFCs or HCFCs in the building cooling system. ■ The massing and orientation of the building was optimized by computer energy simulation.

Team

CLIENT Town of Canmore ARCHITECTURE Marshall Tittemore Architects MECHANICAL/ ELECTRICAL Keen Engineering Co. Ltd. STRUCTURAL ENGINEERING Cascade Engineering Group Ltd. LANDSCAPE Landplan Associates Ltd.

▼ Seawater Cooling System
▼ Rear View with Green Roof
▶ Sun Shading Device
  Photos: James Steeves

ENERGY CENTRE
BEDFORD INSTITUTE OF OCEANOGRAPHY

DARTMOUTH, NOVA SCOTIA, 2003

Public Works and Government Services Canada commissioned the design of the BIO Energy Centre to complement and showcase its unique seawater cooling system. The innovative cooling system replaces conventional refrigeration, reducing power consumption and producing approximately 400,000 kg less greenhouse gas emissions annually.

BIO hosts a public open house annually, which showcases the unique mechanical systems within the Energy Centre and also supports the existing educational process. The Energy Centre was awarded a Lieutenant Governor's Design Award (Citation) in 2003 and that recognition has generated broader industry awareness of the facility's green building strategies.

The Energy Centre at BIO is the first Federal building in Canada to incorporate a 'green' sod-covered roof. As such, the Green Roof is not only an innovative green building feature, but a visible demonstration of the Federal Government's commitment to sustainable development. The building integrated photovoltaic (BIPV) panel installation, which supplies electricity to open the clerestory windows and provides free natural ventilation, is also one of the first of its kind in Canada.

▼ Photovoltaics Detail
Photos: James Steeves

Highlights

■ A low-maintenance, sod-covered green roof is comprised of a 150-millimetre soil base and Kentucky blue grass turf. The green roof protects a waterproof membrane from harmful ultraviolet rays, provides superior insulation, mediates storm water flow rates, naturally filters over 100 kilograms of dust from the air annually and supports local flora and fauna. ■ A state-of-the-art seawater cooling system draws naturally cool water from a 30-metre depth in Bedford Basin and provides virtually free air conditioning. ■ Building materials contain a high per-centage of natural and recycled materials, including mineral wool insulation and metal panels made of zinc. Materials were chosen with downstream recycling in mind. ■ The Federal Government's 'Supportive Workplace' initiative is reinforced by the provision of natural daylighting and natural ventilation for workers. An eave overhang and sun-shading device mediate solar gain through the day. ■ Building integrated photovoltaic panels (BIPVs) provide electricity to open the clere-story glazed units for free, natural ventilation.

Team

CLIENT Public Works Government Services Canada ARCHITECTS WHW Architects Inc. MECHANICAL/ELECTRICAL SNC Lavalin Inc.

▾ Earth Residence South View
Photo: Robert Burley/Design Archive

YMCA ENVIRONMENTAL LEARNING CENTRE
KITCHENER-WATERLOO, ONTARIO, 2002

Three new groups of buildings on this 70-acre site represent a remarkable demonstration of a comprehensive and ambitious embodiment of green architecture and site planning. They include the first two of eight proposed off-grid straw bale cabins, a year-round off-grid earth-sheltered residence which sleeps up to 40 people and an assembly/conference/office building with a dramatic greenhouse. This greenhouse provides much of the building's heating and cooling and also cleanses the toilet waste water to drinking quality.

The complex is an education, recreation and conference centre which operates an integrated environment of natural features, buildings, technologies and programs. The facility acts as a 'green' information source for local people, organizations and businesses. Technologies and strategies are selected on the basis of their affordability at the time of construction or within the foreseeable future. Each building incorporates a unique response to its site character and microclimate to illustrate different 'green' approaches.

▾ Day Centre Exterior with
South Facing Offices,
Solarium and Boiler Room
Photo: Charles Simon

Highlights

■ A Lake Restorer cleans the 22-acre lake, which is shared by cottagers and their septic systems. Designed by Dr. John Todd, inventor of the Living Machine™, it comprises a floating raft housing plants and other biota, which biologically cleanse. ■ A recent donation has enabled the installation of a large wind turbine, delivering more electrical energy than the entire site requires. ■ A non-polluting masonry stove and active solar panels provide full backup heating of space and water in the Earth Residence. ■ Electricity is derived from wind machines, photovoltaic panels and human pedal power. ■ Passive cooling includes earth-sheltering, trellises and a vent stack effect. ■ 96% of wood, including windows, is re-used and carpet is made from recycled pop bottles. ■ A large, south-facing greenhouse houses a Living Machine, which biologically restores toilet and greywater to drinking quality in the Day Centre. ■ Waste management includes a composting toilet and an innovative greywater treatment system using interior planters in the Straw Bale Cabins.

Team

CLIENT Kitchener-Waterloo YMCA ARCHITECTS Charles Simon Architect + Planner MECHANICAL/ELECTRICAL Sustainable EDGE Ltd. STRUCTURAL The Walter Fedy Partnership LANDSCAPE Mike Hensel (formerly MacKinnon Hensel & Associates)

GLENEAGLES COMMUNITY CENTRE

WEST VANCOUVER, BRITISH COLUMBIA, 2003

The District of West Vancouver desired a new community centre in the Gleneagles area and wished to incorporate a sustainable building approach. A gymnasium, a community living space, a fitness centre, an art centre, and childcare and administrative space, are all brought together in a 23,000 sq. ft. architectural framework. The team took a holistic approach in creating a facility that delivers a healthy and comfortable environment for its visitors and staff, while minimizing its impact on the environment.

The project is organized on three levels on a sloping site. By adjusting the cross-sectional topography of the site, all major program components have direct access to complimentary outdoor spaces. The gymnasium volume is a unifying space that rises through all three levels of the building. Glazed walls allow visual connection between the major program components so that the interior of the community centre is animated by the complex variety of simultaneous activities that comprise the social life of the building.

Highlights

■ The thermoactive radiant heating and cooling system uses the Swiss Bâtiment Isotherme concept. Piping is embedded within the tilt-up and cast-in-place concrete structure, so that heated and cooled water can pass through the concrete, allowing the walls and floors to act as radiant surfaces. ■ Ventilation uses a low velocity displacement system, minimizing the negative impact associated with large ducts. ■ Heating and cooling for the mechanical systems is provided by heat pumps in combination with a ground source heat exchanger. ■ The building roof drainage and hard surface storm water runoff is used as a 'designed water feature,' collected by a fountain in the plaza of the building. The overflow from the fountain and runoff from the parking lot are directed to a bio-swale, which flows into a wetland in the neighbouring golf course and then feeds into Larson Creek; a local salmon bearing stream. ■ Energy-efficient lighting, multiple switching options and occupancy lighting sensors provide a reduced energy demand.

Team

CLIENT District of West Vancouver ARCHITECT Patkau Architects PROJECT MANAGER Maurice J. Ouellette Consulting STRUCTURAL Fast + Epp CIVIL Webster Engineering MECHANICAL/ELECTRICAL Earth Tech LANDSCAPE Vaughan Landscape Planning & Design

▾ Entry
▸ Butterfly Roof and Rainwater Sluice
   Photo: Martin Tessler

HAR-EL SYNAGOGUE

WEST VANCOUVER, BRITISH COLUMBIA, 1998

The design of the Har-El Synagogue faced two critical challenges: exposure to extreme urban noise and visual pollution at the intersection of the Trans-Canada Highway and a major urban artery, and the presence of a sensitive salmon creek traversing this urban site.

The L-shaped building located at the north upper side of the south-facing site insulates the site and creek from the highways while controlling run-off from the building and landscaping before safely entering the creek. It also bridges the creek and connects to a parking lot, which is located below creek level to avoid run-off from paved areas. The main green building strategy integrates a storm water management plan protecting the ecology of the site with a layout favourable to passive design while delivering a sacred house of worship.

The design of the Synagogue strengthens the community's social interaction, sense of belonging, and spiritual enrichment. Social and cultural values are embedded in the fabric of a long-lasting architecture.

Highlights

■ The site was challenging: a mountainside at the intersection of two busy highways bisected by a salmon spawning stream. Advantages included central community location and close proximity to public transportation. ■ The compact building footprint aimed to reduce collateral damage and impact to the existing natural features and wildlife habitat of the native landscape. ■ A butterfly roof captures rainwater and releases it into a feature rainwater sluice. Continuous swales were constructed to manage the run-off as it returned to the creek. ■ Exposed concrete and masonry walls and an exposed aggregate floor act as heat sinks. ■ Energy efficient fixtures include power smart/low energy heating and lighting systems, low volume water toilets, showerhead and faucets. ■ Locally harvested and manufactured materials were selected, including Squamish rock from a small community north of the site, and cedar and fir logs from a local company. Concrete blocks with high-recycled content were used throughout. ■ Interpretative information about the protected salmon-spawning habitat raises public awareness.

Team

CLIENT Har-El Synagogue ARCHITECTS Acton Ostry Architects Inc STRUCTURAL Glotman Simpson Consulting Engineers MECHANICAL/ELECTRICAL Stantec Consulting Ltd. LANDSCAPE Stevenson and Associates

◀ Council Chambers
▾ Meeting House
 Photos: Martin Tessler

"We have it all. We have great diversity of people, we have a wonderful land, and we have great possibilities. So all those things combined there's nowhere else I'd rather be."

BOB RAE

RICHMOND CITY HALL

RICHMOND, BRITISH COLUMBIA, 2000

Richmond is one of British Columbia's fastest developing municipalities and the new City Hall supports a long term vision to be situated the as a viable urban centre. The City Hall design was conceived as a civic landscape as opposed to a singular building to maximize environmental efficiency and flexibility in operations and to mitigate the overall massing on the site. Three main elements—the two-storey Meeting House, the circular Council Chamber and the eight-storey administration tower—are configured to define a series of outdoor courtyards, watergardens and terraces for public use.

The design also demonstrates the City's investment in its work force with a supportive work place environment.

Balconies and terraces allow for access to the outdoors. Employees are able to control their environmental comfort level and have access to fresh air with operable windows and a hybrid ventilation system. Fire-exit stairs are fully glazed to minimize elevator use and to encourage interdepartmental communication.

The site plan has been organized to anticipate a 40,000 sq. ft. expansion in the future. The project was awarded the 2002 Governor General's Medal as well as 2001 Lieutenant Governor of British Columbia Merit Award.

Highlights

■ Universal access from all directions is provided for pedestrians, cyclists and cars. ■ The layout of the building is broken down into functional components, allowing for flexibility in operating hours. This, in turn, also allows for more effective and energy-efficient heating, cooling and ventilation. ■ The harvesting of daylight is enhanced through the use of exterior and interior light shelves that reflect daylight further back into the perimeter spaces. The entire lighting system for the site is networked into a programmable, low-voltage lighting control system. ■ Heritage tree groups were retained and indigenous, low-maintenance trees were introduced to the landscaped areas. ■ To lessen the impact on the global ecosystem, materials were selected to provide for longevity and to avoid contaminants and minimize maintenance. ■ Balconies provide physical and psychological access to outdoors on every floor. ■ Enhanced circulation uses perimeter-glazed stairs with appealing views to encourage use of stairs.

Team

CLIENT City of Richmond ASSOCIATED ARCHITECTS Hotson Bakker Architects/ Kuwabara Payne McKenna Blumberg Architects, Associated Architects for Richmond City Hall LANDSCAPE Phillips Farevaag Smallenberg Inc. STRUCTURAL Bush Bohman & Partners MECHANICAL DWT Stanley, Tescor Pacific Energy Services ELECTRICAL R.A. Duff & Associates ACOUSTICS Barron Kennedy Lyzun & Associates Ltd.

▸ Firehall in Surroundings
Photo: Martin Tessler

SPRING CREEK FIREHALL

WHISTLER, BRITISH COLUMBIA, 2005

Located on a steeply sloped mountainside near the world class Whistler ski resort, the Spring Creek Fire Hall achieves LEED® Silver Certification and features simple concrete wood-frame construction to blend in with its natural community-oriented setting. Its use of recycled building materials and green building strategies reflects the Resort Municipality of Whistler's concern for protecting and minimizing impact to its natural setting. The facility features a green roof of indigenous grasses and drought tolerant plants, which help to capture rainwater and reduce solar gain during summer months.

Other features include, post consumer/post industrial recycled content including recycled formwork and rebar, natural ventilation, storm water return, snow retention as insulation, non SFC based refrigerant HVAC & R system, dual-flush low-water toilets, green power certificates, low-toxicity (low VOC points) interior materials, local material sourcing and end-of-trip amenities for bicycles. As the first building in the Whistler area to achieve LEED® Certification and a popular facility for school tours, the facility serves as an important educational "case study" for green design.

▼ Three Bay Garage and Training Tower
Photo: Martin Tessler

Highlights

■ Silt and sediment fencing was used and a retaining wall was built to prevent loss of soil during construction. ■ Rock excavated from the site was used to construct the retaining wall on site and reused on neighbouring construction projects. ■ The valley trail allows for alternative transportation modes. A secure bicycle rack, change rooms with showers and priority parking spaces for vehicles that carpool are provided. ■ The roof is planted with local indigenous grasses and drought tolerant plants, attracting native wildlife. ■ The only exterior lighting is that needed for safety, access and building identification. ■ Over 75% of the materials used were manufactured locally. Of these more than 65% were extracted, harvested, or recovered within 500 miles of the project. ■ The location of window placement, size of windows, type of glass, roof overhang and the location of rooms in the building all allow occupants to control their environment. ■ The sheet metal supplier used new software and a plasma cutting to reduce the amount of material cost, increase productivity and reduce the amount of waste being sent to landfill.

Team

CLIENTS British Columbia Building Corporation, Resort Municipality of Whistler ARCHITECT Hughes Condon Marler: Architects STRUCTURAL C.Y. Loh Associates MECHANICAL Keen Engineering Co. Ltd. ELECTRICAL R.A. Duff Ltd. LANDSCAPE Vagelatos Associates Landscape CIVIL C.J. Anderson Civil Engineering Inc.

"You wait for fate to bring about
the changes in life which you should
be bringing about by yourself."
DOUGLAS COUPLAND

▾ Staircase Referencing
St. John's European Origins
Photo: Jim Dow

▾ South Elevation
Photo: Manasc Isaac Architects

▸ East Facing Atrium
Photo: Jim Dow

ST. JOHN AMBULANCE PROVINCIAL HEADQUARTERS
EDMONTON, ALBERTA, 2005

St. John Ambulance, a charitable institution with a 900 year history, is renowned for its first aid training. First established in Alberta in 1922, its new state-of-the-art building houses both the Edmonton branch and the Alberta headquarters. St. John's Board of Directors and staff requested a facility that was an experience more than a building. They also wanted a prominent facility that was open and engaged with the city. The result is an iconic building that is plugged into the life of the city via an inviting forecourt and three-storey atrium. The south-facing forecourt is used by students during the day and community skateboarders during the evening.

The building's ability to realize 50% energy savings at the same cost of a regular building is a first for Alberta. At the end of the building's life—approximately 500 years—every component of the facility's construction can be reused. Many of this building's design elements were designed to be un-bolted. The result is a building with very low operating costs, superior health and comfort conditions for occupants, and reduced impact on the local environment.

◀ Sunshades Designed and Manufactured by Manasc Isaac Architects Ltd.
Photo: Jim Dow

Highlights

■ 96% of construction waste was diverted from landfill. ■ Most building materials are fully recyclable at the end of the building's life and all materials and assemblies contain little or no Volatile Organic Compounds. ■ Natural daylight is maximized by means of light-shelves, energy efficient lighting system and occupancy sensors on selected fixtures. A custom-designed exterior Sunshade system controls the amount of natural light entering the building and minimizes the glare inside. ■ A natural ventilation process is enhanced through a 'stack effect.' ■ Night sky illumination is minimized to avoid visual pollution. ■ Potable water use was reduced by lavatory faucets with infrared sensors, dual-flush toilets and waterless urinals. ■ A storm water management system minimizes run-off. ■ Heat-reducing landscape and reflective exterior materials limit internal and external heat gain, while high performance fenestration Visionwall™ controls heat-gain and heat-loss. ■ Edmonton's very first LEED® Silver Certified Building

Team

CLIENT St. John Ambulance ARCHITECTS Manasc Isaac Architects Ltd. STRUCTURAL Earth Tech MECHANICAL Keen Engineering ELECTRICAL Keen Engineering CIVIL GPEC Consulting LANDSCAPE Carlyle & Associates

◀ Interior of Main Public Concourse
▼ Entry to Cancer Radiation Treatment Rooms
Photos: Klik Photography

THUNDER BAY REGIONAL HEALTH SCIENCES CENTRE

THUNDER BAY, ONTARIO, 2004

Built as a new greenfield hospital in Ontario, the facility embraces the qualitative, humanistic aspects of building design by recognizing the combined benefits of the science and art of healing. Understanding that it is impossible to detach from nature without also compromising human spiritual existence, the primary objectives for this 375 bed, 600,000 sq. ft. hospital are to create a more humanistic environment for patient care, to respond to the rugged natural context, and to promote sustainable design initiatives such as passive solar gains and storm water regeneration.

The Thunder Bay Regional Health Sciences Centre was the first hospital in Ontario to receive approval for the use of wood as a primary structural element. It was previously forbidden by prevailing building and fire codes. The dramatic three-storey wood and glass walkway references the northern vernacular with over 1100 glue-laminated members, some over 65 feet long. Successfully responding to the changing needs of its community, the facility functions as a local hospital and also services a rural population within a region covering approximately the area of France.

◄ Main Building Entry at Night
Photo: Klik Photography

Highlights

■ This is the first hospital in Canada to incorporate direct light skylights in Cancer Radiation Treatment Rooms without compromising user or patient safety. ■ Building orientation and intentional sunshades realize passive solar energy gains and reduce the long-term overall running costs. To date the main public concourse uses virtually no heat in the winter and no cooling in the summer. ■ Only 35 of the site's 60 acres are used for the building with the remaining area consisting of a system of wetlands, natural drainage channels and undisturbed brush.

■ On-site, interconnected system of aerated wetlands divert and cleanse storm water run-off before returning it to indigenous cold-water fish breeding grounds. ■ Unites the historic, amalgamated communities of Port Arthur and Fort Williams for healthcare purposes, and serves as a community gathering point via its central geographic position. ■ Providing a positive civic and healing environment, the design contributes to the overall psychological well being of patients, staff and the community.

Team

CLIENT Thunder Bay Regional Health Sciences Centre; Cancer Care Ontario; Northwestern Ontario Regional Cancer Centre ARCHITECTS Completed by Salter Farrow Pilon Architects Inc. of which Farrow Partnership Architects Inc. is one of two successor firms. ASSOCIATE ARCHITECTS Kuch Stephenson Gibson Malo INTERIOR DESIGN Salter Farrow Pilon Interiors LANDSCAPE Schollen and Company Inc., Kuch Stephenson Gibson Malo MECHANICAL/ELECTRICAL/SECURITY/ VERTICAL H.H. Angus & Associates Ltd. STRUCTURAL Michelson/Cook Engineering Joint Venture CIVIL Wardrop Engineering

▾ Interior Top Floor
▸ Exterior Roof
  Photos: Mark Truze

TORONTO MILITARY FAMILY RESOURCE CENTRE

TORONTO, ONTARIO, 2003

The Toronto Military Family Resource Centre is located on the perimeter of Parc Downsview Park, a National Urban Park. It is the first new building to be built along the Park's perimeter since its inception.

While previous building projects of this type had been built to 'Minimum Military Standards,' a new and elevated appreciation of the needs of military spouses and their families began to gain force in Defence thinking. This lead to the full participation and advocacy of community families, staff and volunteers in the design development process.

A project evolved that would provide space for a complexity of internal and external programs.

The facility includes childcare programs, a youth centre, referral and counselling services, adult training and language education facilities, a recycling centre, a library, multipurpose rooms, playgrounds, gardens and a community meeting place.

The environment is complex and rich, underlain by a simple and transparent geometry that binds a rich palette of steel, timber, brick and concrete into a fabric reminiscent of forms found in nature.

Highlights

■ The project utilizes a rich variety of renewable and reusable materials, and building fabrication includes plans for deconstruction. ■ Operable windows are interconnected with a passive stack-effect technology. Other energy saving comes from shading devices, organic shading, and windbreak schemes. ■ The generous supply of interior and exterior glazing minimizes artificial lighting requirements and promotes communal interaction. ■ Heating includes in-floor hydronics supplemented by a fresh air ventilation and cooling system. Monolithic, super-insulated wall and roofing systems provide for an abundance of thermal resistance and also eliminate interstitial cavities. The inclusion of this feature aids in the prevention of mold and bacteria growth.

Team

CLIENT Department of National Defence ARCHITECTURE/ENGINEERING Public Works and Government Services Canada STRUCTURAL Totten Simms Hubicki Associates ENVIRONMENTAL ASSESSMENT Defence Construction Canada

RESIDENTIAL
CASE STUDY AND FEATURED PROJECTS

Canada's landscape varies from urban centres to prairies and forests, while the weather includes humid summers and bitterly cold winters. This has served as the foundation for a wide variety of sustainable approaches to residential design. Local materials include trees, rock, straw and earth, all of which have been used as the basis for innovative structural design.

The homes represented here are built on islands, in urban centres, in forests, by protected salmon breeding streams, and by lakes. However, they reflect the commitment of individual owners to pursue a more sustainable lifestyle by building a custom residential dwelling. Issues confronted in these unique projects include allergy sensitivities, respect for the surrounding environment and personal comfort.

The economic demands and challenges of residential design have partially impeded the adoption of sustainable practices in multiple-unit housing and tract subdivision development. Increasingly, however, agencies like Canadian Mortgage and Housing Corporation, local authorities like the Toronto Regional Conservation Authority and towns like Milton are attempting to address the issue of sustainable housing through planning projects. Even large scale residential developers such as Tridel and Minto are confronting and tackling this issue. Our case study project, a model sustainable condominium interior created by Peter Busby, is part of this trend to experimentation. It explores the integration of sustainable design into mass-produced housing at the scale of the housing unit. In the coming years major planning projects documented in our Community Planning section will provide the impetus for increased sustainability in residential construction.

◄◄ Sustainable Condo Exterior
Photo: Martin Tessler

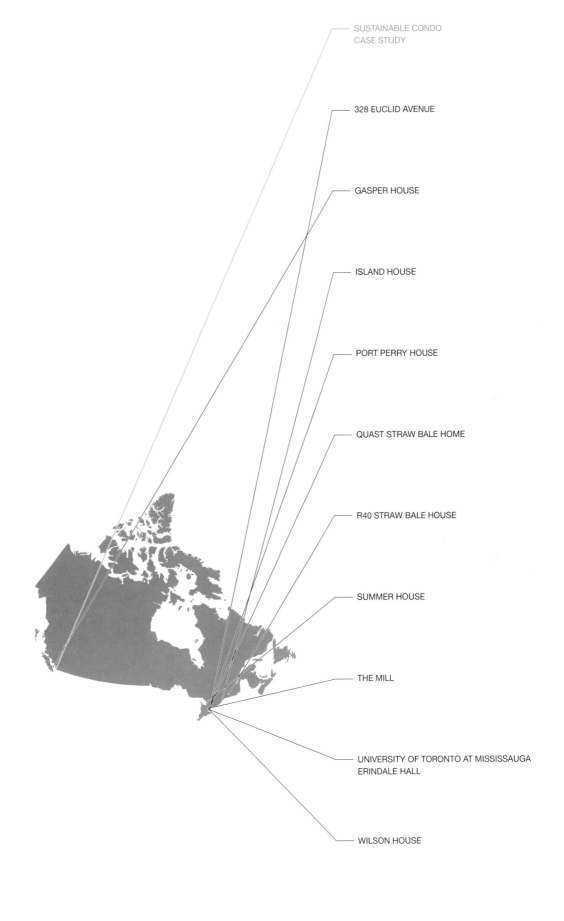

SUSTAINABLE CONDO
CASE STUDY

328 EUCLID AVENUE

GASPER HOUSE

ISLAND HOUSE

PORT PERRY HOUSE

QUAST STRAW BALE HOME

R40 STRAW BALE HOUSE

SUMMER HOUSE

THE MILL

UNIVERSITY OF TORONTO AT MISSISSAUGA
ERINDALE HALL

WILSON HOUSE

CLIENT EcoSmart Foundation ARCHITECTS Busby Perkins+Will
ENGINEERING Keen Engineering STRUCTURAL Fast & Epp DEVELOPERS
The Shelter Group CONSTRUCTION Ledcor Construction EXHIBIT
DESIGNERS D. Jansen & Associates INTERIOR DESIGN Penner &
Associates Interior Design

RESIDENTIAL CASE STUDY

SUSTAINABLE CONDO

TRAVELLING EXHIBIT, 2004

The Sustainable Condo is an award-winning showcase of innovative Canadian products and technologies that can help create a financially sound, higher comfort and environmentally responsible dwelling. Busby Perkins+Will brought together a team of consultants to create this interactive, dynamic exhibition featuring leading edge green building technologies and concepts. All available in the current marketplace, these help to reduce environmental impacts and resource consumption.

The Sustainable Condo educates visitors about today's main environmental issues: energy, water and materials consumption; general health and well-being; and land-use practices. As visitors tour the Condo, they learn about new methods to mitigate personal environmental impact and live a greener lifestyle. The majority of the Condo's materials are renewable, recyclable, durable, non-toxic, and derived from local and recycled-content sources.

The Condo was first unveiled at GLOBE 2004, an international environmental forum and tradeshow held bi-annually in Vancouver. It has since been exhibited at other public venues and will tour through to the 2010 Vancouver Olympics. An EcoSmart™ project, it is a collaboration between the Government of Canada and over 45 Canadian partners and sponsors.

Highlights

■ Energy efficient appliances used—dishwasher, fridge and washer/dryer—are 10-40% more efficient than conventional models. ■ Advanced glazing systems incorporate photovoltaic panels, integrated shading devices and high-performance glazing. ■ In-floor radiant heating and cooling systems use energy storage capacity of concrete structural system. ■ Dual-flush toilet and low-flow showerheads prevent water waste. ■ The XeroFlor green roofing system decreases the rate and volume of rainwater runoff, reducing urban heat effect. ■ Forestry Stewardship Council wood for the millwork comes from sustainably harvested forests and flooring is constructed from reclaimed fir. ■ Organic cotton, hemp and wool contribute to the overall comfort and health of the occupants. ■ Natural ventilation and daylighting are maximized.

"The central problem of architecture is space. Space is essential for the individual and for the community. This is equally true for the small space (the capsule) as well as for the large space (the city)."

JUSTUS DAHINDEN

▸ Live Space with
Entertainment Unit
▸ Dress Space with Flyash
Concrete Tile
▸ Sleeping Space with
Natural Fibre Bedding,
Mattress and Carpet
▾ Dining Space with
Breathing Wall/Solarium
▾ Cleansing Space with
Dual-Flush Toilet
and Low Flow Shower
▾ Work Space with Home
Office and Interior Blinds
Photos: Courtesy of
Busby Perkins+Will

About half of the world's population is living in cities. In thirty years' time this may rise to as much as three-quarters. The Sustainable Condo Project was designed to address this and other challenges of urban growth, providing sustainable options for what has become the dominant form of urban dwelling: the condominium.

The Sustainable Condo is an exhibition that displays innovative green technologies and showcases sustainable products. All of the products featured in the exhibit are currently available and are produced primarily by Canadian companies. In addition to informing visitors on products and technologies, the Condo illustrates sustainable practices and design principles.

As visitors tour the exhibit, they are provided with demonstrations and literature explaining these principles and how they can be applied to condominium construction. Despite the growing need for a more sustainable way to produce and live in urban housing, there is currently no condo development or business strategy to address this need. The unique goal of the Sustainable Condo is to target the average homebuyer, and illustrate, educate, and help create the conditions favourable to the successful development of this new housing type.

By specifically addressing the home-buyer as well as the green building community, The Sustainable Condo fosters a market transformation towards more sustainable urban living. It directly challenges the innovation barriers of the building industry, which tend to more risk-adverse and conservative approaches, duplicating previous designs that were commercially successful.

▲ Kitchen
Photo: Martin Tessler

▶ Bed with Built in Storage
▼ Condo Exterior
   Photos: Martin Tessler

Showcased Products and Technologies

The Sustainable Condo is the result of a collaborative effort involving over 40 suppliers of innovative products and technologies. The intention of the project was to showcase actual sustainable building products and techniques and demonstrate how they can be applied to other projects. The following is a list of the firms involved:

Advanced Glazing Systems Ltd.
BC Hydro Power Smart
Greater Vancouver Regional District (GVRD)
Lafarge North America Inc.
Teck Cominco Metals Ltd.
Bang and Olufsen Burrard Street - A Division of Commercial Electronics Ltd.
George Third & Son
Midland Appliance
StructureCraft Builders Inc.
Arc Structures Inc.
ArtCraft Display Graphics Inc.
Bernstein & Gold
Bridge Electric Corp.
Canadian Eco-Lumber Co-op

Caroma USA Inc.
Collin Campbell & Sons Ltd.
Design West
Ecco Heating Products Ltd.
Fred Welsh Ltd.
Garibaldi Glass Industries Inc.
Grohe Canada Inc.
Hemlock Express
Herman Miller Canada
InfoEnergy Inc.
Inform Interiors Inc.
Jenn-Air
Light Resource
Morane Industries Ltd.
MP Lighting
Natura World Inc.

Nysan Shading Systems Inc.
Ornamentum Furniture
Pacific Online
Print and Run
Rider Computer Services
roost homeware
SED Technologies
Shaw Contract
small medium large
Sonia
Telus
The Canadian Institute for Market Intelligence (CIMI)
this is it. design inc
Xero Flor Canada Ltd.

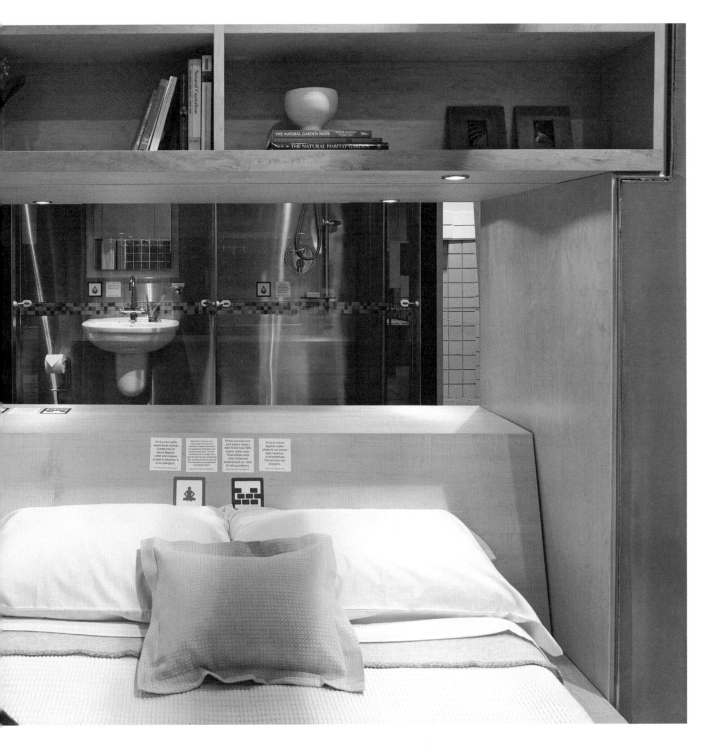

Awards

2005

■ Architectural Institute of British Columbia Innovation Award, The Sustainable Condo
Project ■ Royal Architectural Institute of Canada Award of Excellence for Innovation in
Architecture ■ Royal Architectural Institute of Canada Award of Excellence, Architectural
Firm ■ Canadian Wood Council, Wood Works, Architect Award

2004

■ Canadian Institute of Energy (BC), Energy Research & Development Award ■ Ethics in
Action Firm Award for Environmental Excellence (Medium-Sized Firm Category)

▾ Exterior Entrance
▸ Staircase and Skylight
Photos: Ben Rahn

328 EUCLID AVENUE

TORONTO, ONTARIO, 2005

328 Euclid Avenue is an urban infill site in downtown Toronto. Dean Goodman & Janna Levitt designed the house for their own use on a standard 20 foot wide downtown lot. Their intention was to build a small house of approximately 1,550 sq. ft., which would use a pragmatic approach to green building practices.

The house was laid out and sized to suit a family of four. It is two stories high with a basement and utilizes all of this space to maintain a small footprint on the lot. The layout anticipates the changing needs of a family with teenagers and considers the way in which the house might evolve over time as the children grow up and leave home. Though modest in size, the main floor has a large open floor plan of approximately 16' x 55' with large sliding doors at the front and back. This coupled with a 12 foot ceiling height contributes to the feeling of a generous interior larger than its actual size. Large windows allow for excellent natural light throughout the entire house and provide a sense of space, which helps to moderate the long dark Toronto winter. Bedrooms and workspaces are located on the second floor and basement to give maximum sound separation between the floors.

◂ Kitchen Open to Living Room
Photo: Ben Rahn

Highlights

■ To help keep the house cool in summer, green roofs are used and are planted with native Ontario plant species. These are draught resistant and attract birds and butterflies. ■ The addition of large operable windows and ceiling fans moderate the need for air conditioning and keep the house comfortable in summer. ■ The strategic location and size of windows has eliminated the need for additional electrical lighting during daylight hours. ■ All floors including the basement use exposed polished concrete, which serves as heat sinks for cooling in summer and heating in winter. ■ The heating system is an 'on demand' gas fired hot water system using a single boiler for radiant floor heat as well as for domestic hot water.

Team

CLIENTS Dean Goodman & Janna Levitt
ARCHITECTS Levitt Goodman Architects Ltd.
CONSTRUCTION MANAGERS Boszko and Verity Inc.

▾ Kitchen
▸ Living Area
Photo: Jens Fischer

GASPER HOUSE

SALT SPRING ISLAND, BRITISH COLUMBIA, 2004

The large, solid forms of Gasper House echo the rock face site. It has a compact design with modular walls and reusable forms; the durable earth walls could last 1000 years. The homeowners' primary goal was to create a home that would improve their health, which in turn became the basis for all decision-making throughout the building process. The use of walls and concrete roof tiles that block micro and radio waves is an example of this consideration. High indoor air quality includes the use of solid wood cabinetry, milk paint and natural oil finishes and the avoidance of all toxic materials. The rammed earth walls are insulated with an integral core of foam insulation, a technique developed by Terra Firma that is the first of its kind. Engineered for stability that can withstand a major earthquake, the walls include steel reinforcing and a small amount of cement. The Gasper House received a gold CARE award for Best Single Family Home under 2,000 sq. ft. and the Environmental Achievement CARE Award from the Canadian Home Builders Association.

Highlights

■ Positioning the house on a downhill site rather than an uphill one with a better view in order to avoid microwaves and radio waves. Two-foot thick earth walls and a concrete tile roof also block micro/radiowave pollution. ■ The homeowners wired with AC/DC low EMR wiring to avoid electromagnetic pollution. The electrical and mechanical room is separated from the main building. ■ The design includes solar power and a gravity-fed rainharvest system. ■ No plywood and dry- wall was used due to the toxicity of the glues in these products and processes. ■ The only finishes used were milk paint and natural oils. ■ The concrete floor was poured without steel reinforcing. Tests show that metal in floors disrupts the magnetic forces of the earth. Instead of steel, fibre mesh was used to strengthen the floors. ■ Environmentally friendly appliances such as a low flush toilet, and a low-voltage fridge were used.

Team

ARCHITECTS Terra Firma Builders Ltd.
BUILDERS Terra Firma Builders Ltd.
FINISHINGS the clients

▾ Exterior with Pond
  Photo: Howard Sutcliffe

ISLAND HOUSE

THOUSAND ISLANDS, ONTARIO, 2004

This single-family, 2000 sq. ft. residence is located on one of the Thousand Islands in the St. Lawrence River. The architects wanted to retain the openness of this agrarian landscape while providing their clients with privacy and a splendid view.

Created as a new site within an existing site, construction began with pouring a 200-foot long concrete retaining wall, which informed the section of the residence and the larger site simultaneously. The entire five-acre site was hydro seeded with a local clover mix, which is harvested by a local farmer several times a year. The surrounding clover meadow and the green roof complement each other and blur the notion of building roof and ground plane. The green roof, which covers fully 1700 sq. ft., serves to redefine and balance the relationship between landscape, building and water on this site.

This project was one of six recipients of a 2004 Green Roof Award of Excellence in North America. It was the only Canadian example and the only project located in an agrarian landscape.

"Perhaps an igloo
is innovative.
After that everything
else is a little pale."
BRIGITTE SHIM

Highlights

■ Both the upper and lower green roofs use a Sopranature green roof system and occupy 1,700 sq. ft. of surface area. The plant list for the upper green roof is a wildflower meadow with a mix of local indigenous flowers. ■ The green roof is integrated into the site concept and the building concept. ■ The green roof seeks to redefine and balance the relationship between landscape, building and water on this site. ■ On the St. Lawrence River side the project opens up onto a large water garden with indigenous water lilies and bullrushes.

Team

CLIENT Kevin and Carol Reilly ARCHITECT Shim-Sutcliffe Architects STRUCTURAL Blackwell Engineering MECHANICAL Toews Systems Design CONTRACTOR Peabody and Sheedy Construction GREEN ROOF DESIGNER Soprema Canada GREEN ROOF LANDSCAPE Top Nature

"Organic buildings are
the strength and lightness
of the spiders' spinning,
buildings qualified by light,
bred by native character to
environment, married to
the ground."
FRANK LLOYD WRIGHT

▾ Dining Room
▸ Green Roof
▸ Building Exterior Corner Detail
Photos: Breathe Architects

PORT PERRY HOUSE
PORT PERRY, ONTARIO, 2004

Designed by architect Martin Liefhebber, Port Perry House is a simple three-storey cube clad with birch plywood. A modest 1700 sq. ft. residence, it provides maximum output while requiring minimum input. The house is sited to maximize the use of trees to regulate temperature by shading the house naturally in the summer and sheltering from the wind in winter. During the summer, a flat roof adorned with perennials keeps the house cool and comfortable while maximum passive solar gain is achieved in the winter months through south-facing windows.

By varying orientation, layout, shape, and material composition, the holistic, sustainable design eliminates the need for purchased energy as well as costly, compensatory appliances to heat/cool the home. The floors are heated by hot water from solar panels and by sun shining directly through glass. This reduces dependence on fossil fuels and altogether eliminates the need for a furnace, saving over $1000 per year in energy costs.

◂ Building Exterior with Walkway
Photo: Breathe Architects

Highlights

■ The stiff engineered wood post and beam structure carries the concrete floors and permits large expanses of glazing to enable passive solar heating. In-floor heating serves as backup. ■ A green roof provides added insulation in the winter and enough cooling in the summer that air-conditioning is not required. ■ 12" Truss joists typically used for floor and roof construction are used vertically for the walls creating a curtain wall type of system that minimizes thermal bridging. ■ Triple-glazed windows are treated with a special coating for maximum heat gain in winter without the usual nighttime heat loss. ■ Open spaces allow maximum winter sunlight penetration throughout the house. ■ Water and sewage provisions are taken care of through natural processes.

Team

ARCHITECT Martin Liefhebber, Breathe Architects STRUCTURAL Read Jones Christoffersen CONTRACTOR Keith Nelson MILLWORK Mark McCabe LANDSCAPING Peter Kaiser

▼ Tying Bales
▶ Bale Wall Detail
Photos: Loghman Azar

QUAST STRAW BALE HOME
OAKVILLE, ONTARIO, 2006

Conceived as a challenge to design a modern spacious home within the limitations of straw bale construction, Quast Straw Bale Home is the first straw bale home to be built in Oakville, Ontario.

Straw bale is an innovative building material that is superior in energy efficiency, environmentally safe and both simple and easy to work with. Employing a natural by-product of farming, straw bale construction is completely biodegradable and very economical. Its increased insulating qualities provide improved living conditions: it allows for the installation of significantly smaller heating and cooling systems than conventional wall systems. Straw bale walls have also proven to be exceptionally fire resistant. The thickness and subtle curves of the material have a special beauty and character that can easily be modified according to the creative aspirations of the home's inhabitants. A drawback is the requirement of a conventional structural solution to act as a primary framing system; the method is still in its growing stage when it comes to being accepted by modern building codes.

Working with its lack of acceptance as a structural material, the design of Quast Straw Bale Home uses a hybrid system combining infill straw bale walls with a traditional post and beam framing system.

Highlights

■ The infill straw bale walls are a natural by-product of farming. They provide insulation, are fire-resistant, economical and completely biodegradable. ■ Natural ventilation brings fresh air throughout the space. ■ Open spaces allow for maximum day lighting. ■ Radiant heating avoids dependency on fossil fuels. ■ Non-toxic internal and external finishes are used. ■ Reusable and reconstituted wood products, and salvaged materials are used throughout. ■ A kiva fireplace made from lightweight masonry burns wood or ceramic gas logs. ■ Overhangs are used to shade the house from the southern sun and to protect the bale walls from excessive rain, while allowing the winter sun to penetrate.

Team

OWNERS Michael and Loraine Quast
ARCHITECT Loghman Azar LINE Architect Inc.
STRUCTURAL Yoles Partnership Ltd. BUILDERS Quast Family, Mike Holmes, Harry White and Ben Polly

▾ Living Area Looking East
▸ Kitchen with Strawboard Cabinetry
Photos: Robert Burley

R40 STRAW BALE HOUSE
MONTREAL, QUEBEC, 1999

This two and a half storey 2000 sq. ft. single family house was conceived as a demonstration project with the fundamental objective of designing an affordable, comfortable, ecological home. It is a prototype demonstrating the architectural potential of straw bale construction and the potential of urban densification on small lots. This house design is characterized by a holistic approach incorporating affordability and sustainability.

The principal objective of this pilot project was to introduce sustainable design, and specifically straw bale construction, to the Canadian urban context. Based on the development of an accessible, affordable building technique combining straw bales with 2x4" studs, the house also features a straw bale insulated slab-on-grade, as well as other innovative, ecological materials and techniques. Most significant was the simplicity and accessibility of the building process.

A second objective was to encourage the revitalization of inner-city neighbourhoods through the construction of housing on undersized lots. In the context of a grant provided by the ACT program, Julia Bourke worked closely with the City of Montreal's urban planners to provide supporting research for changing restrictions on such developments.

◀ Building Exterior
Photo: Robert Burley

Highlights

■ The slab-on-grade foundation maximizes accessibility and interaction between the interior space and the garden. This significant thermal mass at the ground floor level also benefits from a passive solar gain. ■ The sloped roof is covered with galvanized steel and insulated with blown cellulose. ■ The interior layout maximizes natural ventilation, winter solar gains, flexibility and efficiency. ■ The project is located on a small lot, only 36 ft. deep, on an abandoned street. All trees were preserved. ■ Straw bale infill walls pro-vide R-40 insulation, two-hour fire resistance, low-embodied energy and carbon sequester-ing. ■ 2x4 light wood balloon frame-studs are flush with the interior; a first for strawbale construction. ■ High lime content stucco is used inside and out with pigment incorpo-rated for durability. ■ Low-E argon-filled double-glazed windows are used. ■ Radiant hot water provides in-floor heating. ■ Non-toxic, natural wood and concrete finishes include tree resin, linseed oil, milk paint, and bee's wax.

Team

ARCHITECTS/ENGINEERS Julia Bourke Architecture Inc. BUILDING TEAM Julia Bourke, Simon Jones, family and friends, Michel Bergeron (straw bales), CRIB construction (framing), Paul Holding (cabinetry)

"Only when architect,
bricklayer and tenant
are a unity, or one and
the same person, can we
speak of architecture."
FRIEDENSREICH HUNDERTWASSER

▾ Living Area with Wood
  Burning Stove
▸ Kitchen/Dining Area with
  Screened Porch
  Photo: Jacek Vogel

SUMMER HOUSE
MUSKOKA, ONTARIO, 1999

Conceived as an experimental model for a sustainable summer place, the Summer House's functional program and detailing are reduced to an elemental level and maintenance-free materials are in standard manufactured sizes. The house is aligned to fit between the existing trees and granite boulders, and is oriented north/south to celebrate early morning and late afternoon sun, and to encourage natural ventilation by the prevailing winds.

Retreat on Skeleton Lake was developed from the idea of a skeleton, in a form of a traditional 'long house', using a simple light wood-frame structure. Exterior walls are clad with single glazing and wood fibre-cement boards in colour and texture matching rocks, resisting moisture, fire and rodents. Being seasonal, the house is not winterized: the exterior skin forms the interior finish. All openings are finished without frames so glazing and doors are attached directly to structural elements.

The result is an economical yet sophisticated house that demonstrates how a rethinking of the design and construction of a summerhouse can provide effective sustainable solutions. This reorientation could prevent the gradual erosion of our remaining places of wilderness, introduce 'nature' into the daily rituals of users, and encourage the development of lasting environmental ethics.

The project received the 1999 Ontario Association of Architects Award of Excellence for its architectural and environmental qualities.

Highlights

■ The structure is elevated above the existing grade on concrete piers to minimize its impact on the existing drainage patterns. ■ Services are kept simple and unobtrusive: cables are buried beneath the concrete steps of the approach, water is pumped from the lake, wastewater drains to a leaching pit. ■ The kitchen area contains only what a seasonal house requires: a counter top with a sink and built-in electrical range, a small fridge and open shelves. ■ The washroom contains only a shower and a sink, as a separate outhouse is provided nearby. ■ Exterior walls are clad with either single glazing or 5/8" wood fiber-cement boards which resist moisture, fire and rodents. Left unpainted, the colour and texture of these boards match the granite rocks on site. ■ Corrugated galvanized metal is used over the entire roof (the fiberglass corrugated panels cover the porch area) and on the side walls of the house's south end. ■ All of the house's openings are finished without the use of frames; window glazing and doors are attached directly to the structural elements that form openings. ■ The house, being seasonal, is not winterized, and its exterior skin consequently forms the finish of the interior.

Team

CLIENT Barbara, Jacek and Kaija Vogel
ARCHITECT Vogel Architect team - Barbara Vogel, Jacek Vogel, Rino Filippelli
STRUCTURE David Laird, Robert Halsall and Associates Ltd. CONTRACTOR Bud Doucette and Sons Construction Ltd.

▾ Exterior with Courtyard and Solarium
Photo: Charles Simon

THE MILL

EDEN MILLS, ONTARIO, 2003

This project involved the adaptive re-use of a seriously threatened 1842 stone mill, which was destroyed by two fires. Built for nineteenth century waterpower, the mill has been recycled for twenty-first century solar power. Preservation of this landmark heritage structure in the centre of a picturesque village includes appropriate contemporary technologies. As a mixed-use live/work building (home/office/sculpture studio/apartment), emphasis on flexible design allows for adaptive re-use and long-term fiscal and social viability.

Embodying the principles of low energy, loose fit, and long life, primary energy strategies exploit natural systems. These include micro-climatic design and passive heating, cooling and ventilation.

Reconstruction of the historic millpond is a remarkable community effort achieved through the creation of a private land trust by the owners which ensures that the private amenity is enjoyed and maintained by the villagers.

◀ Livingroom, Low-E
Triple-Glazed Windows
Overlooking Millpond
Photo: Margaret Belisle
and James Eager

Highlights

■ Passive solar heating through solarium (fan extraction) and south-facing windows. ■ Vent stack cooling through the solarium provides night flushing of the entire house, office and studio. The same strategy cools the apartment through clerestory windows and is further tempered through earth coupling. ■ A novel application of active solar collectors within the solarium together with a boiler backup provides domestic hot water. ■ Provision has been made for building integrated photovoltaic collectors and accessing hydropower from the restored millrace.

■ Use of local and in-place materials as well as adaptive re-use exploit embodied energy. ■ A high-performance building envelope includes window selection, extreme care in avoiding thermal bridging and a continuous 'wrap' of exterior insulation. ■ There is extensive use of roof gardens: plants are used for water retention, shade, air cleansing and cooling, and soil stabilization. ■ Extreme care is taken in ensuring zero pollution of the adjacent river system, which flows to the nearby primary source of the City of Guelph's drinking water.

Team

ARCHITECT Charles Simon Architect and Planner MECHANICAL ENGINEERING Enermodal Engineering ELECTRICAL ENGINEERING Peter R. Meridew Consultants Ltd. STRUCTURAL ENGINEERING O.T. Baggio & Associates

▾ Tower Cluster with Glazed Corridor
▸ Main Stair Hall
   Photos: Michael Awad

UNIVERSITY OF TORONTO AT MISSISSAUGA ERINDALE HALL

MISSISSAUGA, ONTARIO, 2003

This residence embraces its spatial and temporal role as a place of transition for first time university students. Integrating built form with innate natural site attributes, the 197-bed facility is designed to create a locus of collegial society that will support and enrich the quality of student experiences, whether pursuing studies alone or socializing in groups. Inserted into a 'rift' in the forest, a remnant of the Credit River Valley landscape, the building is designed to realize the dream of a 'northern campus' that the Erindale founders imagined as a particularly Canadian experience of university community.

Located on an area of disturbed landfill left by old utility buildings, the new building bends and undulates to minimize impact on its landscape context; the ever-changing forest landscape is made an integral part of the experience of interior spaces.

Collective facilities for residents are concentrated on the ground floor along the length of a colonnade and separated from it by areas of butted glass alternating with massive stone panels. Pocked and fossilized panels of strata limestone contrast with slick reflective glass and recall the nearby Credit River's transit through time and space.

◀ View of Colonnade
Photo: Tom Arban

Highlights

■ The primary exterior and interior building materials have been selected for durability, serviceability, natural richness and tactility. ■ An aggressive approach to energy efficient design has reduced the building's overall energy consumption and resulted in full CBIP funding. ■ Daylighting and amenity of collective and private areas are maximized by generous areas of spectrally selective glazing. ■ Storm water is not discharged into municipal storm sewers but routed through landscaped swales and retained on site to recharge an adjacent protected natural wetland area. ■ Large areas of floor to ceiling glazing in public areas at the base of the building allow not only for views through the building to the treed areas on the other side, but provide enhanced security by reducing the potential for blind areas. ■ Bedrooms are designed to enhance privacy and acoustic separation. ■ Large windows with openers maximize daylighting, natural ventilation and sensory contact with the landscape. ■ Integration of student residents into the campus reduces vehicular traffic.

Team

CLIENT University of Toronto ARCHITECTS Baird Sampson Neuert Architects STRUCTURAL Yolles Partnership Inc. MECHANICAL/ELECTRICAL Crossey Engineering Ltd. LANDSCAPE Janet Rosenberg + Associates Landscape Architects Inc. GEOTECHNICAL Shaheen & Peaker Ltd. BUILDING ENVELOPE Dr. Ted Kesik, P. Eng BUILDER Ledcor Construction Ltd.

▾ Kitchen Greenhouse
▸ Interior Bridge
  Photos: Breathe Architects

WILSON HOUSE

MONO MILLS, ONTARIO, 2003

The house and the metamorphosis of its owner are a model for sustainable living. Wilson House is an 'instrument for change' that proves we can thrive without being destructive to the environment. The Wilsons' main goal was to live in a house that is powered by the sun, wind and rain using an array of energy-efficient, earth-friendly technologies without sacrificing modern conveniences. They were willing to explore high and low tech solutions.

As the house took shape the client became so enthusiastic, he created a website devoted to his emerging definition of 'Natural Living'. Deeply moved by the design of his new home, he also wrote a book and produced a movie about the experience. John Wilson now conducts events on his property such as workshops on how to make changes to one's way of life and Sunfest—an open house which 1800 people attended in 2003. This house received the National Post/Design Exchange award for sustainability and is included in the 2005 Living Spaces Exhibition being shown in Canada's major centres.

Highlights

■ Local, natural materials are used. ■ The straw bale insulated walls are fully biodegradable. ■ Ten individual solar panels were installed. The Wilson House further generates its own electricity through the use of a wind turbine allowing the grid supply meter to run backwards. ■ The house has no furnace or air-conditioning and zero emissions, yet proves to be comfortable during all seasons.

■ The house is energy autonomous; therefore power outages have no impact. ■ Over the useful life of the wind turbine, it can offset approximately 1.2 tons of air pollutants and 200 tons of greenhouse gasses. Excess energy is essentially sold back to the grid. ■ A green roof contributes energy efficiency and the recycling of rain water.

Team

CLIENT John Wilson, NaturalLifeNetwork. com ARCHITECTS Martin Liefhebber, Breathe Architects STRUCTURAL Read Jones Christoffersen CONTRACTOR Colin Richards, Kolapore Construction Inc. ELECTRICAL Phantom Electron Corp

CATALOGUE AND
RESOURCES

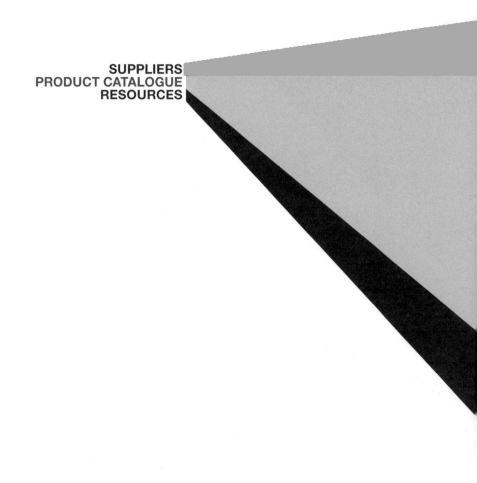

SUPPLIERS
PRODUCT CATALOGUE
RESOURCES

SUPPLIERS	198
INTERFACE FLOORING SYSTEMS	205
SARNAFIL LTD.	206
C-S GROUP	208
AQUATECH SALES & MARKETING INC.	210
ARMSTRONG	
CANFOR	211
CENTURY WOOD	
CGC INC.	212
DELTALOK INC.	
ELEVATED LANDSCAPE TECHNOLOGIES	213
ENVIROSHAKE	
FALCON WATERFREE TECHNOLOGIES	214
FORBO FLOORING	
HEAT MIRROR SUNLITE	215
INLINE FIBERGLASS	
KAWNEER COMPANY CANADA	216
KONE	
OWEN SOUND LEDGEROCK LIMITED	217
SHAW CONTRACT GROUP	
DUSTING DIVAS	218
GENERAL PAINT CORPORATION	
HOK CANADA INC.	
PRELCO	
ROBERTS COMPANY CANADA LTD.	219
SARAMAC INC.	
WATERLOO BIOFILTER SYSTEMS INC.	
CANADA GREEN BUILDING RATING SYSTEMS	220
LEED® CERTIFIED BUILDINGS	222
DESIGN CHARRETTES	223
GREEN BUILDING ALLIANCE	224
SUPPORTERS OF THE SB08 TORONTO BID	226
ARCHITECT DIRECTORY	228
ORGANIZATIONS	234

SUPPLIERS

Accurate Dorwin
1535 Seel Ave
Winnipeg, MB R3T 1C6
tel 204.982.8370
info@accuratedorwin.com

Adams and Kennedy
tel 613.822.6800
info@wood-source.com

Advanced Glazing Systems Ltd.
High performance glazing systems
8315 Riverbend Crt
Burnaby, BC V3N 5E7
tel 604.521.4449
www.advancedglazing.com

AFG Industries Ltd.
Low E-coated glazing with high
performance spacer bar
75 Doney Cr
Thornhill, ON L4K 1P6
tel 905.738.9400

Airolite Co.
Sun shades
114 Westview Ave
Marietta, OH 45750
tel 740.373.7676

Air Quality Solutions
Bio-filter green wall
55 Callander Dr
Guelph, ON N1E 4H6
tel 519.820.5504
info@naturaire.com
www.naturaire.com

American Standard
Low-fluid toilets
2480 Stanfield Rd
Mississauga, ON L4Y 1S2
tel 905.949.4800

Amtico
Tile
440-B Britannia Rd E
Mississauga, ON L4Z 1X9
toll free 1.800.479.0190
flooring@american-biltrite.com

Anderson Windows
Windows
46 Cheryl Cr
Sundridge, ON P0A 1Z0
tel 705.384.5341

**Aquatech Sales &
Marketing Inc.**
High Efficiency Boilers
4390 Paletta Crt
Burlington, ON L7L 5R2
tel 905.631.5815
www.aquatech.ws
See Product Catalogue

Ardex Engineered Cements Inc.
Carpet Adhesive
400 Ardex Park Dr
Aliquippa, PA 15001
tel 724.203.5000
info@ardex.com
www.ardex.com

Argus Controls
Digital control system
for greenhouses
1281 Johnston Rd
White Rock, BC V4B 3Y9
toll free 1.800.667.2090
argus@arguscontrols.com
www.arguscontrols.com

Armstrong World Industries
2500 Columbia Ave
P.O. Box 3001
Lancaster, PA 17604
toll free 717.397.0611
www.zv.com
See Product Catalogue

Arrlin Interior Supply
Pyrok building boards
9 Meteor Dr
Etobicoke, ON M9W 1A3
tel 416.798.9200

Aspmaxcess
QC
tel 514.915.3577
www.aspmaxcess.com

Atlas Carpet Mills
Carpet
2200 Saybrook Ave
Los Angeles, CA 90040
tel 323.724.9000
www.atlascarpetmills.com

BASF
Foam insulation
345 Carlingview Dr
Toronto, ON M9W 6N9
toll free 1.866.485.2273
www.basf.ca

Bay Resource Group Inc.
toll free 1.866.646.6519

Benjamin Moore & Co. Ltd.
Low VOC eco-logo certified paints
26680 Gloucester Way
Aldergrove, BC V0X 1A0
tel 604.857.0600
www.benjaminmoore.ca

BPB Westroc
2424 Lakeshore Rd W
Mississauga, ON L5J 1K4
tel 905.823.9881
www.ca.bpb-na.com

Camino Modular Systems
Tate access floor
89 Carlingview Dr
Toronto, ON M9W 5E4
tel 416.675.2400
www.camino-access-floors.com

Canadian Eco-Lumber Co-Op
FSC wood and reclaimed wood
150 14480th Knox Way
Richmond, BC V6V 2Z5
tel 604.278.4300
www.ecolumber.ca

Can-Cell Industries
Cellulose loose-fill
thermal insulation
14715 - 114th Ave
Edmonton, AB T5M 2Y8
toll free 1.800.661.5031
info@can-cell.com
www.can-cell.com

Canfor Panel and Fibre
430 Canfor Ave
New Westminster, BC V3L 5G2
toll free 1.800.363.8873
inquiries@canforpfd.com
www.canforpfd.com
See Product Catalogue

Canlyte Inc.
Agili-T Lightolier fully
addressable lighting system
3015 Louis A Amos
Lachine, QC H8S 1A1
tel 514.636.0670
www.canlyte.com

Carmanah Technologies
Photovoltaics panels
#5 – 556 Brune Dr.
Barrie, ON L4N 9P6
toll free 1.800.300.3037
www.carmanah.com

Caroma USA, Inc.
Low-flow washdown toilet
134-15236 36th Ave
South Surrey, BC V3S 2B3
toll free 1.800.605.4218
dkirkpatrick@caromausa.com
www.caromausa.com

CCI Industries Ltd.
Concrete masonry block
9420 52nd St SE
Calgary, AB T2P 2G6
tel 403.279.8810
www.cci-industries.com

**Cement Association of
Canada Headquarters**
Eco-smart concrete
60 Queen St
Ottawa, ON K1P 5Y7
tel 613.236.9471
headquarters@cement.ca
www.cement.ca

Century Wood
Reclaimed wood
6305 2nd Line
Fergus, ON N1M 1N0
tel 519.787.3768
sales@centurywood.com
www.centurywood.com
See Product Catalogue

CGC Inc.
Bunting Coady Architects
350 Burnhamthorpe Rd W, 5th Flr
Mississauga, ON L5B 3J1
tel 905.803.5600
webmaster@cgcinc.com
www.cgcinc.com
See Product Catalogue

Clivus Multrum Inc.
Waterless composting toilets
15 Union St
Lawrence, MA 01840
toll free 1.800.425.4887
www.clivusmultrum.com

Cloverdale Paint
VOC compliant interior paint
6950 King George Hwy
Surrey, BC V3W 4Z1
tel 604.596.6261
helpdesk@cloverdalepaint.com
www.cloverdalepaint.com

Colin Campbell & Sons Ltd.
Wool carpet
1428 W 7th
Vancouver, BC V6H 1C1
tel 604.734.2758
www.naturescarpet.com

Columbia Forest Products
Plywood
222 SW Columbia St
Portland, OR 97201
tel 503.224.5300
www.columbiaforestproducts.com

Con-Force Structures Ltd.
Flyash concrete
7900 Nelson Rd
Richmond, BC V6W 1G4
tel 604.278.9766
con-force@con-force.xom
www.con-force.com

Conserval Engineering Inc.
Solar systems
200 Wildcat Rd.
Toronto, ON M3J 2N5
tel 416.661.7057
info@solarwall.com
www.solarwall.com

Coolar Electric
GeoThermal
47901 Calton Line
Aylmer, ON N5H 2R4
tel 519.773.8951

C/S Group
Sunshade device
895 Lakefront Promenade
Mississauga, ON L5E 2C2
tel 905.274.3611
www.c-sgroup.com
See Product Catalogue

Cunningham Brick Co.
Post-industrial waste clay
701 N Main St
Lexington, NC 27292
tel 336.248.8541
www.cunninghambrick.com

Daubois Inc.
Stucco
6155 Grandes-Prairies Blvd
Saint-Leonard, QC H1P 1Z5
tel 1.800.561.2664
info@daubois.com
www.daubois.com

Deltalok
Vegetated retaining wall system
125 Charles St
North Vancouver, BC V7H 1S1
tel 604.980.6116
main@deltalok.com
www.deltalok.com
See Product Catalogue

Dinoflex Manufacturing Ltd.
Recycled rubber sport flooring
5590 – 46th Ave S.E.
Salmon Arm, BC V1E 4S1
toll free 1.877.713.1899
sales@dinoflex.com
www.dinoflex.com

**D. Litchfield Demolition &
Used Building Materials**
Mackey Partnership
3046 Westwood St
Port Coquitlam, BC V3C 3L7
tel 604.522.1736
demo@dlitchfield.com
www.dlitchfield.com

Dofasco Inc.
Corrugated galvanized steel panels
1330 Burlington St E Box 2460
Hamilton, ON L8N 3J5
tel 905.544.3761
www.dofasco.ca

Domco Inc.
1001 Yamaska St E
Farnham, QC J2N 1A1
toll free 1.800.363.9276
www.domco.com

**Dordan Mechanical
Contractors Ltd.**
Ground source heat pump
HVAC system
300 Mill St, Unit 7
Kitchener, ON N2M 5G8
tel 519.742.6650
info@dordanmech.com
www.dordanmech.com

Dow Bioproducts
Woodstalk fibreboard
toll free 1.800.441.4369
www.dow.com/bioprod/

Duochem
Duodeck traffic coating
1250 Graham Bell
Boucherville, QC J4B 6H5
toll free 1.888.577.6421
sales@duochem.com
www.duochem.com

Durisol Inc.
67 Frid St
Hamilton, ON L8P 4M3
tel 905.521.0999
durisol@durisol.com
www.durisol.com

Dusting Divas
Cleaning products
P.O. Box 46010
2642 Quadra St
Victoria, BC V8T 4E1
tel 250.391.4058
divas@dustingdivas.com
www.dustingdivas.com
See Product Catalogue

Ecco Heating Products Ltd.
Heat pumps and exchangers
19700 Landmark Way
Langley, BC V1M 1A1
tel 604.530.2748
www.eccohtg.com

Eco-House Natural Products
Silicate dispersion paint
P.O. Box 220 Station A
Fredericton, NB E3B 4Y9
toll free 1.877.326.4873
www.eco-house.com

Elevated Landscape
Technologies Inc.
Green roof
245 King George Rd Suite #319
Brantford, ON N3R 7N7
toll free 1.866.306.7773
info@eltgreenroofs.com
www.eltgreenroofs.com
See Product Catalogue

Engineered Air
Enthalpy Wheel
1401 Hastings Cr SE
Calgary, AB T2G 4C8
tel 403.287.2590
www.engineeredair.com

Enviro-Drain Inc.
12568 33rd Ave NE
Seattle, WA 98125
tel 206.363.0316

Enviroshake
Roofing tiles
650 Riverview Dr, Unit 1
P.O. Box 1462
Chatham, ON N7M 5W8
toll free 1.866.423.3302
info@enviroshake.com
www.enviroshake.com
See Product Catalogue

ERV Parent Ltd.
Resilient flooring
5 Otter St
Winnipeg, MB R3T 0M7
tel 204.475.3555
wpg@ervparent.com
www.ervparent.com

EuroLine Windows Inc.
PVC tilt and turn windows Brugmann
series-81
7620 MacDonald Rd
Delta, BC V4G 1N3
toll free 1.800.337.8604
www.euroline-windows.com

Expanko Cork Co.
Cork tiles
3135 Lower Valley Rd
Parksburg, PA 19365
toll free 1.800.345.6202
sales@expanko.com
www.expanko.com

Falcon Waterfree Technologies
Waterless urinal
1593 Galbraith Ave S.E.
Grand Rapids, MI 49546
toll free 1.866.975.0174
info@falconwaterfree.com
www.falconwaterfree.com

Fisher & Ludlow
(Division of Harris Steel)
Aluminum sunshades
750 Appleby Line
P.O. Box 5025
Burlington, ON L7R 3Y8
tel 905.632.2121
info@fisherludlow.com
www.fisherludlow.com

Floorworks Int. Ltd.
Carpet
365 Dupont St
Toronto, ON M5R 1W2
tel 416.961.6891

Forbo Linoleum Inc.
Flooring
tel 416.661.2351
www.forbolinoleumna.com
See Product Catalogue

The Garden Watersaver
Rain barrels
8260 Dalemore Rd
Richmond, BC V7C 2A8
tel 604.274.6630
dan@gardenwatersaver.com
www.gardenwatersaver.ca

GE Lighting Ltd.
Wattstopper
tel 580.634.0151
www.gelighting.com/na

General Paint Corp.
Z-Coat HP3000 Semi-gloss
950 Raymur
Vancouver, BC V6A 3C5
tel 604.253.3131
www.generalpaint.com
See Product Catalogue

Gillis Quarries
2895 Wenzel St
Winnipeg, MB R2E 1H4
toll free 1.800.540.0988
www.tyndallstone.com

Good Shepherd Wool Insulation
R.R #3
Rocky Mountain House
AB T4T 1A1
tel 403.845.6705
stan@goodshepherdwool.com
www.goodshepherdwool.com

Goodfellow Inc.
225 Goodfellow St
Delson, QC J5B 1V5
toll free 1.800.361.6503
info@goodfellowinc.com
www.goodfellowinc.com

Grosvenor North America
Technologies Inc.
Ecoresin Partition, 3form
1311 Howe St, 2nd Floor
Vancouver, BC V6Z 2P3
tel 604.602.0566
info@grosvenorna.com
www.grosvenorna.com

Groundheat Systems
International Inc.
15450 Yonge St
Aurora, ON L4G 1P2
tel 416.410.0586
www.groundheat.com

Haworth
www.haworth.com

Healthiest Home and
Building Supplies
384 Richmond Rd
Ottawa, ON K2A 0E8
tel 613.715.9014
www.thehealthiesthome.com

Herman Miller
Workplace Resource
462 Wellington St W
Toronto, ON M5V 1E3
tel 416.366.3300
fax 416.366.2100
toronto_info@hermanmiller.com
www.hermanmiller.com/canada

Homestead House
Paint Company
Authentic milk paint
95 Niagara St
Toronto, ON M5V 1C3
tel 416.504.9984
Info@Homesteadhouse.ca
www.homesteadhouse.ca

Hydrotech Membrane Corporation
Green roof
10951 Parkway Blvd
Ville D'anjou, QC H1J 1S1
tel 514.353.6000
info@hydrotechmembrane.ca
www.hydrotechmembrane.ca

Ice Kube Systems
Frontier refrigeration
41 St. Paul Blvd
West Saint Paul, MB R2P 2W5
tel 204.255.5959
www.icekubeystems.com

ICI Canada Paints
Low-VOC primer/latex
2600 Steeles Ave W
Thornhill, ON L4K 1A1
tel 905.738.0080
www.icipaintsinna.com

Inline Fiberglass Ltd.
Fibreglass window frames
30 Constellation Ct
Toronto, ON M9W 1K1
tel 416.679.1171
info@inlinefiberglass.com
www.inlinefiberglass.com
See Product Catalogue

InterfaceFLOR Commercial
Carpet
233 Lahr Dr
Belleville, ON K8N 5S2
toll free 1.800.267.2149 x2128
www.interfaceflor.ca
www.interfacesustainability.com
See Product Catalogue

Interstyle Ceramic & Glass Ltd.
Recycled glass tiles
3625 Brighton Ave
Burnaby, BC V5A 3H5
info@interstyle.ca
www.interstyle.ca

Invisible Structures Inc.
Storm water management
toll free 1.800.233.1510
sales@invisiblestructures.com
www.invisiblestructures.com

I-XL Masonry Supplies Ltd.
Marler Architects
3595 East 1st Ave
Vancouver, BC V5M 1C2
tel 604.299.0270
ix-l@ixlgroup.com
www.ixlbrick.com

James Hardie Siding Products
Hardiplank
26300 La Alameda, Suite 250
Mission Viejo, CA 92691
toll free 1.888.542.7343
info@JamesHardie.com
www.jameshardie.com

Johns Manville
Batt insulation 50% recycleable
P.O. Box 5108
Denver, CO 80217-5108
toll free 1.800.654.3103
www.jm.com

Frank Jonkman & Sons Ltd.
High & low mechnically driven window
ventilation system
R.R. #4
Brantford, ON L3Z 2A6
toll free 1.800.566.5626
www.jonkman.com

K & M Bamboo Products
Eco-logo certified tongue and groove
floor planks
300 Esna Park Dr
Unionville, ON L3R 0E5
tel 905.947.1688
info@silkroadflooring.com
www.silkroadflooring.com

Kawneer
Curtain wall
info@kawneer.com
www.kawneer.com
See Product Catalogue

**Klimatrol Environmental
Systems Ltd.**
Radiant in-slab heating
and cooling system
10 A Bram Ct
Brampton, ON L6Y 2N4
tel 905.454.1742
klimatro@idirect.com
www.klimatrol.com

Kone Inc.
Mackey Partnership
80 Horner Ave
Toronto, ON M8Z 4X8
tel 416.252.6151
www.kone.com
See Product Catalogue

**Lafarge Canada Inc. – Brookfield
Cement Plant**
Flyash concrete
1 West Pearce St, 7th Floor
Richmond Hill, ON L4B 3K3
tel 905.764.5260
www.lafargenorthamerica.com

Lees Carpets
Carpet with unibond RE
tel 514.425.2908
www.leescarpets.com

**Legacy Vintage Building
Materials & Antiques**
Peterson
540 Division St
Cobourg, ON K9A 1A1
tel 905.373.0796
www.legacyvintage.com

LGI (Lighting Group Inc.)
Fluorescent lighting
9040 Leslie
Thornhill, ON L4B 3M4
tel 905.886.8967
Boates.LGI@Lighting.net
www.premier-lighting.net

Lithonia Lighting
Fluorescent lighting
1 Lithonia Way
Conyers, GA 30012
tel 770.922.9000
www.lithonia.com

Loewen
Doors and windows
77 Hwy 52 West
Box 2260
Steinbach, Manitoba R5G 1B2
toll free 1.800.563.9367
www.loewen.com

Lutron Electronic Co. Ltd.
toll free 1.888.588.7661
www.lutron.com

Madsen Custom Cabinets
Refinished wood panels
618 Whitetail Rd
Whitehall, MT 59759-9639
tel 406.287.5664

Mansfield Plumbing Products
EcoQuantum dual-flush toilet
150 E 1st
Perrysville, OH 44864
tel 419.938.5211
www.mansfieldplumbing.com

Mantei Woodcraft Ltd.
Refinished wood panels
5935 6th St NE
Calgary, AB T2K 5R5
tel 403.295.0028
www.manteiwoodcraft.com

Mapei Inc. Canada
Tile grout
2900 Francis-Hughes
Laval, PQ H7L 3J5
toll free 1.800.426.2734
www.mapei.com

Marvin Windows and Doors
Wood and fiberglass doors
and windows
1455 Courtney Park Dr
Mississauga, ON L4T 1A1
tel 905.670.5052
www.marvin.com

Meteor Plywoods Ltd.
Waferboards and plywood
4 Kenview Blvd
Brampton, ON L6T 5E4

Milliken
tel 647.223.2889
www.milliken.com

New City Resources Inc.
Plastic boards
250 Baseline Rd E
Bowmanville, ON L1C 1A4
tel 905.697.3888

Noug-Art Inc.
Terrazzo floors
107 Tycos Dr
Toronto, ON M6B 1W3
tel 416.249.6581

Novus Lighting
385 Saint-Hubert
Laval, QC H7G 2Y8
tel 450.629.4944
www.novuslighting.com

Nysan Shading Systems Inc.
Interior shading devices (PVC free);
mechanical and operable
window systems
#1 115 28th St SE
Calgary, AB T2A 5K4
tel 403.204.8675
sales@nysan.com
www.nysan.com

Omnilumen Technical Products
Site lighting
80 West Beaver Creek
Thornhill, ON L4B 1H3
tel 905.886.8454

Ontario Ready Mix Ltd.
Flyash concrete
21 Goodmark Place
Etobicoke, ON M9W 6P9
tel 416.674.8237

OSI Hard Surfaces
Tile and stone
tel 416.679.9100

Osram Sylvania Ltd.
Lighting
2001 Drew Rd
Mississauga, ON L5S 1S4
tel 905.673.6171
www.sylvania.com

Otis Canada Inc.
Energy efficient elevator
710 Dorval Dr
Oakville, ON L6K 3V7
tel 905.842.6847
www.otis.com

Owen Sound Ledgerock Ltd.
Regionally quarried limestone
Owen Sound, ON N4K 1A1
tel 519.376.0366
info@ledgerock.com
www.ledgerock.com
See Product Catalogue

Owens Corning Canada
Glass fibre insulation
toll free 1.800.533.3354
www.owenscorning.com

Pacific Timber Tech Inc.
Reclaimed flooring, sheathing plywood
1151 West 8th Ave
Vancouver, BC

P.J. White Hardwoods Ltd.
Wood
1200 E Kent Ave
Vancouver, BC V5X 2X8
tel 604.327.0241
www.pjwhitehardwoods.com

Panel Source International
PureKör
101 18th Rayborn Cr
Saint Albert, AB T8N 5C1
tel 780.458.1007
info@panelsource.net
www.panelsource.net

Patcraft Commercial Carpet
Dagenais LeTourneux
toll free 1.800.713.6697
www.patcraft.com

Patterson-Kelley
High efficiency boilers
P.O. Box 458
100 Burson St
East Stroudsburg, PA 18301
toll free 1.877.728.5351

Peri Formwork Systems
Reusable modular concrete formwork
45 Nixon Rd
Bolton, ON L7E 1K1
tel 905.951.5400
www.peri.ca

Permaquik Corporation
Planted roof systems
6178 Netherhart Rd
Mississauga, ON L5T 1B7
tel 905.564.6100
perma@interlog.com
www.permaquik.com

Playtech Distributors Inc.
Grass and gravel pave material
12031 Twigg Rd
Richmond, BC V6V 1M5
tel 604.324.2734
playtechdistinc@yahoo.com

Polyurithane Foam Systems Inc.
Spray foam insulation
440 Conestogo W
Waterloo, ON N2L 4E2
tel 519.884.0688

PPG Canada Inc.
Solarban 60
81 Bluewater Rd
Bedford, NS B4B 1H4
tel 902.835.7281
corporateinfo@ppg.com
www.corporateportal.ppg.com

Prelco Inc.
Fritted glass
94 Blvd Cartier
Rivière-du-Loup, QC G5R 2M9
toll free 1.800.463.1325
sales@prelco.ca
www.prelco.ca
See Product Catalogue

Primco Ltd.
Resilient flooring
14320 112th Ave
Edmonton, AB T5M 2T9
tel 780.454.0316
www.primco.ca

Rayette Forest Products
Exterior grade wood sheet goods
tel 416.661.0831

React Energy Corp.
#103-2800 107 Ave SE
Calgary, AB T2Z 3R7
tel 403.273.0109
www.reactenergy.ca

Rehau Incorporated
1501 Edwards Ferry Rd
Leesburg, VA 20176
toll free 1.800.561.9609
www.rehau-na.com

Rempel Brothers Concrete Ltd.
High content flyash concrete
#203 – 20353 64th Ave
P.O. Box 3160
Langley, BC V3A 4R5
tel 604.525.9344
info@rempelbros.com
www.rempelbros.com

Richelieu Panel Products
Nevamar laminate
2600 Viking Way
Richmond, BC V6V 1N2
tel 604.273.3108
www.panel-products.com

Roberts Company Canada Ltd.
Low emission adhesive
2070 Steeles Ave E
Brampton, ON L6T 1A7
toll free 1.800.840.9422
www.qep.com
see Product Catalogue

Roxul Inc.
Stone wool insulation
551 Harrop Dr
Milton, ON L9T 3H3
tel 905.878.8474
www.roxul.com

Saramac Inc.
3145 Chdes 40th Arpents
Lachenaie, QC H8S 1K9
tel 450.966.1000
info@saramac.com
www.saramac.com

Sarnafil
1260 Lakeshore E
Mississauga, ON L5E 3B8
tel 905.271.7009
www.sarnafilus.com
See Product Catalogue

Selmar Lab
Recycled and reused
laboratory casework
3513th-199A St
Langley, BC V3A 1J3
tel 604.514.0595

Shaw Contract Group
www.shawfloors.com
See Product Catalogue

Sico Inc.
2505 de la Métropole
Longueuil, QC J4G 1E5
toll free 1.800.463.7426
info@sico.com
www.sico.com

Siemens Building
Technologies Inc.
2 Kenview Blvd.
Brampton, ON L6T 5E4
tel 905.799.9937 x2509
www.siemens.com

Sika Canada
Sika floor 3S
6915 Davand Dr
Mississauga, ON L5T 1L5
tel 905.795.3177
www.sikacanada.com

Sikkens
VOC compliant exterior
wood stain
toll free 1.866.745.5467
www.nam.sikkens.com

Silentaire Manufacturing Ltd.
Mechanical air handling units
tel 832.327.7452

Sloan Valve Company
10500 Seymour Ave
Franklin Park, IL 60131-1259
tel 847.671.4300
Info.411@sloanvalve.com
www.sloanvalve.com

Solace Energy
4025 East Hastings St
Burnaby, BC V5C 2J1
tel 604.291.0342
www.solaceenergy.com

Solarco Manufacturing Ltd.
Vacuum tube solar collectors
2 Matilda St
Toronto, ON M4M 1L9
tel 416.466.3111
info@solarcosystems.com
www.solarcosystems.com

Soprema
Green roof systems
1640 rue Haggerty
Drummondville, QC .J2C 5P8
toll free 1.800.478.8163
www.soprema.ca

Specialty Interior Systems
Acoustical ceiling tiles

Specified Lighting Systems
tel 604.874.2226

Spheral Solar Power
25 Reuter Dr
Cambridge, ON N3E 1A9
tel 519.650.6513
www.spheralsolar.com

Steelcase Canada
tel 905.475.5678
www.steelcase.com

Steels Industrial Products
Building envelope membrane
and insulation
Bldg. 8, 15050 – 54A Ave
Surrey, BC V3S 5X7
tel 604.576.3111
info@steels.com
www.steels.com

Structurlam Products Ltd.
Glulam structural members
2176 Government St
Penticton, BC V2A 8B5
tel 250.492.8912
sales@structurlam.com
www.structurlam.com

Sunlite Insulating Glass
Exterior glazing
1416 Bonhill Rd
Mississauga, ON L5T 1L3
tell 905.564.8235
info@sunlite-ig.com
See Product Catalogue

Tandus Canada
Habitat carpet tile
Unit 5, 2820 Argentia Rd
Streetsville, ON L5N 3J6
tel 905.542.0229
www.tandus.com

Taylor Munro Energy
Systems Inc.
Solar water heating panels
11-7157 Honeyman St
Delta, BC V4E 1E2
tel 604.946.4433
info@taylormunro.com
www.taylormunro.com

Teknion
Workstation furniture
tel 416.661.1577
info.can@teknion.com
www.teknion.com

Tembec Inc.
10 chemin Gatineau, C.P. 5000
Temiscaming, QC J0Z 3R0
tel 819.627.3321
www.tembec.com

Temp-Cast Enviroheat
Wood masonry heaters
3324 Yonge St
P.O. Box 94059
Toronto, ON M4N 3R1
toll free 1.800.561.8594
staywarm@tempcast.com
www.tempcast.com

Temp-Coat
Liquid acrylic insulation
toll free 1.800.950.9958
info@temp-coat.com
www.tempcoat.com

Thermotech Windows
Windows
42 Antares Dr
Ottawa, ON K2E 7Y4
tel 613.225.1101
www.thermotechwindows.com

Timber Systems Ltd.
Glued laminated timber
120 Bollock Dr
Markham, ON L3P 1W2
tel 905.294.7091
timber@timsys.com
www.timsys.com

Tremco Ltd.
220 Wicksteed
Toronto, ON M4H 1G7
tel 416.421.3300

Vanport Steel International Inc.
1417 N.E. 76th St, Suite G-1
Vancouver, WA 98665
toll free 1.800.288.9279
sales@vanport.com
www.vanport.com

Venmar Ventilation Inc.
Heat recovery wheel
550 Lemire Blvd
Drummondville, QC J2C 7W9
toll free 1.800.567.3855
www.venmar.ca

Verdir Systems Inc.
Green walls
Unit 6, 2009 Abbotsford Way
Abbotsford, BC, V2S 6Y5
toll free 1.888.837.3470
info@verdirsystems.com
www.verdirsystems.com

Visionwall Corporation
Vision wall
17915-118th Ave
Edmonton, AB T5S 1L6
toll free 1.800.400.8633
marketing@visionwall.com
www.visionwall.com

Waterloo Biofilter Systems Inc.
Waste water treatment systems
P.O. Box 400, 143 Dennis St.
Rockwood, ON N0B 2K0
tel 519.856.0757
wbs@waterloo-biofilter.com
See Product Catalogue

Water Matrix
Waterless urinals
331 Trowers Rd, Unit 3
Woodbridge, ON L4L 6A2
toll free 1.800.668.4420
maryc@watermatrix.com
www.watermatrix.com

Western Archrib
Glued laminated timber
4315 92nd Ave
Edmonton, AB T6B 3M7
tel 780.465.9771
gen@westernarchrib.com
www.westernarchrib.com

Weyerhaeuser Canada
Low-VOC/non-formaldehyde
MDF coloured panels
te 604.661.8408
www.weyerhaeuser.com

Windows Unlimited
Vinyl windows
108 Lime St
St. Johns, NFLD A1C 4H8
tel 709.722.9800

WIRSBO
Radiant floor heating
655 Park St
Regina, SK S4N 5N1
tel 306.721.2449
www.wirsbo.com

Wise Energy
info@wiseenergy.ca
www.wiseenergy.ca

Yetmans Sheet Metal
269 Conception Bay Hwy
Conception Bay South,
NL A1W 5J9
tel 709.744.2300

Your Solar Home
299 Applewood Cres., Unit 4
Vaughan, ON L4K 4E7
toll free 1.866.556.5504
info@yoursolarhome.com
www.yoursolarhome.com

Zenon Environmental Inc.
Grey water
3239 Dundas St W
Oakville, Ontario L6M 4B2
tel 905.465.3030
www.zenon.com

Zimmcor Inc.
High performance glazing
and curtain wall
250 Bowes Rd
Concord, ON L4K 1J9
tel 905.738.9500

Zinko
Green roof systems
international@zinko.de

INTERFACEFLOR COMMERCIAL

With a rich history of product design and innovation, InterfaceFLOR Commercial is the world's leading manufacturer of modular, soft-surfaced floorcovering. InterfaceFLOR Commercial has pioneered the concept of non-directional modular floorcovering which InterfaceFLOR offers as the i2™ collection of products. This collection of products—over 70 styles, installs with less waste, requires no attic stock for refurbishment, and multiple dye-lots can be used in any installation. InterfaceFLOR is deeply immersed in the corporate promise: Mission Zero and to make InterfaceFLOR a sustainable corporation by leading a worldwide effort to design sustainable manufacturing and development processes. Over 75% of our new styles re-

cently launched contain PLA, (polylactic acid) a renewable resource, InterfaceFLOR continues to lead the industry with sustainable building products that range from bold patterns, to bright colours to tailored sophistication. Proscenium Collection—a hybrid style is setting the stage using a combination of linear and geometric elements, the patterns in this collection are designed to create an accent area or brighten up an entire room. The Proscenium Collection includes 8 patterns that can be used alone or in combination with each other. Most styles feature a unique shape or pattern over the signature Proscenium Collection plaid effect of the Opening Night style.

Address
InterfaceFLOR Commercial
233 Lahr Dr
Belleville, ON K8N 5S2

Contact
toll free 1.800.267.2149 x2128
www.interfaceflor.ca
www.interfacesustainability.com

GREEN VEGETATED ROOF

SARNAFIL LTD.

Green roofs are roof systems that incorporate vegetation on top of the roof assembly with the added advantages of storm water run-off control, increased roofing membrane life, sound insulation and aesthetic appeal.

Sarnafil's durable roofing membrane is specially designed to remain watertight in extreme conditions, such as those possible under a vegetated roof. Reflective roofing, such as Sarnafil's EnergySmart Roof®, or a vegetated roof using a Sarnafil Green Roof System, meets the design criteria for one point under Sustainable Sites Credit 7: Heat Island Effect: Roof, Req. 2, which states: "Use ENERGY STAR compliant (highly reflective) AND high emissivity roofing (emissivity of at least 0.9 when tested in accordance with ASTM 408) for a minimum of 75% of the roof surface; OR install a "green" (vegetated) roof for at least 50% of the roof area. Combinations of high albedo and vegetated roof can be used providing they collectively cover 75% of the total roof area".

ENERGY SMART LEED®

Whether your project is new construction or renovation, energy efficient roofing is an important point to consider—and Sarnafil makes it easy.

With over 40 years experience providing high quality, proven performance roofing systems combined with the knowledge gained from working on many LEED® buildings, Sarnafil is uniquely qualified to help you with your roofing needs.

Knowledgeable technical representatives, valuable LEED® experience, and an energy efficient membrane make Sarnafil the best choice for architects, specifiers and building owners seeking to create their own high performance building. The potential payback comes in many forms: reduced environmental impact and improved building standards for the future, to name a few.

Address
1260 Lakeshore Rd E
Mississauga, ON L5E 3B8

Contact
tel 905.271.7009
toll free 1.800.268.0479
canadainfo@sarnafilus.com

*Design with the
elements in mind.*

C|S GROUP

C-S GROUP

C/S Pedisystems Entrance Grilles and Mats – Construction Specialties Company

In LEED® 2.1 EQ Credit 5, Architects/ designers are encouraged to place permanent entryway systems (grilles, grates, etc.) to capture dirt and other particulate matter at all high volume entries. Specifying a C/S Pedisystems helps prevent poor indoor air quality due to tracked in dirt and reduces the amount of cleaning chemicals used in building maintenance. Further, it assists in prolonging the life of other textile and hard surface finishes in the building.

C/S Peditred has been tested to meet the Carpet and Rug Institute criteria for indoor air quality. Aluminum components are manufactured from 80 – 100% recycled aluminum (30% post consumer). C/S Pedisystems offers many options to keep your entrance clean, safe and beautiful.

Address
895 Lakefront Promenade
Mississauga, ON L5E 2C2

Contact
Wayne Browning
tel 905.274.3611
toll free 1.888.895.8955
wbrowning@c-sgroup.com

C/S Interior Wall Protection – Construction Specialties Company

Nothing is more sustainable than not building. The second best solution is to build with the building's life cycle in mind. Specifying materials that protect walls, corners and finishes from damage allows the building to maximize its life cycle.

C/S Acrovyn Wall Protection provides environmentally friendly wall and door protection systems to assist in sustainable design: ■ PVC Free Wall Protection – Acrovyn 3000 is a complete protection system free of PVC, dioxin formers, phalates and brominated or halogenated fire retardants; it is also completely recyclable. ■ LEED® 2.1 MR Credit 6 – Rapidly Renewable Materials:

C/S offers a line of hard wearing bamboo handrails. ■ LEED® 2.1 MR Credit 7 – FSC Certified Wood: Acrovyn Renaissance handrails, crashrails, bumper guards and corner guards can be specified to be made from FSC Certified Wood. ■ LEED® Indoor Environmental Quality Credit 4.2: All C/S wood products are finished with low-VOC waterborne stains, paints and finishes. C/S also offers environmentally friendly (no VOC) powder coat finish for selected wall protection products.

Recycled Materials: All C/S aluminum products are manufactured from 80 – 100% recycled aluminum (30% Post Consumer). Consider Acrovyn 3000 on your next LEED® or sustainable building project.

C/S Sun Control Systems – Construction Specialties Company

In LEED® 2.1 EQ credit 8.1 and 8.2 architects/designers are encouraged to provide building occupants with a connection between indoor and outdoor spaces through the introduction of daylight and views into regularly occupied areas of the building. This desire can produce other design challenges. Permanent exterior and interior shading is a technology that can, with properly designed shading elements, limit solar heat gain in summer months and utilize it for supplemental heating in winter. In addition, the need for artificial light can be reduced at all times. Incorporating shading into a building's design can lead to lower

initial lighting and HVAC costs as well as long term operational cost.

C/S offers the widest array of passive solar control solutions to reduce solar heat gain and glare in interior spaces including exterior shading and interior lightshelves. C/S has the ability to provide expert consultancy to architects in the design of sun control solutions based on building orientation, time of day/time of year criteria.

With over 35 years of experience in the sun control business we have compiled a comprehensive list containing websites and publications that are current and educational. Contact Construction Specialties Company for information on C/S Sun Controls.

AQUATECH SALES & MARKETING INC.

High Efficiency Natural Gas Condensing Hot Water Boiler. Utilizing recuperative heat exchange technology to scrub the flue gas of the available latent heat energy and convert it back into the heating water increases the operating efficiency and thermal performance of the appliance as high as 97%. Fan assisted combustion technology combined with referenced gas / air operation ensure low emmission production and infinitely proportional load profile operation throughout its operating range for individual and multiple unit installations. Lon Works compatible intelligence for interoperability language integration into building automation systems make this unit desireable for new construction and retrofit opportunities.

Address
4390 Paletta Crt
Burlington, ON L7L 5R2

Contact
Darryl Singleton,
National Sales Manager
darryls@aquatech.ws

LOCHINVAR INTELLI-FIN.

ARMSTRONG

Armstrong World Industries, the world's largest producer of acoustical ceilings, has introduced its Ceiling Recycling Program in Canada. The closed loop program is the first of its kind to offer recycling as an earth-friendly alternative to disposing of old ceilings.

The Armstrong Ceiling Recycling Program enables building owners to ship old ceilings from renovation projects to an Armstrong ceiling plant as an alternative to landfill disposal. Under the program, Armstrong even pays freight costs for shipping the old ceilings (30,000-square-foot minimum), which it uses as raw materials in the manufacture of new, high-performance acoustical ceilings.

Address
2500 Columbia Ave
P.O. Box 3001
Lancaster, PA 17604

Contact
toll free 1-877-ARMSTRONG
www.armstrong.com/environmental

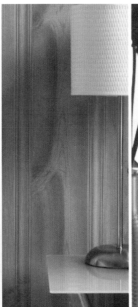

CANFOR

Canfor Panelwoods™ are compressed hardboard panels made with residual wood fibres extracted exclusively from post consumer waste and forest industry byproducts. No ureaformaldehyde resin is used in the manufacturing process and only water based paints are used in the finishing process. Canfor Panelwood™ carry the Green Cross certificate from Scientific Certification Systems for 100% recycled and recovered content. Panelwoods are a unique, attractive and economical alternative to solid wood, veneer, drywall, paint and wallpaper, as well as for interior masonary looks in brick and stone. They are durable, easy to clean, dent resistant and easy to install.

Address
430 Canfor Ave.
New Westminster, BC V3L 5G2

Contact
Doug Ross
toll free 1.800.363.8873
doug.ross@canfor.com

CENTURY WOOD

Welcome history into your home or cottage. Surround yourself with the rich character and ageless ambience of century old wood. By reclaiming beautifully aged wood from vintage buildings, Century Wood Products are the perfect choice for both restoration and the introduction of unique character to new designs. Capture the beauty of the past and take it with you into the future.

Century Wood Products is recognized for quality flooring. We offer plank flooring in a wide selection of species, sizes and finishes. Heart Pine, White Pine, and Douglas Fir are among the many species we offer.

For your next project choose Century Wood Products.

Address
Marsville R.R. #3
Orton, ON L0N 1N0

Contact
Bill Van Veen
millers@centurywood.com

CGC INC.

The manufacturing process for FIBEROCK®
AQUA-TOUGH™ products combines gypsum and paper fibers to create a variety of
high-performance panels used in multiple
applications, including interior wall panels,
floor underlayments and exterior sheathings.

Engineered for strength and resistance
against both water and mold, FIBEROCK®
AQUA-TOUGH™ panels offer excellent
sustainability. FIBEROCK® AQUA-TOUGH™
Underlayment panels are a great alternative to wood-based products, most notably
lauan, which is harvested from endangered,
old-growth forest.

FIBEROCK® AQUA-TOUGH™ panels
contain no VOC's and are made from 95
percent recycled materials. Specifically, 85
percent of content in these panels comes
from recaptured gypsum and 10 percent is
from post-consumer recycle paper fiber.

Address
350 Burnhamthorpe Road W
Mississauga, ON L5B 3J1

Contact
www.cgcinc.com

DELTALOK INC.

Ecological Engineering. The Deltalok System
provides a simple, innovative solution for
erosion control, slope stability and earth
wall applications. The patented Deltalok
System combines proven engineering and
bio-engineering principles in the delivery of
naturally vegetated bio-technical solutions.
The Deltalok System promotes and sustains
vegetative growth through the interlocking
GTX bags, creating an indigenous appearance and protecting the plants root zone.
Construction is simple, requiring minimal site
preparation and no specialized equipment.
From shoreline stabilization to geogrid reinforced walls and slopes where a natural
solution is desired.

'Build it Green' with Deltalok.

Address
125 Charles St
North Vancouver, BC V7H 1S1

Contact
Bruce Stickney
Sales Manager
tel 604.980.6116
info@deltalok.com
www.deltalok.com

THE DELTALOK SYSTEM

ELEVATED LANDSCAPE TECHNOLOGIES INC.

Green roofs and living walls have been found to have extensive properties which contribute to the sustainability of green buildings. In addition to improving air quality and reducing the Urban Heat Island Effect, green roofs and living walls reduce water pollution through storm water absorption and retention, they conserve energy helping to reduce greenhouse gas emissions and they create biodiversity conservation opportunities. ELT Easy Green™ can replenish this much needed green amenity space in downtown environments using our LEED® friendly, innovative green roof and living wall technologies, available across North America.

Address
245 King George Rd. Suite 319
Brantford, ON N3R 7N7

Contact
toll free 1.866.306.7773
info@elteasygreen.com
www.elteasygreen.com

ELT EASY GREEN™

ENVIROSHAKE

Enviroshake® composite engineered roofing provides homeowners with the best of both worlds, accurately replicating the desirable look of a "silvered" taper-split cedar roof while offering the durability and maintenance free features everyone desires and expects in a quality premium roof. No topical treatments are required. There are no painted or granular coatings to peel, lift or wear away over time. It is 95% derived from recycled materials. Enviroshake® will not rot, warp, crack or blister and is backed by a 50 year non-prorated and transferable warranty.

Wellington Polymer Technology Inc. is an ISO 9001:2000 registered company.

Address
650 Riverview Dr, Unit 1
P.O. Box 1462
Chatham, ON. N7M 5W8

Contact
Brian Eberle
toll free 1.866.423.3302
www.enviroshake.com

QUALITY ENGINEERED ROOFING

FALCON WATERFREE TECHNOLOGIES

The Falcon Waterfree urinal is a revolutionary system that saves an annual average of 40,000 gallons per urinal. Waterfree urinals are more hygienic and resistant to vandalism than flush urinals. Without flush valves, plumbing repairs and emergencies are eliminated. Several models are available that earn LEED® points and Green Globes points. Falcon Waterfree urinals are in use around the world, in stadiums and arenas, schools and universities, airports and every type of commercial and institutional facility.

Address
1593 Galbraith Ave SE
Grand Rapids, MI 49546

Contact
tel 616.954.3570
fax 616.954.3579
info@falconwaterfree.com

WATERFREE URINALS

FORBO FLOORING

Marmoleum has been distinguished with the widest range of environmental quality labels in resilient floor coverings, from Australia, Austria, Sweden, the Netherlands and Germany. Marmoleum meets growing concerns worldwide about the use of renewable materials. Marmoleum is made from natural renewable raw materials, and features inherent bactericidal properties that make it the ideal floor where respiratory concerns are present. Marmoleum also has natural anti-static properties to repel dust and dirt, making it easy to maintain a clean and healthy environment.

Address
25 Pollard St
Richmond Hill, ON L4B 1A8

Contact
Scott Day
tel 1.866.661.2351
fax 416.661.5362
scott.day@fl-na.com
www.forbolinoleumna.com

MARMOLEUM GLOBAL 2

HEAT MIRROR SUNLITE

Sunlite's Heat Mirror® insulating glass provides the ultimate in thermal performance (U-value 1.05 W/m²*°K to U-value 0.399 W/m²*°K / U-value 0.186 BTU/(hr*ft2*°F) to U-value 0.070 BTU/(hr*ft2*°F)) From Passive Solar to Solar Control applications, Sunlite custom fabricates today's curtainwall / window assemblies for optimum daylighting and energy savings.

Sunlite's glazing dramatically reduces energy consumption via insulation, solar control and natural daylighting. Reducing energy usage lowers green house gas emissions. Eliminating condensation on glass and effectively controlling the natural ventilation via operators improves indoor air quality. Elevated comfort levels, both physical and psychological, are paramount for building occupants. Sunlite's glazing solutions speak to these evolving human needs.

Address
1416 Bonhill Rd
Mississauga, ON L5T 1L3

Contact
Sales
tel 905.564.8235
http://sunlite-ig.com

INLINE FIBERGLASS

Inline's technological advances extend far beyond simply making products with superior physical characteristics such as strength, design flexibility and stability. The company's products and technology are also rapidly becoming recognized as having a minimal impact on our environment in terms of the low embodied energy incorporated in their manufacturing. This is further enhanced by the products' innate long-term durability and stability. All of these characteristics combined with tremendous energy savings result in a material that satisfies the ever more important requirement that today's products not only be the best choice for the job but also the best choice for the planet.

Address
30 Constellation Crt
Toronto, ON M9W 1K1

Contact
Larry Bidner
lbidner@inlinefiberglass.com

KAWNEER COMPANY CANADA

Kawneer's 7500 Wall was designed with energy conservation as the first priority. The glass reinforced nylon 24mm and 49mm ISOWEB thermal breaks combined with double or triple glazing offers significant savings in HVAC capital costs and annual energy costs.

This high performance system leads the way in energy conservation providing reduced pay-back time periods. The 7500 Wall is ideal for storefronts, strip window, window/wall and curtain wall applications. There are optional high performance vents, casements and doors to compliment the system. 7500 Wall offers an efficient energy conservation alternative to earlier generation curtain wall systems.

Address
1051 Ellesmere Rd
Scarborough, ON M1P 2X1

Contact
Ray Mount
Ray.Mount@Kawneer.com

KONE

Kone is the acknowledged leader in sustainable elevator design, manufacture, installation and maintenance. The Kone EcoSystem family of elevator products use next generation KONE EcoDisc® hoisting machines that are highly energy efficient, remarkably lightweight and space-efficient. The KONE EcoDisc® hoisting machine has an optimized power factor, so the motor consumes less power and produces less heat than traditional traction elevators. Energy savings can be 40% to 60% when compared to standard in-class solutions. Cost effective, the reduced starting current demand lets you use smaller mainline feeder and emergency generators.

Address
80 Horner Ave
Toronto, ON M8Z4X8

Contact
Leo Redmond
Vice President, NEB
tel 416.252.6151

ELEVATORS AND ESCALATORS ECOSYSTEM

OWEN SOUND LEDGEROCK LIMITED

The Company quarries large dolomitic limestone blocks for the production of dimensional stone products. The blocks are extracted from the quarry by way of sawing or drilling. No explosives or chemicals are used in the process. Products made from the naturally occurring mineral dolomite are high-density and hard wearing. The compressive strength of the material ranges between 12,000 PSI to 38,000 PSI depending on the stone type. Absorption of water is typically rated lower than 1% and often as low as .02%. Dolostone building construction can last for centuries. Building components made from less durable materials will be replaced many times during the life cycle of a building. Products made by Owen Sound Ledgerock Limited include Building Wall Stone/ Custom Cut Stone for Architecture/ Floor Tile and Slabs/ Limestone Wall Panels/ Landscape Stone.

Address
P.O. Box 445, RR5
Owen Sound, ON N4K 5P7

Contact
tel 519.376.0366
info@ledgerock.com
www.ledgerock.com

SHAW CONTRACT GROUP

EcoWorx is the industry's first 100% sustainable, non-PVC carpet tile backing. Shaw received acknowledgement for EcoWorx from the U.S. Environmental Protection Agency as a recipient of the Presidential Green Chemistry Challenge Award. The honor recognizes Shaw for developing a carpet tile that may be sustainably recycled and has less embodied energy than traditional PVC carpet tiles, while maintaining equal or greater performance. EcoWorx contains 40 percent recycled content, has been assessed by the MBDC Design Protocol as safe for human health and the environment, and passes CRI Green Label Plus requirements for low emissions. To view EcoWorx-backed products, visit www.shawcontractgroup.com.

Address
50 Torbay Rd
Markham, ON L3R 1G6

Contact
Harvey Salzman
tel 905.513.1011

ECOWORX

DUSTING DIVAS

Dusting Divas non-toxic cleaning products are made ethically with Nature's most powerful purifying agents. They are effectively used by people with kids, pets, allergies or chemical sensitivities. Ask about our specials on bulk sizes and New Home Owner Appreciation Gifts!

Address
P.O. Box 46010
2642 Quadra St
Victoria, BC V8T 4E1

Contact
tel 250.391.4058
divas@dustingdivas.com

GENERAL PAINT CORPORATION

Z-Coat is a 100% acrylic interior finish with VOC levels under 10 grams / litre. Master Painters Institute approved.

Z-COAT

Address
950 Raymur Ave
Vancouver, BC V6A 3L5

Contact
Chris Lonsdale
tel 604.253.3131
clonsdale@generalpaint.com

HOK

Architecture / interior design / planning: Sustainability as a core value integrated into all of our practice areas, service offerings and regional offices, globally.

Address
720 King St W, Suite 505
Toronto, ON M5V 2T3

Contact
Terri Robinson
tel 416.203.9993 x 2237
fax 416.203.9992
terri.robinson@hok.com
www.hok.ca

PRELCO

Prelco offers a full range of energy efficient glass having a significant impact on the energy performance levels of a building.

THERMALITE

Address
32 Coulter Cres
Trenton, ON K8V 3G1

Contact
Jens Harnest
tel 613.394.6952
jens.harnest@prelco.ca

ROBERTS CONSOLIDATED INDUSTRIES

Roberts worldwide Environmental Commitment ensures the industry of Environmentally Safe flooring installation adhesives that also combat the growth of mold and mildew.
www.roberts-consolidated.com

Address
2070 Steeles Ave
Bramalea, ON L6T
1A7

Contact
tel 905.791.4444
fax 905.791.1998
www.qep.com

ENVIRONMENTALLY SAFE FLOORING ADHESIVES

SARAMAC INC.

Saramac has been a leader for more than 25 years in the precast concrete and masonry panels. The durability and the versatile design make it a number one choice to enhance and enliven any architectural project. With all its other inherent characteristics, the precast concrete is a leading sustainable product that makes a better environment.

Address
3145 Chemin des 40 Arpents
Lachenaie, QC J6V 1A3

Contact
Caroline Alain, Robert Venne
info@saramac.com

WATERLOO BIOFILTER SYSTEMS INC.

Waterloo Biofilter is "sustainable sewage infrastructure" for cottages to small villages, with; low energy use, easy servicing, confirmable treatment, recoverability, and robustness with modern chemicals.

Address
143 Dennis St
Rockwood, ON N0B 2K0

Contact
tel 519.856.0757
info@waterloo-biofilter.com
www.waterloo-biofilter.com

CANADIAN GREEN BUILDING RATING SYSTEMS

Building rating systems have originated as a way of rewarding the producers of new buildings (developers and design team) and managers of existing buildings for doing the right thing in improving the energy and environmental performance of buildings. The rating systems identify the best practices and superior performance and thereby encourage a market transformation to wider application of such measures in buildings.

Canada has been fortunate to have had several green building assessment systems. This has allowed for the cross fertilization of ideas and has fostered healthy competition, which, in turn, has motivated research and development, ultimately benefitting the marketplace. In Canada, two national systems, LEED® and Green Globes have achieved significant market penetration. In addition, the GB tool, a research assessment protocol has been a major contributor to theoretical assessment investigations and has explored issues that high performance buildings must address. Through its international events, GB tool has benefited from contributions by international experts and has served as a laboratory for assessment tools. Other approaches have also been explored in Canada. The ISO 14000 approach was considered but was generally found to be too onerous for most buildings operations. In light of the above, it is no surprise that Canada has gained a reputation for being a hotbed of activity in the field of building assessments. Whilst some have argued that diversity could lead to confusion, there appears to be a general consensus among the systems with respect to the objectives of green buildings and best practices. This was greatly aided by a harmonization study by the Government of Canada for the two main systems: LEED® and Green Globes. Meanwhile, as the science of building green evolves, some issues are debated, and all systems continue to refine themselves, based on their research and development and with a view to enhancing their user-friendliness.

LEED® Canada for New Construction and Major Renovations version 1.0 is an adaptation of the US Green Building Councils (USGBC) Leadership in Energy and Environmental Design Green Building Rating System (LEED®), tailored specifically for Canadian climates, construction practices and regulations. LEED® recognizes leading edge buildings that incorporate design, construction and operational practices that combine healthy, high-quality and high-performance advantages with reduced environmental impacts. They provide a voluntary, consensus-based, market-responsive set of criteria that evaluate project performance from a whole-building, whole-life perspective, providing a common understanding for what constitutes a "green building."

The Prerequisites and Credits are organized in the five principal LEED® categories:
Sustainable Sites
Water Efficiency
Energy and Atmosphere
Materials and Resources
Indoor Environmental Quality

An additional category, Innovation & Design Process, addresses sustainable building expertise as well as design measures not covered under these five environmental categories. Project ratings are certified by the CaGBC based on the total point score, following an independent review and audit of selected Credits of documentation submitted by a design and construction team. With four possible levels of certification (certified, silver, gold and platinum), LEED® is flexible enough to accommodate a wide range of green building strategies that best fit the constraints and goals of particular projects.

The other system in Canada, Green Globes is offered not only for retrofits and new buildings but has gained wide acceptance for the assessment of existing buildings. In 2004, it was adopted by BOMA Canada as a national program for evaluation of energy and environmental performance of existing buildings and was re-branded as BOMA Go Green Comprehensive. Green Globes was also launched in USA in 2004 by the not-for-profit Green Building Initiative, which also works with the National Association of Home Builders and local building associations to promote residential green building guidelines developed by the NAHB.

Green Globes is similar to LEED® in many ways but differs from LEED® in the following respects:

It is a questionnaire-based, online method, which automatically generates a report, which can then be edited as needed.

Green Globes emphasizes the integrated design process. With questionnaires for each stage of the design process, it helps to integrate principles of green architecture at every stage of project delivery.

The automated reports (one for each stage of project delivery) list the achievements of a design and offer ratings in seven areas: project management, site, energy, water, resources, emissions and effluents and indoor environment.

The reports also provide detailed recommendations for improving the project along with web links to additional resources.

Green Globes serves as a design guidance and self assessment tool. It also offers independent third-party verification leading to certification. Ratings are given from one to five green globes.

Leadership in Energy and Environmental Design Canada (LEED® Canada):
http://www.cagbc.org

Green Globes:
www.greenglobes.com
www.bomagogreen.ca
www.thegbi.org

LEADERSHIP IN ENERGY AND ENVIRONMENTAL DESIGN (LEED®) CERTIFIED BUILDINGS IN CANADA

The following is a listing of current LEED® certified buildings in Canada as posted November 10th, 2005 on the Canada Green Building Council www.cagbc.org

Hughes Condon Marler:
Architects Office Renovation
Vancouver, British Columbia
LEED-CI® Silver
Hughes Condon Marleer Architects

BC Cancer Agency Research Centre
Vancouver, British Columbia
LEED® Canada Gold
IBI Group / Henriquez Partners,
Architects in Joint Venture

EMS Headquarters and Fleet Centre
Cambridge, Ontario
LEED® Canada Gold
McCallum Sather Architects Inc.

Stratus Winery
Niagara-on-the-Lake, Ontario
LEED® Canada Silver
Andrew Inc. Architect

Cardel Place and Library Facility
Calgary, Alberta
LEED® Gold
Gibbs Gage Architects (in Association
with Barry Johns {Architecture} Limited)
Associate Architect: Cannon Johnston
Architecture Inc.

Surrey Transfer Station
Surrey, British Columbia
LEED® Silver
CEI Architecture Planning Interiors

Mountain Equipment Co-op (MEC) Winnipeg
Winnipeg, Manitoba
LEED® Gold
Prairie Architects Inc.

Canmore Civic Center
Canmore, Alberta
LEED® Silver
Marshall Tittemore Architects

St. John Ambulance Headquarters
Edmonton, Alberta
LEED® Silver
Manasc Isaac Architects

Crowfoot Library
Calgary, Alberta
LEED® Certified
Cohos Evamy ARchitects

Spring Creek Firehall
Whistler, British Columbia
LEED® Silver
Hughes Condon Marler: Architects

Technology Enterprise Facility III (TEF III)
Vancouver, British Columbia
LEED® Silver
Chernoff Thompson Architects

Alberta Urban Municipalities
Association Building Expansion
Edmonton, Alberta
LEED® Certified
Manasc Isaac Architects Ltd.

City of Vancouver National Works Yard
Vancouver, British Columbia
LEED® Gold
Omicron Architecture Engineering Construction
Services Ltd.

The Semiahmoo Library & RCMP District Office
Surrey, British Columbia
LEED® Silver
Musson Cattell Mackey Partnership (MCMP),
Darrell J. Epp Architect, Norson Construction

Vancouver Island Technology Park
Victoria, British Columbia
LEED® Gold
Bunting Coady Architects
& Idealink Architecture

White Rock Operations Building
White Rock, British Columbia
LEED® Gold
Busby + Associates Architects

DESIGN CHARRETTES

Sustainable Buildings Canada (SBC) has been showcasing the integrated design process through the delivery of design Charrettes. In the context of sustainable buildings, a Charrette is an intensive brainstorming session that uses the integrated design process to examine and consider alternative design configurations for new or existing buildings. Integrated design differs from traditional design approaches by using a more iterative approach to decision-making—one in which a variety of design options might be considered as part of a desire to maximize the outcome with respect to building performance. Typically, overarching environmental goals are established at the beginning of the process and the design team works together to examine ways of meeting those goals.

In the integrated design process, the makeup of the design team is expanded beyond that of the more typical owner/architect/engineer approach. A facilitator is added and broader ranges of expertise are engaged as part of the process. Energy and environmental software simulations are often used to aid in the process and there is likely to be multiple iterations before the design team completes its deliberations.

The integrated design process works equally well for both new and existing buildings and SBC has successfully delivered Charrettes for a wide variety of buildings including new and existing offices, multi-family units, industrial facilities, sports complexes, community centres and hospitals. The process was also applied at the community scale when SBC undertook a Charrette for the Regent Park social housing development in Toronto. In all cases, the resulting plans and outcomes represented significant environmental design performance—a testament to the exciting possibilities using the integrated design process.

GREEN BUILDING ALLIANCE

The Green Building Alliance was established in 2004 to provide leadership and support for the development and advancement of sustainable building and development practices in Toronto, Canada and urban areas around the world. The GBA is composed of four organizations which include: the Toronto and Region Conservation Authority, the Canadian Urban Institute, Sustainable Buildings Canada and the Canada Green Building Council (Toronto Chapter).

We are working to create a culture of sustainability and efficiency among municipalities, builders, developers and other stakeholders. Our efforts are directed at creating the necessary regional and local capacity required to effect market transformation for the rapid application of sustainable building and development practices. At the national scale, the GBA is working with academia, industry, government and special purpose research organizations to broaden the impact and effectiveness of educational and outreach initiatives. Globally, the GBA is functioning as a hub to connect Canadian industry and activities with communities around the world to promote innovation and encourage knowledge exchange.

We are well positioned to help identify, disseminate and advance strategic programs and projects, as well as form collaborative partnerships that will contribute to the acceptance and enhancement of sustainable building and development practices.

To achieve our mandate, the GBA is engaged in a variety of initiatives which will:

Advance the business case for building in a sustainable manner

Contribute to creating public and private incentive programs and policies

Encourage new financing, monitoring and evaluation mechanisms

Address regulatory and non-regulatory barriers

Acknowledge the champions in sustainable building and development

Market the advantages and success stories

Link public and private sector agencies involved in sustainable development

Share knowledge and products

Showcase the best examples

For more information on the Green Building Alliance, please visit www.greenbuildingalliance.org

Since its formation in 1957, the Toronto and Region Conservation Authority (TRCA) has prepared and delivered programs for the management of renewable natural resources within nine Toronto region watersheds. The TRCA, through its extensive partnerships, is working to incorporate environmental features that lower energy and water demand and construct buildings that will benefit future generations.

The Canadian Urban Institute (CUI) is an independent, not-for-profit urban think tank dedicated to enhancing the quality of life in urban areas in Canada and around the world. Since 1992, the CUI has provided thought leadership and strategic support for industry and government priorities in the areas of knowledge management, energy conservation, sustainable buildings and communities and brownfield redevelopment.

Sustainable Buildings Canada (SBC) is a non-profit organization formed in 2003 to provide an array of services and opportunities for individuals and organizations interested in furthering the concepts of higher environmental performance in the buildings sectors. SBC offers strategic advice, training and assistance for incorporating sustainable development practices in both new and existing buildings in the commercial/institutional and residential sectors.

The Canada Green Building Council is a broad-based inclusive coalition of representatives from different segments of the design and building industry formed to accelerate the design and construction of green buildings. The Council is responsible the design, implementation and monitoring of the Leadership in Energy and Environmental Design (LEED®) rating system.

SUPPORTERS OF THE SB08 TORONTO BID

INDUSTRY

Lino Luison
Vice President
Opportunity Development
Enbridge Gas Distribution

Mark Mitchel
Vice President and General Manager
Keen Engineering

Chris Sherriff-Scott
Senior Vice President
Minto Urban Communities

Richard Lu
Chief Conservation Officer
Toronto Hydro (consortium)

Dino Carmel
Chief Operating Officer
Tridel

Alex Speigel
Director of Development
Context

David Sisam
Principal
Montgomery Sisam Architects Inc.

PROFESSIONAL

Adrian Van Wijk
President
Association of Canadian
Industrial Designers

Gary Hewson
President
Association of Registered
Interior Designers

Chuck Stradling
Executive Vice President
Building Owners & Managers
Association of the GTA

Paul Evans
Partnership Director
INREB, Farady Partnerships
Building Research Establishment

Ron Shishido
President
Canadian Institute of Planners

Linda McPhee
Director
Canadian Wood Council

Wayne Dawnson
Vice President
Ontario Region Cement
Association of Canada

Mike Yorke
Vice President
Central Ontario Regional Council of
Carpenters, Drywall and Allied Workers

Shai Spetgary
Executive Director
Environmental Markets Association

Bob Goodings
President
Ontario Society of
Professional Engineers

Julie Di Lorenzo
President
Greater Toronto Home Builders'
Association

Cathie Macdonald
Convener
National Executive Forum on
Public Property

Randy Roberts
President
Ontario Association of Architects

Linda Irvine
President
Ontario Association of
Landscape Architects

Don May
President
Ontario Professional Planners Institute

John Cartwright
President
Toronto and York Region
Labour Council

Temple Harris
President
Toronto Construction Association

Andy Manahan
Development Promotion Representative
Universal Workers Union Local 183

SCIENCE & TECHNOLOGY

John English
Dean
British Columbia, Institute
of Technology

Sarah Wakefield
Director
Centre for Urban Health Initiatives

Joni Seager
Dean
Faculty of Environnmental Studies
York University

Ted Brandon
Training Officer
Fleming College

Frank Cunningham
Principal
Innis College, University of Toronto

Malcolm Clendenning
President
Nunavut Arctic College

Andy Anderson
Profesor
Ontario Institute for Studies
in Education

John Meligrana
Assistant Professor
School of Urban
and Regional Planning
Queens University

George Kapelos
Professor
Department of Architectural
Science Ryerson University

Larry Rosia
Dean
Sait Polytechnic

William Humber
Chair
Centre for Built Environment
Seneca College

Jean Bilodeau
Visiting Scholar
Centre for Built Environment
Seneca College

Mark Kingwell
Professor
Trinity College
University of Toronto

Thomas Homer-Dixon
Professor
Trudeau Centre for Peace
and Conflict Studies

Andre Sorensen
Professor
Department of Geography
University of Mississauga

Edward Relph
Professor
University of Toronto at Scarborough

Harry Ruda
Professor
Advanced Nanotechnology
University of Toronto

Paul Young
Professor and Chair
Department of Civil Engineering
University of Toronto

Ingrid Stefanovic
Director
Division of the Environment
University of Toronto

Danny Harvey
Professor
Faculty of Geography
University of Toronto

Rodney White
Director
Institute for Environemental Studies
University of Toronto

Nasser Ashgriz
Professor
Mechanical and Industrial Engineering
University of Toronto

Eric Haldenby
Director
School of Architecture
University of Waterloo

NGO

Margaret Zeidler
President
Urbanspace Property Group

Mark Vanderheyden
Chairman of the Board
ONEIA

Ian Morton
Executive Director
Canadian Energy Efficiency Alliance

Ersilia Serafini
Executive Director
Clean Air Foundation

Eva Ligetti
Executive Director
Clean Air Partnership

Anne Parker
Executive Director
Communities of Tomorrow

Steven Peck
President
Green Roofs for Health Cities

Robert Kerr
Executive Director
International Council for Local
Environmental Initiatives

Martin Collier
Acting General Manager
Moving the Economy

Quentin Chiotti
Air Programme Director
Pollution Probe

Naofumi Hida
Director
Japan Local Government Centre
New York

FEDERAL

Gordon McIvor
Vice President
Public and Government Affairs
Canada Lands Company

Dino Chiesa
Chairman
Canada Mortgage
and Housing Corporation

Tony Genco
President
Parc Downsview Park

Stéphane Dion
Former Minister
Minister of Environment

Pierre Pettigrew
Former Minister
Ministry of Foreign Affairs

André Juneau
Former Deputy Minister
Ministry of Infrastructure

John Efford
Former Minister
Ministery of Natural Resources

Morad Atif
Director, Indoor Environment Chairman
International Energy Agency
National Research Council

Glen Murray
Chair
National Round Table on the
Environment and Economy

ONTARIO

Brad Graham
Assistant Deputy Minister
Minister of Public Infrastructure
and Renewal

Dwight Duncan
Minister
Ministry of Energy, Ontario

J.S. Burke
Deputy Minister
Ontario Minister of Municipal Affairs
and Housing

MUNICIPAL

Pat Vanini
Executive Director
Association of Municipalities of Ontario

Robert MacIsaac
Mayor
City of Burlington

Hazel McCallion
Mayor
City of Mississauga

David Miller
Mayor
City of Toronto

Dianne Young
Executive Director
Ontario Exhibition Place

James Knight
Chief Executive Offficer
Federation Canadian Municipalities

Joyce Savoline
Regional Chair
Halton Region

Arlene Campbel
General Manager
The National Trade Centre
at Exhibition Place

Patrick Guran
Chief Conservation Officer
PowerStream

Nick Tunnacliffe
Commissioner of Planning
Region of Peel

Bill Fisch
Regional Chair and CEO
Regional Municipality of York

Rob Maxwell
Acting Executive Director
Toronto Atmospheric Fund

Blair Peberdy
Vice President
Toronto Hydro

John Livey
Mayor
Town of Markham

Gord Kratz
Mayor
Town of Milton

ARCHITECT DIRECTORY

Acton Ostry Architects Inc.
Acton Ostry Architects emphasizes design solutions that ensure the provision of long-term social contributions to the communities in which they exist. Design is practiced with a responsible response to the ecology of the site and program, treating each solution as the product of its place, history, materiality and user needs. As a result, successful sustainable architecture continuously evolves to serve the public and invoke civic pride, surviving any cultural, economic and/or technological shifts over time.

1637 W. 5th Ave
Vancouver, BC V6J 1N5
tel 604.739.3344
fax 604.739.3355
www.actonostry.ca

Adamson Associates Architects
Established in 1934 in Toronto by Gordon Sinclair Adamson, the firm has been prominent internationally for many decades, and responsible for numerous high-profile projects in Canada, North America and England. It was already known by the 1970s for its early adoption of energy-saving heating and cooling systems.

55 Port St E
Mississauga, ON L5G 4P3
tel 905.891.8666
fax 905.891.1403
www.adamson-associates.com

Architects Alliance
Architects Alliance offers architecture, planning and urban design services to clients in Canada, the US and overseas. Sixty architects, designers, planners and technologists support a broad scope of practice, from academic and institutional buildings to large-scale residential and mixed-use developments. Sustainable design—incorporating architectural innovation and advanced building science—is central to the practice. Sustainable principles are incorporated into all of the projects, both for their practical benefits and as a matter of principle.

317 Adelaide St W Suite 205
Toronto, ON M5V 1P9
tel 416.593.6500

Atelier in Situ
Atelier in situ is the recipient of the Prix de Rome of Canada and Grand Prix of excellence in architecture of the Order of the Architects of Quebec (1997). The firm has worked since 1995 to define an architectural practice that widens the traditional limits of intervention by integrating a trans-disciplinary approach. Through installations and traditional projects questions are raised concerning the changeable perceptions in time and in space, using architecture as a medium of analysis and criticism.

55 Mont-Royal ave W Suite 700
Montreal, QC H2T 2S6
tel 514.393.9397
www.insitu.qc.ca

Baird Sampson Neuert Architects
Baird Sampson Neuert Architects is dedicated to excellence in design of the built environment and service to the community. Its engagement with the design of buildings, urban design, public space, and environmental sustainability arises out of its interest in human society and the integration of architecture and landscape design. BSN has developed an unusual capability to conduct research and to provide innovative design solutions in response to building programs. The firm's projects have received numerous awards for design excellence, technical achievement and energy efficiency and have been acknowledged internationally in academic and popular publications, journals and juried exhibitions.

35 Britain St Third Floor
Toronto, ON M5A 1R7
tel 416.363.8877
fax 416.363.4029
www.bsnarchitects.com

Breathe Architects
Breathe Architects' principal; Martin Liefhebber has been instrumental in advancing green design through his built projects for more than two decades. By eliminating reliance on fossil fuels, the use of renewable resources is emphasized, as are source manufacturers that do not reduce the value of the environment or affect our client's health.

177 First Ave
Toronto, ON M4M 1X3
tel 416 469 0018
fax 416 469 0987
www.breathebyassociation.com

Bregman + Hamann Architects
Through its 50-year history, B+H has designed award-winning buildings, and collaborated with top international architects on significant projects from the Toronto Dominion Centre to the Royal Ontario Museum. The ability to work in diverse sectors at a range of scales is a hallmark of B+H's work, which includes commercial, mixed use, institutional, renewal, planning, hospitality, retail, health care, residential, and transportation projects.

481 University Ave Suite 300
Toronto, ON M5G 2H4
tel 416.596.2299
www.bharchitects.com

Bruce Mau Design, Inc.
Bruce Mau founded his studio in Toronto in 1985. Since then, Bruce Mau Design, Inc. (BMD) has grown to a staff of forty and has gained international recognition for its expertise and innovation across a wide range of projects achieved in collaboration with some of the world's leading architects and institutions, artists and entrepreneurs, writers, curators, academics and businesses.

Collaboration is the studio's wellspring. Clients come to BMD with ambitions that can be built on, whether in book design, visual identity and branding, environmental graphics, programming and exhibitions, or product development. BMD approaches these collaborations not as accounts, but as ongoing projects.

Bruce Mau Design is part of the MDC Partners network, one of the world's foremost multi-disciplinary communication firms.

197 Spadina Ave Unit 501
Toronto, ON M5T 2C8
tel 416.260.5777
www.brucemaudesign.com

Busby Perkins+Will
Established by Peter Busby in 1984, Busby Perkins+Will are a full service design, planning, and architectural consulting practice deeply committed to: sustainability and green building design; creating modern, functional, and flexible spaces; utilizing the latest, most efficient technology to meet our client's needs; and providing the highest degree of personal service possible. As a medium-sized diversified practice, there is involvement in a range of projects, from industrial design to large comprehensive site planning. Busby Perkins+Will has the largest portfolio of completed green projects in Canada and is considered to be one of North America's leading green architecture firms.

1220 Homer St
Vancouver, BC V6B 2Y5
tel 604.684.5446
fax 604.684.5447
www.busby.ca

Bunting Coady Architects

Bunting Coady Architects is an innovative architectural practice based in Vancouver, BC with a reputation for high performance buildings and sustainable development. Specializing in innovative and developing technologies related to environmental design and energy engineering, their design philosophy has always been to create places and spaces in which people can live and work successfully. The firm has 8 LEED® accredited professionals.

Suite 300-171 Water St
Vancouver, BC V6B 1A7
tel 604.685.9913
fax 604.685.0694

Charles Simon Architect & Planner

Founded in 1970, the firm has vigorously pursued pioneering 'green' strategies in its architectural and community design work for over three decades. Architecture and planning projects vary in size and complexity from small renovations to large building complexes, neighbourhoods, new cities and regional development patterns. Its future-oriented approach has led to a strong emphasis on research work in a variety of environmental, social and physical areas. Charles Simon's pioneering work in a variety of fields has resulted in a number of "firsts", including Canada's first engineered passive solar house and its largest passive solar housing project.

221 Barden St
Eden Mills, ON N0B 1P0
tel 519.856.9921
fax 519.856.9921
www.simon-archplan.com

Corbett Cibinel Architects

A corporate partnership, Corbett Cibinel Architects practices architecture as a medium-size consulting office offering personalised service to institutional and commercial clients. Formed in October 1991, the firm has grown into a respected design studio with an international reputation for green building expertise. The firm attracts clients looking for leading edge solutions to building projects.

420A Stradbrook Ave
Winnipeg, MB R3L 0J8
tel 204.989.8910
fax 204.989.8920
www.corbettcibinel.com

Daoust Lestage Inc

Daoust Lestage Inc. has been active in the field of urban design and architecture since 1988, offering a full range of multidisciplinary expertise. The firm's approach rests on a careful understanding of the space or site's historical and current characteristics (the genius locci) in order to anchor the proposed contemporary interventions in the intrinsic qualities of their surroundings.

Through urban operations and architectural schemes, the firm is committed to the creation of significant quality and simplicity in environments at all scales.

3575 St-Laurent Blvd, Office 701
Montreal QC H2X 2T7
tel 514.982.0877
fax 514.982.0878
www@daoustlestage.com

Diamond and Schmitt Architects

Diamond and Schmitt Architects has received national and international recognition for sustainable architecture that achieves design excellence and displays an understanding of the communities in which the projects are located. The firm was established in 1975 and is comprised of 70 design professionals with 11 LEED® accredited professionals.

384 Adelaide St W Suite 300
Toronto, ON M5V 1R7
tel 416.862.8800
fax 416 862.5508
www.dsai.ca

Farrow Partnership Architects

Farrow Partnership Architects is a leading design firm offering innovative and comprehensive architecture, interior, masterplanning, and environmental design services with a specialty in health sustainability. Research plays a critical factor in their portfolio; they have received numerous awards, publications, conference presentations and prestigious research grants.

134 Peter St Suite 200
Toronto, ON M5V 2H2
tel 416.979.3666
fax 416.979.3680
www.farrowpartnership.com

Fiset Miller Bourke architectes

Fiset Miller Bourke architectes combines an innovative vision with over 35 years experience, a critical philosophy anchored in the reality of practice, and a design sensibility as refined at the level of urban planning as at the intimate scale of interior design. In 1998, Julia Bourke joined the Fiset Miller team as partner, contributing to the firm her broad theoretical and practical experience as well as a particular expertise in ecological, affordable design and construction techniques.

460 Saint-Catherine St W Suite 303
Montréal, QC H3B 1A7
tel 514.931.7501
fax 514.931.7503
www.fisetmillerbourke.com

Grant Diemert Architect

Established in Owen Sound, Grant Diemert was part of the team responsible for the development of the Escarpment Centre of Ontario, an interpretive centre for the Niagara Escarpment. He was also involved in the Grey Roots Visitor and Heritage Centre in Grey County Ontario, and the E'Terra Inn, which won the Green by Design Award.

Grant Diemert
tel 519.376.1975
gm.diemert@bmts.com

Hotson Bakker Boniface Haden Architects

Hotson Bakker Boniface Haden Architects offers a wide range of services to both public and private sector clients in the fields of architecture, planning, urban design, and interior design. With a staff of 30 people, the firm has the expertise and the resources to complete projects at all scales and complexities. Significant emphasis is placed on the quality of design in buildings and the creation of both interior and outdoor spaces that people truly enjoy.

406-611 Alexander St
Vancouver, BC V6A 1E1
tel 604.255.1169
fax 604.255.1790
www.hotsonbakker.com/offices.html

Hughes Condon Marler Architects (HCMA)
HCMA is a highly proficient Vancouver-based architectural firm of over 30 people with a passion for innovative and sustainable architectural solutions. Since the founding of our predecessor firm in 1976, we have worked with a range of clients and completed a diversity of RAIC award-winning projects and LEED® buildings. Our portfolio of work includes public and private institutions; educational facilities; urban town centers; museums and libraries; community centers; health care facilities; recreational and sports facilities; corporate offices; single family/ multi-family dwellings; and residential developments.

#300 – 1508 West Second Ave
Vancouver, BC V6J 1H2
tel 604.732.6620
fax 604.732.6695

**IBI Group / Henriquez Partners,
Architects in Joint Venture**
This 13 year-old joint venture combines the creative skills of Henriquez Partners Architects, a nationally recognized design practice, with the extensive design, technical and management resources of IBI Group, an international multi-disciplinary consulting practice. The IBI/Henriquez collaboration believes in a design process that embraces a "listening attitude" and strives to achieve a balance between program aspirations and budget; vision and practicality. The IBI/Henriquez joint venture has successfully completed over thirty projects.

Suite 700 – 1285 W. Pender St
Vancouver, BC V6E 4B1
tel 604.683.8797

Jacques Plante Architect
A graduate of the Massachusetts Institute of Technology in Cambridge, Jacques Plante is particularly interested in the design of performance centres such as theatres, circuses, cinemas and concert halls. His work includes consideration of green architecture and the social impact of aesthetics. A member of the Ordre des architectes du Québec since 1982, he received the title Grand Nom de l'Architecture from Université Laval in 2002.

479 rue Jeanne-d'Arc
Québec, QC G1S 2R9
tel 418.694.6979

**Jodoin Lamarre Pratte
and associates architects**
Established in 1958, the firm is recognized for its reliability as witnessed through the dedication of its numerous institutional and corporate clients with whom a lasting relationship has been founded, some spanning over two decades. The basis of this recognition is a respectful approach to clients' needs in order to meet their functional, financial as well as aesthetic requirements. The architectural approach taken by the firm relies on knowledge and expertise developed in four aspects of its professional practice: design, technology, cost and quality control.

3200 rue Rachel E
Montréal, QC H1W 1A4
tel 514.527.8821

**Kuch Stephenson Gibson Malo,
Architects and Engineers**
Formed in 2002 with the merger of two Thunder Bay firms, Kuch Stephenson Gibson Malo includes architects, engineers and interior designers. They have been involved in the development of the Aviation Centre of Excellence at Confederation College as well as Thunder Bay's École secondaire catholique de La Vérendrye– built with wood in order to focus on energy conservation.

131 Court St N
Thunder Bay, ON P7A 4V1
tel 807.345.5582
fax 807.345.4093
www.ksgm.ca

**Kuwabara Payne McKenna
Blumberg Architects (KPMB)**
KPMB was founded in 1987 by Bruce Kuwabara, Thomas Payne, Marianne McKenna and Shirley Blumberg. Their portfolio encompasses cultural, civic, educational, hospitality and performing arts projects located across Canada and, increasingly, in the United States and Europe.
    The work has received over 70 awards, including 9 Governor General's awards and has been published internationally, including in the Contemporary World Architect series by Rockport Publishers (1997) and The Architecture of Kuwabara Payne McKenna Blumberg Architects by Birkhauser (2004).

322 King St. W, Third Floor
Toronto, ON M5V 1J2
tel 416.977.5104
fax 416.598.9840
www.kpmbarchitects.com

Levitt Goodman Architects Ltd.
Levitt Goodman Architects has a proven commitment to providing excellent buildings with a high degree of design expertise. They have received recognition for their architectural work in many forums such as receiving the prestigious 1999 Governor General's Medal of Excellence in Architecture, the 2001 Peter J. Marshall Municipal Innovation Award of Excellence, a 2004 CMHC Best Housing Practices Award and an Urban Institute Brownie Award for best urban conversion project of a brownfield site.

16A Plymouth Ave
Toronto, ON M6J 1Z1
tel 416.922.3131
fax 416.922.3116
www.levittgoodmanarchitects.com

LINE Architect Inc.
LINE was formed in 1990 and offers expertise in designing energy efficient and sustainable architectural solutions. Art, science and technology are brought together to create memorable and viable architecture. LINE's work was showcased by Canada Government, Wood Council, Enbridge, the National Post, the Toronto Star and in design conferences for its innovations in sustainable design.

366 Adelaide St E Suite 333
Toronto, ON M5A 3X9
tel 416.955.9938
fax 416.955.9939
www.linearchitect.com

**L'OEUF (L'Office de l'eclectisme
urbain et fonctionnel)**
L'OEUF, founded in 1992, is a firm with a broad and diversified architectural practice. Sensitive to political and ecological issues that are often excluded from professional concerns, L'OEUF has developed a reputation for sustainable architecture. This expertise is based upon maintaining a balance between appropriate technologies, economic feasibility, architectural expression and environmental impact of a project. As architects, the members of l'OEUF. see themselves as the stewards of a built environment that is dignified, human, pleasing, useful and sustainable.

642 rue de Courcelle 402
Montreal, QC H4C 3C5
tel 514.484.7745
fax 514.484.8897
www.loeuf.com

Manasc Isaac Architects Ltd.

Manasc Isaac Architects Ltd. Is an innovative, award-winning, experienced architectural firm, practicing locally, nationally, and internationally. Dedicated to a client-centered planning, design and construction approach to architecture, the firm has earned a reputation for sustainable, high-quality, technically outstanding buildings. Manasc Isaac Architects are the leading LEED® accredited architectural firm in Alberta.

10225 – 100 Ave
Edmonton, AB T5J 0A1
tel 780.429.3977
fax 780.426.3970
www.miarch.com

Markson Borooah Architects Inc.

Operating under two principals—Ronji Borooah and Jerome Markson—the firm has worked in Toronto for five decades. With experience in architecture, urban design and planning, their projects are committed to the integration of neighbourhoods with the urban fabric.

161 Eglinton Ave E Suite 600
Toronto, ON M4P 1J5
tel 416.322.3887
fax 416.322.3941
www.mbarchitects.ca

Marshall Tittemore Architects

Led by principals Bill Marshall and Tom Tittemore, the award-winning Calgary based firm of Marshall Tittemore Architects has a guiding principle that results in innovative spaces for a diversity of clients: 'Living and Learning' is the process behind every memorable place that they create.

301, 215 – 10th Ave SW
Calgary, AB T2R 0A4
tel 403.264.8700
fax 403.264.8029
www.mtalink.com

Montgomery Sisam Architects Inc.

Established in 1978, Montgomery Sisam Architects has developed a reputation for design excellence that has been recognized by over 30 regional, national and international design awards. The firm's approach to design begins with the essential role buildings play in our everyday lives and their potential to provide healthy and enriching places for living. Montgomery Sisam's designs enhance the activities they house and contribute positively to the communities in which they are located. The firm is committed to designing buildings that function efficiently, are environmentally sustainable, and have a positive influence on the people who inhabit them.

35 Britain St
Toronto, ON M5A 1R7
tel 416.364.8079

Consortium MTF
(Studio MMA, Lyse M Tremblay, architecte and Duschenes & Fish/DFS architects)

Brought together as a consortium for the design of the Mountain Equipment Coop store in downtown Montreal, the firms and architects involved are all established in the province of Quebec and share a commitment to green architecture.

Studio MMA

7275 St. Urbain, Suite 403
Montreal, Quebec H2R 2Y5
tel 514.338.3451
www.studiomma.ca

Lyse Tremblay, Architect

tel 450.448.5836

Duschenes and Fish/DFS Architects

1425 René-Lévesque W, Suite 1001
Montréal, Québec H3G 1T7
tel 514.879.1708
fax 514.861.6219
www.dfsarch.com

Musson Cattell Mackey Partnership Architects

Since 1965, Musson Cattell Mackey Partnership has provided architectural and interior design services in support of their clients' aspirations, both in the private sector and in the public realm. A passion for design and creativity is combined with reliability in project delivery.

1600 Two Bentall Centre
555 Burrard St Box 264
Vancouver, BC V7X 1M9
tel 604.687.2990
fax 604.687.1771
www.mcmparchitects.com

Oleson Worland Architect

Oleson Worland Architects is a Toronto based firm established in 1984. With an emphasis on the integration of architecture with landscape architecture, their projects have garnered the Governor General's Medal for Architecture, the President's Award of Excellence from the American Society of Landscape Architects and four City of Toronto Architecture & Urban Design Awards.

192 Spadina Ave Suite 400
Toronto, ON M5T 2C2
tel 416.365.1414

P3 Architecture

P3 Architecture was formed in 1996 and traces its roots back to 1954. Currently our award winning firm has offices in Regina and Saskatoon (Saskatchewan) with 20 staff, including 5 registered architects. Sustainable design is a cornerstone of our work and forms the starting point for all of our projects.

Regina Office:
201-1945 Scarth St
Regina, SK S4P 2H1
tel 306.757.1669

Saskatoon Office:
348 3rd Ave S
Saskatoon, SK S7K 1M5
tel 306.651.4660
www.p3arch.com

Patkau Architects Inc.

Patkau Architects was founded in 1978 and is based in Vancouver, British Columbia, Canada. There are currently three principals: John Patkau, Patricia Patkau and Michael Cunningham, and three associates: David Shone, Peter Suter and Greg Boothroyd.

Projects vary in scale from gallery installations to urban planning, from houses to major urban libraries, from glassware and furniture design to research into sustainable practise and the future of educational technologies.

1564 West 6th Ave
Vancouver, BC V6J 1R2
tel 604.683.7633
fax 604.683.7634

Phillip Sharp Architect Ltd.

Firmly committed to serving clients with special needs, Phillip Sharp Architects' work for the Environmentally Hypersensitive ranges from low-cost, multi-unit developments to custom homes, additions, renovations, and consultations on commercial and institutional projects, as well as initiatives financed by the National Research Council and Canada Mortgage and Housing Corporation. The firm has been published internationally in the popular press, in conference papers, and in architectural and academic journals.

68 Hopewell Ave
Ottawa, ON K1S 2Z1
tel 613.730.4950
fax 613.730.0479

Public Works and Government Services Canada (PWGSC)

As the buyer and property manager for the Government of Canada, PWGSC plays a leading role in sustainable development. Committed to ensuring a cleaner environment for all Canadians, all new government buildings are designed and constructed to use less electricity and reduce greenhouse gas emissions.

150 Burnham St
Cobourg, ON K9A 2W6
tel 416.590.8270
fax 416.512.5535

PWL Partnership

A leading Vancouver-based landscape architectural firm with over thirty years of experience, PWL Partnership has been involved in the planning and design of public and private open spaces for clients across Canada, the U.S. and China.

Birks Place
900 - 688 West Hastings St
Vancouver, BC V6B 1P1
tel 604.688.6111
fax 604.688.6112

RHL Architects Inc.

RHL Architects is a firm of consulting architects that has provided a wide range of planning and architectural services for over fifty years. Specializing in educational facilities, they also have extensive experience with recreational, institutional, health care, custom homes, and corporate/commercial projects.

1179A King St W Suite 300
Toronto, ON M6K 3C5
tel 416.203.7677
fax 416.203.7679

Robert Burgers Architects

RBA Inc. is the consulting practice started by Robert Burgers. Robert began RBA Inc. in 1973, prior to which he was in partnership with Buttjes Burgers Sammarco Architects whose numerous awards firmly established the firm in the international and commercial field. Prior to the partnership Robert collaborated in the design of Paris's Front de Seine (1967), an extensive urban renewal in France. RBA's projects reflect the environmental and cultural conditions of the locale in which they are built. Technological innovations in building and materials are balanced with an intimate understanding of human behavior and desires.

107 - 657 Marine Dr
West Vancouver, BC V7T 1A4
tel 604.926.6058
fax 604.926.9141
info@rbaarchitects.com

Saia Barbarese Topouzanov, architectes

Established in 1968, the firm offers experience in projects ranging from cultural, sports and community facilities, to housing, commercial complexes and educational institutions. Highly acclaimed and recognized for its commitment to quality, the firm received numerous awards and mentions, namely: two Governor General's Medal, many Awards of Excellence from the Québec Order of Architects, Save Montréal and the Royal Architectural Institute of Canada. Its projects have been published both nationally and internationally.

Les architectes Tétreault Parent Languedoc et associés + Saia Barbarese Topouzanov, architectes
401 Notre-Dame St E
Montréal, QC H2Y 1C9
tel 514.848.0808
fax 514.844.6824

Shim-Sutcliffe Architects

Brigitte Shim and Howard Sutcliffe are partners as well as collaborators. They have created a firm and a life around their shared passion for architecture, landscape and furniture. Shim-Sutcliffe Architects, is located in Toronto, Canada. The city's diversity and ethnicity make it a vital metropolis reflective of both global and North American sensibilities. The work references both the city and its landscape within the urban core of Toronto and the many particular landscapes around it. The studio shares ideas through drawings, models, and discussion with the numerous remarkable clients who have put their faith in them over the last decade.

441 Queen St E
Toronto, ON M5A 1T5
tel 416.368.3892
fax 416.368.9468
www.shim-sutcliffe.com

Smith Carter Architects and Engineers Inc.

Established in 1947, Smith Carter is one of Canada's largest integrated architectural and engineering practices. From offices in Winnipeg, Calgary, Ottawa and Atlanta, they provide services and solutions to architecture, engineering, planning, interior design, and landscape architecture for highly complex and technical building types in the global environment.

1600 Buffalo Place
Winnipeg, MB R3T 6B8
tel 204.477.1260
fax 204.477.6346

Stantec Architecture Ltd.

Established in 1954, Stantec Architecture specializes in the design of airports; attractions; commercial and residential buildings; health care and research facilities; community, industrial, and transportation projects; educational environments; and hospitality, retail, and mixed-use developments. With a multi-disciplined team of experienced professionals, they provide clients with creative and integrated solutions.

500-477 Mount Pleasant Rd
Toronto, ON M4S 2L9
tel 416.596.6666
fax 416.596.7892
www.stantec.com

Studio MMA, Atelier d'architecture (Mamfredis Miners Architects)

Studio MMA, Atelier d'architecture is a young Montréal firm whose practice includes many urban projects. The firm is committed to the integration and promotion of sustainable design principles and a collaborative approach. In its design work, Studio MMA is constantly seeking a balance between appropriate technologies and stimulating architectural expressions.

7275 St. Urbain Suite 403
Montreal, QC H2R 2Y5
tel 514.388.3451
fax 514.388.1172
www.studiomma.ca

Sustainable EDGE Ltd.

Sustainable EDGE Ltd. was founded in February 2003 through collaboration between Allen Kani Associates (AKA) and The Mitchell Partnership (TMP) to offer a comprehensive service in sustainable design and engineering. Sustainable EDGE, an Ecological Design and Green Engineering practice, extends AKA's 20 years of expertise in multi-disciplinary sustainable design. Through an integrated design process, they work with design teams toward achieving a sustainable product.

285 Yorkland Blvd
Toronto, ON M2J 1S5
tel 416.488.4425
fax 416.499.7446
www.s-edge.com

Dermot J. Sweeny Architects Inc.

Sweeny Sterling Finlayson and Co. (SSF&Co) is a new multidisciplinary practice that builds on the strengths of two well-known and respected Toronto design firms: Dermot J. Sweeny Architects Inc. and Sterling Finlayson Architects. Architects and urban designers, they provide expertise in architecture, interior design, land use planning, universal accessibility and sustainable design principles, development of financial analysis and project management.

Creating buildings focused on human comfort and practical effectiveness has led to design solutions that mesh energy efficiency and environmental sustainability with the market demands required in commercial buildings.

468 Wellington St W Second Floor
tel 416.971.6252
fax 416.971.5420

Syverson Monteyne Architecture Inc. (SM-Arc)

The origination of SM-Arc in 1994 was motivated by the desire to learn through building. Most of the firm's work is situated in and around Winnipeg. Conjuring an authentic response to the local context has been the inevitable result of keeping it real. We strive to make buildings that help people to live lightly on the planet.

607 - 70 Arthur St
Winnipeg, MB R3B 1G7
tel 204.947.3155
fax 204.947.3161
www.sm-arc.com

Terence Williams Architect Inc.

Located in Victoria, BC, Canada, Terence Williams Architect Inc. specializes in architecture, interior and urban design. For a number of years the practice has been recognized for its commitment to sustainable planning and design. Terence Williams Architect inc. (TWA) is pleased to announce the merger of its firm with Busby Perkins+Will (BPW).

102 - 2957 Jutland Rd
Victoria, BC V8T 5J9
tel 250.384.7878
fax 250.384.7872
twilliams@twarchitects.ca

Les architectes Tétreault Parent Languedoc et associés (TPL+A)

TPL+A is a leading Québec architectural firm founded in 1970, with achievements in all fields of the built environment: healthcare facilities, museums, penitentiaries, educational buildings, industrial and residential projects. Offering architectural and related services: feasibility studies, technical and functional programs, legal and technical opinions, and preventive maintenance, TPL+A has received numerous awards and mentions, namely the Special Citation in Sustainable Development from the Québec Order of Architects for the Central Library of the Cheikh Anta Diop University in Dakar, Senegal, and many awards of excellence from the Québec Order of Architects.

401 Notre-Dame St E
Montréal, QC H2Y 1C9
tel 514.848.0808
fax 514.844.6824

Vogel Architect

Vogel Architect is an architectural firm established in 1990 by Jacek Vogel and Barbara Vogel. VA has won a number of prestigious awards, competitions and commissions including various Canadian embassies. VA is organized as a design studio, and on large projects often operates in collaboration with other architectural firms. VA innovative projects represent a bioclimatic approach to architectural design and commitment to sustainability.

33 Bernard Ave
Toronto, ON M5R 1R3
tel 416.944.1846
vogelarch@sympatico.ca

WHW Architects

Based in Halifax, WHW Architects is a leading architectural practice in Atlantic Canada. The Firm was founded in 1946 and has completed over 1600 commissions. Current members of both USGBC and CaGBC, WHW is a Green Building leader with 2 projects LEED® registered and 8 LEED® Accredited Professionals on staff.

1640 Market St
Halifax, NS B3J 2C8
tel 902.429.5490
fax 902.429.2632
www.whwarchitects.com

Young + Wright Architects Inc.

Young + Wright Architects Inc. is recognized as a design firm with strong commitment to environmental design and green building. The firm has a mandate to create architecture that will reduce our clients' environmental footprint. Young + Wright Architects are widely recognized nationally and internationally for their achievements in the area of sustainable design with LEED® Accredited Professionals. Their contributions include serving on the Board of Directors for the Canada Green Building Council, and chairing the OAA Committee on the Environment.

172 St. George St
Toronto, ON M5R 2M7
tel 416.968.3522
fax 416.960.3310
www.ywarch.ca

Zeidler Partnership

With a triple commitment to the client, their employees and the urban environment, Zeidler Partnership is large enough to take on major projects and a wide variety of work including masterplanning, project management and systems development. They have received over 100 national and international awards for their work.

315 Queen St. W Suite 200
Toronto, ON M5V 2X2
tel 416.596.8300
fax 416.596.1408
www.zrpi.com

ORGANIZATIONS

NATIONAL

Canada Foundation for Innovation
The Canada Foundation for Innovation (CFI) is an independent corporation created by the Government of Canada to fund research infrastructure. The CFI's mandate is to strengthen the capacity of Canadian universities, colleges, research hospitals, and non-profit research institutions to carry out world-class research and technology development that benefits Canadians.
www.innovation.ca

Canada Green Building Council (CaGBC)
CaGBC exists to accelerate the design and construction of Green Buildings across Canada.
www.cagbc.ca

Canadian Environmental Network
CEN facilitates networking between environmental organizations and others who share its mandate—To Protect The Earth And Promote Ecologically Sound Ways Of Life.
www.cen-rce.org

David Suzuki Foundation
Since 1990, the David Suzuki Foundation has worked to find ways for society to live in balance with the natural world. Focusing on four program areas—oceans and sustainable fishing, forests and wild lands, climate change and clean energy, and the web of life—the Foundation uses science and education to promote solutions that help conserve nature.
www.davidsuzuki.org

EcoAction
Since 1995, Environment Canada's EcoAction Community Funding Program has provided financial support to community groups for projects that have measurable, positive impacts on the environment.
www.ec.gc.ca/ecoaction

EcoDesign Resource Society
A not-for-profit organization which promotes environmentally responsible ('green') design, planning and development practices through research, education and communication.
www.vcn.bc.ca/edrs

Ecoportal Canada
A guide to environmental directories, portals and networks in Canada.
www.planetfriendly.net/ecoportal.html

Evergreen
A national non-profit environmental organization with a mandate to bring nature to our cities through naturalization projects.
www.evergreen.ca

Planetfriendly.net
Bringing Canadians together over planet friendly ideas.
www.planetfriendly.net

PlanetVote Canada
A comprehensive election portal, with a focus on environment, peace and sustainability.
www.PlanetVote.net

Pollution Probe
A Canadian environmental organization dedicated to achieving positive and tangible environmental change.
www.pollutionprobe.org

Sierra Club of Canada
SCC has developed four major national campaigns: Health & Environment, Protecting Biodiversity, Atmosphere & Energy, and Transition to a Sustainable Economy.
http://sierraclub.ca

Sustainable Buildings Canada
Working to implement innovative solutions to mitigate climate change, while serving the building industry.
www.sbcanada.org

Sustainable Development Technology Canada (SDTC)
A not-for-profit foundation that finances and supports the development and demonstration of clean technologies which provide solutions to issues of climate change, clean air, water quality and soil, and which deliver economic, environmental and health benefits to Canadians.
www.sdtc.ca

Sustainability Now
Objectives are to increase awareness on sustainability and to find ways to make it common practice in engineering.
www.sustainability.ca

The Green Pages Canada
Thegreenpages.ca is a national network of eco-minded individuals whose mission is to empower and support students, educators, and communities by connecting them to environmental information for the purpose of making meaningful contributions towards environmental sustainability.
www.thegreenpages.ca

REGIONAL

Buildsmart
Greater Vancouver's source for sustainable building information
www.gvrd.bc.ca/BuildSmart

Green Buildings BC
A provincial initiative enabling BC's education and health care agencies to dramatically increase the performance of their new and existing buildings
www.greenbuildingsbc.com/

The 215 Centre for Social Innovation
A group of 15 organizations that work to catalyze, inform and support innovations to advance the social, cultural, environmental and economic well-being of Canadians.
www.the215.ca

The Sustainable Living Network
A not-for-profit organization in Toronto, Ontario founded to inspire and support movement in individuals and groups towards more sustainable ways of living. Topics stewarded include: permaculture, organic and biodynamic farming and gardening and urban agriculture; natural building; renewable energy; alternative waste treatment systems.
www.sustainablelivingnetwork.org

Toronto Environmental Alliance
With a mission to promote a greener Toronto, TEA works with concerned individuals, community groups, professionals and workers, encouraging the participation of local people on local issues.
www.torontoenvironment.org

Toronto Public Space Committee
Dedicated to protecting our shared common spaces from commercial influence and privatisation.
www.publicspace.ca

York Centre for Applied Sustainability
Promoting the application of sustainability principles and practices throughout society, including in the public sector, the private sector, the civil sector, and in education.
www.yorku.ca/ycas

Toronto and Region Conservation for The Living City
Working with partners to ensure that The Living City is built upon a natural foundation of healthy rivers and shorelines, greenspace and biodiversity, and sustainable communities.
www.trca.on.ca

PRINCIPLES OF
SUSTAINABLE DESIGN

From The Philosophy of Sustainable Design,
Jason F. McClennan

Respect for the Wisdom of Natural Systems:
The Biomimicry Principle

Respect for People:
The Human Vitality Principle

Respect for Place:
The Ecosystem/Bioregion Principle

Respect for the Cycle of Life:
The "Seven Generations" Principle

Respect for Energy and Natural Resources:
The Conservation and Renewable Resources Principle

Respect for Process:
The Holistic Thinking Principle

From Ecological Design,
Island Press 1995.
Sim Van der Ryn with Stuart Cowan

1. Solutions grow from grace

2. Ecological Accounting informs design

3. Design with nature

4. Make nature visible

5. Everyone is a designer

From The Hannover Principles
Design for Sustainability,
Prepared for EXPO 2000, The World's Fair
Hannover, Germany
William McDonough & Partners

1. Insist on the rights of humanity and nature
   to co-exist

2. Recognize interdependence.

3. Respect relationships between spirit and matter.

4. Accept responsibility for the consequences
   of design.

5. Create safe objects of long-term value.

6. Eliminate the concept of waste.

7. Rely on natural energy flows.

8. Understand the limitations of design.

9. Seek constant improvement by the sharing
   of knowledge.

GLOSSARY

Aerated autoclaved concrete
Concrete used in precast building materials such as blocks and floor, roof and wall panels. AAC is a lightweight concrete that provides insulation, structural support and fire resistance in one material.

Active solar
The use of a mechanical system to actively capture and convert solar energy into a usable form of energy.

Air barrier
A barrier strong enough to sustain air pressure placed upon it, but not necessarily vapour permeable.

Brownfield
Abandoned or previously used industrial or commercial land with possible environmental contamination which usually hampers redevelopment. Land with high amounts of pollution or hazardous waste do not fall into the lower contamination concentration usually found in brownfields.

Carbon offset
The reduction of carbon dioxide emissions to offset or cancel out an emissions offender. One company or country might lower its carbon emissions and sell the reduction to companies or countries that produce too much carbon emissions.

Charrette
Refers to a collaboration of designers on a given project or design problem.

Cogeneration
The production of heat and electricity at the same time. Heat is often a byproduct of electricity production and captured, the heat can be transferred to homes or businesses.

CFM
Cubic feet per minute.

CFCs
Chlorofluorocarbons – ozone-depleting chemical compounds with both chlorine and fluorine, formerly used in industry as refrigerants, propellants and solvents.

Evaporative cooling
The use of evaporation—water's change of state becoming a gas—to pull heat away from an object. The method requires less energy than other forms of cooling and is popular in residential and industrial cooling, though the process requires a large water source for evaporation and works best in dry climates.

Geothermal pump
A geothermal exchange heat pump or ground source heat pump uses the constant temperature of the ground to heat or cool a building by transferring the heat from the ground below the frost line (approximately 1 to 2m in depth) using water or a water and antifreeze mixture.

Greywater
Also known as sullage, is wastewater produced from washing dishes, bathing or laundry.

Glulam
Abbreviation for glued laminated beams used as structural timber by gluing several smaller pieces of wood into a stronger structural beam often in a curve or arch.

Greenfield
Undeveloped or underdeveloped land, either land left to nature or currently used for agriculture.

Heat island effect
Also called an urban heat island, a densely populated area will have a higher average temperature than surrounding less dense areas. Surface materials such as concrete and asphalt retain heat from the sun more than organic materials, the overall effect causing higher temperatures.

Heat sink
An environment or object that absorbs and dissipates heat from another object using thermal contact.

High volume ash concrete
Concrete containing high amounts of ash, an industrial by-product of coal burning that replaces Portland cement.

HVAC
Heating, ventilating and air-conditioning. Sometimes called climate control. These functions are closely related and they control the temperature and humidity of air within a building.

HCFCs
Hydrochlorofluorocarbons – compounds where not all hydrogen has been replaced by chlorine or fluorine, somewhat less harmful than CFCs. When chlorine has been entirely eliminated, such compounds are known as hydrofluorocarbons (HFCs) with even fewer environmental effects.

Interstitial
Refers to space between adjacent objects.

IAQ
Indoor air quality.

Light shelf
A horizontal light-reflecting overhang placed most often above eye-level with a window above and below. Light shelves help bring more direct sunlight into a building by bouncing the light off the shelf onto the ceiling while also shading the lower window.

Low-E
Low emmitance

Natural stack ventilation
In larger buildings natural ventilation is achieved by allowing warm air to rise and vent out of a building through upper openings which will draw fresh cool air in through openings on the lower levels. The stack effect refers to the difference in pressure between inside and outside air. Less dense warm air will rise to higher elevations and be displaced by cooler denser air.

Off grid
The construction of dwellings that rely on renewable energy sources rather than traditional utilities such as power, sewer and water supply.

Passive solar
A design system used to manage heat gains through daily sunlight with the aim to reduce the use of conventional heating methods. A passive solar-heated building will also not rely on capturing the solar energy into a mechanical system.

Passive ventilation
Refers to buildings that use very low amounts of energy to heat the space. In archiving a significant reduction in energy consumption, a passive building will not need a traditional central heating and cooling system. A passive system will make use of heat from internal sources such as building occupants and waste heat from electrical devices.

Photovoltaic
PV for short, the use of solar energy to produce electricity through the process of converting photons. Photovoltaic or solar cells are grouped in large panels to capture greater amounts of solar energy.

Planimetric
A two-dimensional representation of geographical space. Cartography or mapping term.

PV screen
see Photovoltaic, as in Photovoltaic screen

PSL
Parallel strand lumber

Rain screen
A wall construction featuring an exterior skin, that acts as a repellant to moisture, and a secondary sealed wall in between which sits insulation that air is permitted to circulate through in order to keep the insulation and wall dry. Trapped moisture causes damage to exterior walls. The rain screen is a barrier used to diminish the forces and pressures attempted to push moisture into the wall. Such walls consist of vented exterior cladding, air flow cavity, drainage layer and water-resistant and airtight support wall.

R-Value
Measure of thermal resistance used to characterize building insulation materials.

Swale
A marshy depression between ridges

Stack effect
The ventilation in buildings that results from thermal differences between indoor and outside temperatures.

Thermal solar panel
A solar panel employing water that is heated using the sun's energy then transferred to storage or used in a radiant heating system.

Thermal flywheel effect
The propensity of a building and its construction materials to remain at a given temperature.

VOC
Volatile organic compounds

VAV
Variable air volume device, used in HVAC systems to control the flow of air.

Waterless urinal
Without water, these urinals allow urine to drain but use a sealant liquid that is lighter than water and which floats at the top of the U-bend drain pipe and helps to prevent odors from being released.

WWF
Welded wire fabric

Xeriscaped
A style of landscape design requiring little or no irrigation.

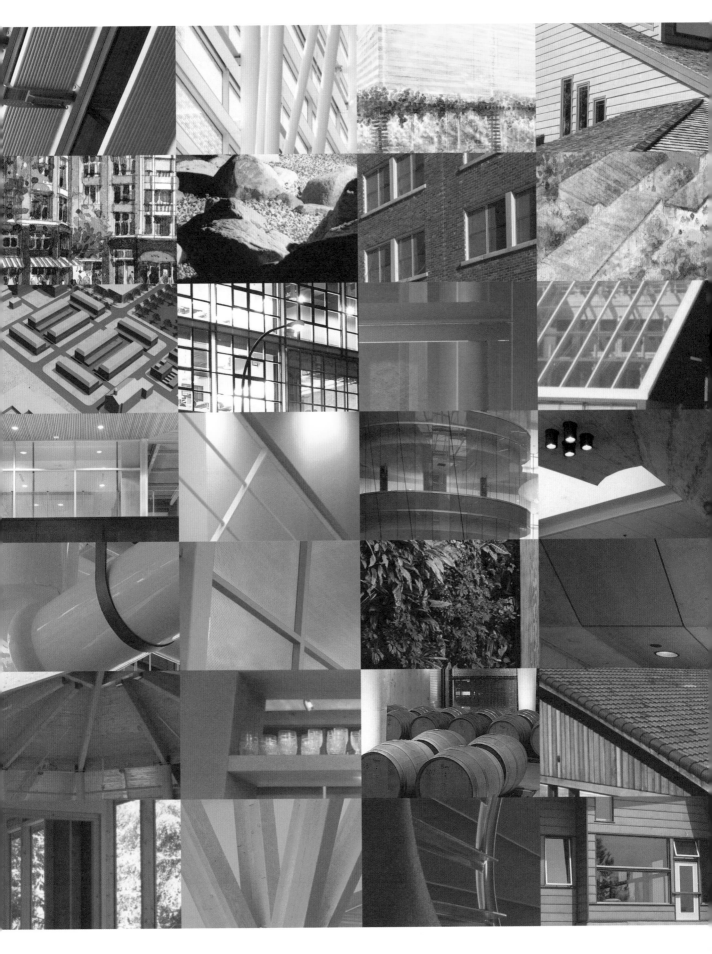